Exploring the shores of Bermuda

Bermuda Island

Reefs

South Shore Beach

Horseshoe Beach

Underwater Bermuda

City of Hamilton

Hamilton's Birdcage

Hamilton's Church Street

St. George

St. George's Water Street

St. George's Harbour

Royal Naval Dockyard

Clocktower Building

Cruise ship terminal at Royal Navy Dockyard

Unique shopping at the Royal Navy Dockyard

Bermuda's many shopping treasures

Bermuda's many pleasures

Beautiful Bermuda

Praise for The Impact Guides

The World's Only Travel-Shopping Series

"YOU LEARN MORE ABOUT A PLACE you are visiting when Impact is pointing the way." – **The Washington Post**

"THE DEFINITIVE GUIDE to shopping in Asia." – **Arthur Frommer**, The Arthur Frommer Almanac of Travel

"THE BEST travel book I've ever read." – Kathy Osiro, **TravelAge West**

"AN EXCELLENT, EXHAUSTIVE, AND FASCINATING look at shopping in the East . . . it's difficult to imagine a shopping tour without this pocket-size book in hand." – **Travel & Leisure**

"BOOKS IN THE SERIES help travelers recognize quality and gain insight to local customs." – **Travel-Holiday**

"THE BEST GUIDE I've seen on shopping in Asia. If you enjoy the sport, you'll find it hard to put down . . . They tell you not only the where and what of shopping but the important how, and all in enormous but easy-to-read detail." – **Seattle Post-Intelligencer**

"ONE OF THE BEST GUIDEBOOKS of the season – not just shopping strategies, but a Baedeker to getting around . . . definitely a quality work. Highly recommended." – **Arkansas Democrat**

"WILL WANT TO LOOK INTO . . . has shopping strategies and travel tips about making the most of a visit to those areas. The book covers Asia's shopping centers, department stores, emporiums, factory outlets, markets and hotel shopping arcades where visitors can find jewelry, leather goods, woodcarvings, textiles, antiques, cameras, and primitive artifacts." – **Chicago Tribune**

"FULL OF SUGGESTIONS. The art of bartering, including everyday shopping basics are clearly defined, along with places to hang your hat or lift a fork." – **The Washington Post**

"A WONDERFUL GUIDE . . . filled with essential tips as well as a lot of background information . . . a welcome addition on your trip." – **Travel Book Tips**

"WELL ORGANIZED AND COMPREHENSIVE BOOK. A useful companion for anyone planning a shopping spree in Asia." – **International Living**

"OFFERS SOME EXTREMELY VALUABLE INFORMATION and advice about what is all too often a spur-of-the-moment aspect of your overseas travel." – **Trip & Tour**

"A MORE UNUSUAL, PRACTICAL GUIDE than most and is no mere listing of convenience stores abroad . . . contains unusual tips on bargaining in Asia . . . country-specific tips are some of the most valuable chapters of the guidebook, setting it apart from others which may generalize upon Asia as a whole, or focus upon the well-known Hong Kong shopping pleasures." – **The Midwest Book Review**

"I LOVED THE BOOK! Why didn't I have this book two months ago! . . . a valuable guide . . . very helpful for the first time traveler in Asia . . . worth packing in the suitcase for a return visit." – Editor, **Unique & Exotic Travel Reporter**

"VERY USEFUL, PERFECTLY ORGANIZED. Finally a guide that combines Asian shopping opportunities with the tips and know-how to really get the best buys." – **National Motorist**

"INFORMATION-PACKED PAGES point out where the best shops are located, how to save time when shopping, and where and when to deal . . . You'll be a smarter travel shopper if you follow the advice of this new book." – **AAA World**

"AN ABSOLUTE 'MUST HAVE' for international travelers." – **Midwest Library Review**

"DETAILED, AND RELEVANT, EVEN ABSORBING in places . . . The authors know their subject thoroughly, and the reader can benefit greatly from their advice and tips. They go a long way to removing any mystery or uneasiness about shopping in Asia by the neophyte." – **The Small Press Book Review**

WHAT SEASONED TRAVELERS SAY, AND STORIES THAT HAVE CHANGED LIVES

"IMMENSELY USEFUL . . . thanks for sharing the fruits of your incredibly thorough research. You saved me hours of time and put me in touch with the best." – **C.N.**, DeKalb, Illinois

"FABULOUS! I've just returned from my third shopping trip to Southeast Asia in three years. This book, which is now wrinkled, torn, and looking much abused, has been my bible for the past three years. All your suggestions (pre-trip) and information was so great. When I get ready to go again, my 'bible,' even though tattered and torn, will accompany me again! Thanks again for all your wonderful knowledge, and for sharing it!" – **D.P.**, Havertown, Pennsylvania

"I LOVE IT. I've read a lot of travel books, and of all the books of this nature, this is the best I've ever read. Especially for first timers, the how-to information is invaluable." – **A.K.**, Portland, Oregon

"THE BEST TRAVEL BOOK I'VE EVER READ. Believe me, I know my travel books!" – **S.T.**, Washington, DC

"MANY MANY THANKS for your wonderful, useful travel guide! You have done a tremendous job. It is so complete and precise and full of neat info." – **K.H.**, Seattle, Washington

"FABULOUS BOOK! I just came back from Hong Kong, Thailand, and Singapore and found your book invaluable. Every place you recommended I found wonderful quality shopping. Send me another copy for my friend in Singapore who was fascinated with it." – **M.G.**, Escondido, California

"THIS IS MY FIRST FAN LETTER TO A BOOK . . . you made our trip to Indonesia more special than I can ever say. I not only carried it in my backpack everyday, I shared it with everyone I met, including a friend in Hong Kong, who liked it so much he kept it and I had to go out and buy another copy for myself when I got back stateside. The book taught us the customs, and through your teachings on how to bargain, I would even draw crowds to watch the Westerner bargain, and some wonderful chats afterwards, always starting off with 'You good bargainer. Where you from?' It was a wonderful trip and we credit your book for making it so. Thank you from my husband and myself, and everyone else we shared your book with." – **N.H.**, New York, New York

"YOU SAVED ME . . . hurry up with the next book so I can find out what I did wrong in Burma!" – **N.H.**, Chiang Mai, Thailand

"I FURNISHED MY HOME IN FLORIDA using your wonderful books. What countries are you doing next?" – **A.A.**, New York City

"I WANT YOU TO KNOW HOW MUCH I ENJOYED YOUR BOOK.
Like many people, I picked up a ton of guide books to China before we took off on our trip in May. However, yours was totally unique, and it was not until we had finished our trip that I fully appreciated everything you covered. It was also the only guidebook I took with us. Your book was the only one that mentioned the Painter's Village in Chongqing. When we arrived in Chongqing early in the morning, our guide told me the village was included in the tour, but several people wanted to skip it and go to the zoo. Fortunately, I was able to lobby the many art lovers on the tour by showing them what you had to say about the village and we did end up visiting it. It was a lovely day and the flowers were in bloom in the gardens surrounding the village. We were greeted warmly and enjoyed visiting some of the artists. I purchased two numbered prints and, although I did not meet the artist, I did get his business card. Once home, the prints were framed and I took a picture of them and wrote to the artist to see what he could tell me about them. Imagine my surprise when several weeks later I received an e-mail from him. His mother and father, both famous artists, lived in the village and his mother had forwarded my letter to their son who now lives in Tokyo. He is a well known illustrator . . . We have been corresponding by e-mail for nearly a year and I have been helping him with his English and in doing his website in English . . . We are looking forward to the day when we can have him visit us in California. Thank you for leading us to one of the highlights of Chongqing for without that experience we would not have found a new and valued friend who has taught us much about China and life under Mao." – **C.S.**, California

"I'VE USED YOUR BOOKS FOR YEARS – *earlier, the book on shopping in Thailand was wonderful and more recently your best of India has been very useful.*" – **S.M.**, Prince George, British Columbia, Canada

"I WOULD JUST LIKE TO SAY HOW MUCH I ENJOY YOUR SE-RIES. *I have been an avid shopper and traveler for many years and it has often been difficult finding even a decent chapter on shopping, let alone an entire book. Your guides are a wonderful contribution to the industry.*" – **H.P.**, Honolulu, Hawaii

"GREAT! *I followed your advice in Bangkok and Hong Kong and it was great. Thanks again.*" – **B.G.**, Los Angeles, California

"WE ADORE ASIA! *We like it better than any other part of the world . . . We have copies of your earlier editions and they are our "Asian Bibles." We also want to compliment you on doing such a masterful research job, especially on what to buy and where. Thanks to you we have some beautiful and treasured pieces from Asia. We could not have done it without your books.*" – **L.C.**, Palm Beach, Florida

"WE TOOK YOUR BOOK *(to China) and had to concur with everything you said. We could hardly believe that 80-90% discounts were in order, but we soon found out that they were!! The Friendship Stores were everything you described. Many thanks for the book, it certainly was a help.*" – **L.G.**, Adelaide, Australia

"AFTER REVIEWING MANY TRAVEL GUIDES, *I chose this book (China) to buy because it gave me not only insight to the same cities I am about to tour, but the how to's as well. With limited time in each city, I can go directly to the "best of the best" in accommodations, restaurants, sightseeing, entertaining, and shopping. It has also supplied me with advice on how to bargain!*" – an Amazon.com buyer

"WE LOVED THE GUIDE. *It's wonderful (Rio and São Paulo). We don't have anything like this in São Paulo.*" – **M.M.**, São Paulo, Brazil

"LOVE YOUR GUIDE *to India. Thanks so much.*" – **B.P.**, Minneapolis, Minnesota

"THANK YOU *so much for the wonderful shopping recommendations on Johannesburg and Namibia. I did want to let you know how grateful we were to have your recommendations with us.*" – **M.S.**, Los Angeles

"I JUST WANTED TO THANK YOU *for your shopping guide to Vietnam and Cambodia. We just spent our month-long honeymoon in Vietnam and it was very helpful to have read your book and to use it as a reference as we went along.*" – **H.F.**, San Francisco

"A MUST HAVE *read for our travel group to Vietnam.*" – **S.B.**, Maryland

"YOU TWO ARE AMAZING! *You have both added so much to our various travels by introducing us to places we never would have seen on our own. Thank you!*" – **C.N.**, DeKalb, Illinois

The Treasures and
Pleasures of Bermuda

By Ron & Caryl Krannich, Ph.Ds

TRAVEL AND INTERNATIONAL BOOKS

Best Resumes and CVs for International Jobs
The Complete Guide to International Jobs and Careers
Directory of Websites for International Jobs
International Jobs Directory
Jobs for Travel Lovers
Mayors and Managers in Thailand
Politics of Family Planning Policy in Thailand
Shopping and Traveling in Exotic Asia
Shopping in Exotic Places
Shopping in the Exotic South Pacific
Travel Planning on the Internet
Treasures and Pleasures of Australia
Treasures and Pleasures of Bali and Lombok
Treasures and Pleasures of Bermuda
Treasures and Pleasures of China
Treasures and Pleasures of Egypt
Treasures and Pleasures of Hong Kong
Treasures and Pleasures of India
Treasures and Pleasures of Indonesia
Treasures and Pleasures of Italy
Treasures and Pleasures of Mexico
Treasures and Pleasures of Paris
Treasures and Pleasures of Rio and São Paulo
Treasures and Pleasures of Santa Fe, Taos, and Albuquerque
Treasures and Pleasures of Singapore
Treasures and Pleasures of Singapore and Bali
Treasures and Pleasures of Southern Africa
Treasures and Pleasures of Thailand and Myanmar
Treasures and Pleasures of Turkey
Treasures and Pleasures of Vietnam and Cambodia

BUSINESS AND CAREER BOOKS AND SOFTWARE

101 Dynamite Answers to Interview Questions
101 Secrets of Highly Effective Speakers
201 Dynamite Job Search Letters
America's Top 100 Jobs for People Without a Four-Year Degree
America's Top Jobs for People Re-Entering the Workforce
America's Top Internet Job Sites
Best Jobs for the 21st Century
Change Your Job, Change Your Life
The Complete Guide to International Jobs and Careers
The Complete Guide to Public Employment
The Directory of Federal Jobs and Employers
Discover the Best Jobs for You!
Dynamite Salary Negotiations
Dynamite Tele-Search
The Educator's Guide to Alternative Jobs and Careers
The Ex-Offender's Job Hunting Guide
Find a Federal Job Fast!
From Air Force Blue to Corporate Gray
From Army Green to Corporate Gray
From Navy Blue to Corporate Gray
Get a Raise in 7 Days
High Impact Resumes and Letters
Nail the Cover Letter!
Nail the Job Interview!
Nail the Resume!
No One Will Hire Me!
Interview for Success
Job Hunting Guide
Job Interview Tips for People With Not-So-Hot Backgrounds
Job-Power Source and Ultimate Job Source (software)
Jobs and Careers With Nonprofit Organizations
Military Resumes and Cover Letters
Moving Out of Education
Savvy Interviewing
Savvy Networker
Savvy Resume Writer

THE TREASURES
AND PLEASURES OF

Bermuda

BEST OF THE BEST IN TRAVEL
AND SHOPPING

RON AND CARYL KRANNICH, PH.DS

IMPACT PUBLICATIONS
MANASSAS PARK, VA

ISBN: 1-57023-231-8

Library of Congress: 2005930829

Publisher: For information on Impact Publications, including current and forthcoming publications, authors, press kits, related websites, online bookstore, and submission requirements, visit www.impactpublications.com.

Publicity/Rights: For information on publicity, author interviews, and subsidary rights, contact the Media Relations Department: Tel. 703-361-7300, Fax 703-335-9486, or email info@impactpublications.com.

Sales/Distribution: All bookstore sales are handled through Impact's trade distributor: National Book Network, 15200 NBN Way, Blue Ridge Summit, PA 17214, Tel. 1-800-462-6420. All special sales and distribution inquiries should be directed to the publisher: Sales Department, IMPACT PUBLICATIONS, 9104 Manassas Drive, Suite N, Manassas Park, VA 20111-5211, Tel.703-361-7300, Fax 703-335-9486, or email info@impactpublications.com.

Contents

Liabilities and Warranties .... **xx**

Preface .... **xxi**

CHAPTER 1
**Welcome to Beautiful
and Predicable Bermuda** **1**
- Tiny and Tidy Upscale Islands   3
- Far Beyond the Caribbean   4
- Seductive and Hassle-Free   4
- Not a Typical Tourist Destination   5
- A Very Special Upscale Place   6
- Exclusive and Predictable   7
- A Prosperous Economy   8
- Getting to Know You   8
- Primary Focus on Treasures   10
- Many Appealing Pleasures   12
- Selecting the Right Place to Stay   13
- Products and Prices   14
- Organize for Bermuda   15
- Beware of Recommended Shops   16
- Expect a Rewarding Adventure   18

PART I
Smart Travel-Shopping

CHAPTER 2
Know Before You Go **21**
- A Short Story of Bermuda   21
- Climate and When to Go   23
- What to Pack and Wear   24
- Required Documents   26
- Arrival, Departure, and Customs   26
- Language and Culture   27
- Time and Business Hours   28
- Safety, Security, and Insurance   29
- Getting There   30
- Tour Groups and Packages   35
- Golf Holidays   36
- Weddings and Honeymoons   37
- Bermuda Tourist Offices Abroad   38
- Local Travel Assistance   41
- Local Transportation   42
- Touts, Hustlers, and Greedy Guides   46

- Money Matters   47
- Tipping   47
- Taxes   47
- Electricity and Water   48
- Family-Oriented Travel   48
- Festivals, Tournaments, and Shows   48
- Useful Websites   50
- Recommended Reading   51
- Anticipated Costs   52
- Cutting Your Costs   54
- Passing U.S. Customs   56

CHAPTER 3
Getting to Know You 58

- Location and Geography   59
- Limestone Construction   60
- Wealthy Waters   60
- A Statistical Profile   61
- Bermuda's Nine Parishes   62
- Bermuda's Three Communities   66

PART II
In Search of Treasures

CHAPTER 4
Shopping Smart 77

- Two Shopping Classes   78
- The Local Shopping Culture   79

CHAPTER 5
Where to Shop 85

- Hamilton   85
- St. George   86
- The Royal Naval Dockyard   87
- Hotel/Resort Shopping Arcades   88
- Shopping Centers   88
- Department Stores   89
- Markets   90
- Cruise Ship Shoppers   90

CHAPTER 6
What to Buy 92

- Jewelry   92
- Watches   93
- Perfumes and Fragrances   94
- Clothing and Accessories   94
- China, Crystal, Tableware, and Glassware   95
- Paintings, Sculptures, and Photography   96
- Crafts, Gifts, and Bermudiana   97

- Antiques and Collectibles   99
- Linens   100
- Luggage and Leather Goods   100
- Foods and Gourmet Products   100
- Liquor and Liqueurs   101

CHAPTER 7
Best Quality Shopping 102
- Hamilton's Best Shops   102
- St. George's Best Shops   119
- Royal Naval Dockyard's Best Shops   122
- Beyond the Towns   126
- 14 Special Shopping Experiences   127

PART III
In Pursuit of Pleasures

CHAPTER 8
Finding Your Best Place to Stay 131
- Costs and Bargains   132
- Selecting Your Best Location   134
- Different Types of Properties   135
- Best of the Best   145

CHAPTER 9
Dining Right 156
- A Changing Dining Scene   156
- Local Cuisine and Best Choices   157
- Dining Tips, Customs, and Issues   158
- Unique Dining Experiences   159
- Bermuda's 36 Best Restaurants   161
- The Quick Restaurant Directory   170
- Pubs, Bars, and Nightly Entertainment   171

CHAPTER 10
What More to See and Do 172
- Sightseeing   172
- Hiking and Birding   177
- Exploring Coves, Bays, and Beaches   177
- Playing Golf and Tennis   179
- Participating in Water Sports   181
- Riding Trails and Beaches By Horse   188
- Being Rejuvenated At Spas   188
- Enjoying Entertainment   190

Index 195
The Authors 200
Feedback and Recommendations 204
More Treasures and Pleasures 205

Liabilities and Warranties

WHILE WE HAVE attempted to provide accurate information, please keep in mind that names, addresses, phone and fax numbers, e-mails, and website URLs do change, and shops, restaurants, and hotels do move, go out of business, or change ownership and management. Indeed, as we go to press, Trimingham's department store, which was a 163 year old institution in Bermuda, closed its door for good. Such changes do occur even in slow changing and highly predictable Bermuda. We regret any inconvenience such changes may cause to your travel and shopping plans.

Inclusion of shops, restaurants, hotels, and other hospitality providers in this book in no way implies guarantees nor endorsements by either the authors or publisher. Recommendations are provided solely for your reference. The honesty and reliability of shops can best be ensured by **you**. It's okay to be a little paranoid when travel-shopping. Indeed, always ask the right questions, request proper receipts and documents, use credit cards, take photos, and observe our 16 shopping smart rules in Chapter 4 as well as on our companion website: www.ishoparoundtheworld.com.

The Treasures and Pleasures of Bermuda provides numerous tips on how you can best experience a trouble-free adventure. As in any unfamiliar place or situation, and regardless of how trustworthy strangers may appear, the watchwords are always the same – *"watch your wallet!"* If it seems too good to be true, it probably is. Any *"unbelievable deals"* should be treated as such.

Preface

WELCOME TO THE TREASURES and pleasures of beautiful Bermuda. Join us as we explore this island's many appealing shops, restaurants, hotels, sites, and entertainment. We'll put you in touch with the best of the best Bermuda has to offer visitors. We'll take you to popular tourist places, but we won't linger long since combining great shopping with terrific dining, sightseeing, and activities is our passion. If you follow us to the end, you'll discover there is a lot more to Bermuda, and travel in general, than taking tours, visiting popular sites, and acquiring an unwelcome weight gain attendant with new on-the-road dining habits.

Bermuda offers wonderful travel-shopping experiences for those who know what to look for and where to go. While it is especially popular its pink beaches, lush golf courses, and numerous watersports and tournaments, for us Bermuda is an important shopping destination offering many attractive imported goods and local products as well as excellent restaurants and resort hotels. Its people, products, sights, and activities may truly enrich your life.

If you are familiar with our other Impact Guides, you know this will not be another standard travel guide to history, culture, and sightseeing in Bermuda. Our approach to travel is very different. We operate from a particular perspective, and we frequently show our attitude rather than just present you with the sterile "travel facts." While we seek good travel value and show you how to significantly cut this high cost of travel to Bermuda (Chapter 2), we're not budget travelers in search of cheap travel experiences.

> ❑ Our approach to travel is very different from most guidebooks – we offer a very different travel perspective and we frequently show our attitude.
>
> ❑ We're not obsessed with local history, culture, and sightseeing. We get just enough history and sightseeing to make our travels interesting rather than obsessive.
>
> ❑ Through shopping, we meet many interesting and talented people and learn a great deal about their country.
>
> ❑ We're street people who love "the chase" and the serendipity that comes with our style of travel.

At the same time, we're not obsessed with local history, culture, and sightseeing. We get just enough of this to make our travels interesting rather than obsessive. When we discuss history, culture, and sightseeing, we do so in abbreviated form, highlighting what we consider to be the essentials. We also assume interested travelers will have that information covered from other resources.

As you'll quickly discover, we're very focused – we're in search of quality shopping and travel. Rather than spend eight hours a day sightseeing, we may only devote two hours to sightseeing and another six hours learning about the local shopping scene. As such, we're very people- and product-oriented when we travel. Through shopping, we meet many interesting and talented people and learn a great deal about their country.

What we really enjoy doing, and think we do it well, is shop. For us, shopping makes for great travel adventure and contributes to local development. Indeed, we're street people who love "the chase" and the serendipity that comes with our style of travel. We especially enjoy discovering quality products, meeting local artists and crafts people, getting good deals, unraveling new travel and shopping rules, forming friendships with local business people, staying in special places, and dining in great restaurants where we often meet the talented chefs and visit their fascinating kitchens. Like Winston Churchill and many other travelers, our travel philosophy is very simple and focused: "*My needs are very simple – I simply want the best of every-*

thing." When we travel, we seek out the best of the best – just like we often do back home.

The chapters that follow represent a particular travel perspective. We purposefully decided to write more than just another travel guide with a few pages on shopping. While some travel guides include a brief and usually dated section on the "whats" and "wheres" of shopping, we saw a need to also explain the "how-tos" of shopping in Bermuda, which we clearly do in Chapter 4. Such a book would both educate and guide you through Bermuda's shopping maze as well as put you in contact with the best of the best in restaurants, accommodations, sightseeing, and other activities. It would be a combination travel-shopping guide designed for people in search of quality travel experiences.

The perspective we develop throughout this book is based on our belief that traveling should be more than just another adventure in eating, sleeping, sightseeing, and taking pictures of unfamiliar places. Whenever possible, we attempt to bring to life the fact that Bermuda has real people and interesting products that you, the visitor, will find exciting. It has many talented artists, craftspeople, and entrepreneurs. When you leave Bermuda, you will take with you not only some unique experiences and memories but also quality products that you will certainly appreciate for years to come.

We have not hesitated to make qualitative judgments about the best of the best in Bermuda. If we just presented you with travel and shopping information, we would do you a disservice by not sharing our discoveries, both good and bad. While we know that our judgments may not be valid for everyone, we offer them as reference points from which you can make your own decisions. Our major emphasis is on quality shopping, accommodations, dining, sightseeing, outdoor activities, entertainment, and in that order. We look for shops which offer excellent quality and styles. If you share our concern for quality shopping, as well as fine restaurants, hotels, and resorts, you will find many of our recommendations useful in planning and implementing your own Bermuda adventure. Best of all, you'll engage in what has become a favorite pastime for many of today's discerning travelers – lifestyle shopping!

Throughout this book we have included "tried and tested" shopping information. We make judgments based upon our experience – not on judgments or sales pitches from others. Our research method was quite simple: we did a great deal of shopping and we looked for quality products. We acquired some choice items, and gained valuable knowledge in the process. However, we could not make purchases in every shop nor do we have any guarantee that your experiences will be the same as ours. Shops close, ownership or management changes, and the shop you visit may not be the same as the one we shopped. The recent (July 2005) demise, after 163 years, of the venerated Trimingham's retail complex testifies to this fact of commercial life. So use this information as a starting point, but ask questions and make your own judgments before you buy. For related information on shopping in Bermuda, including many of our recommended shops, please visit our companion website: www.ishoparoundtheworld.com. For special deals on hotels, cruises, and travel packages, see our discount travel website: www.travel-smarter.com.

Whatever you do, enjoy Bermuda. While you need not *"shop 'til you drop,"* at least shop this place well and with the confidence that you are getting good quality and value. Don't just limit yourself to small items that will fit into your suitcase or pass up something you love because of shipping concerns. Consider acquiring larger items that can be safely and conveniently shipped back home. Indeed, shipping is something that needs to be *arranged* rather than lamented or avoided.

We wish to thank the many people who contributed to this book. They include many shop owners and personnel who took time to educate us on their products and the local shopping, dining, and travel scenes.

We wish you well as you prepare for Bermuda's many treasures and pleasures. The book is designed to be used in the streets, roads, waterways, and beaches of Bermuda. If you plan your journey according to the first three chapters and navigate Bermuda based on the next seven chapters, you should have an absolutely marvelous time beyond just sun and sand. You'll discover some exciting places, acquire some choice items, and return home with many fond memories of a terrific adventure. If you put this book to use, it will indeed become your best friend – and passport – to the many unique treasures and pleasures of Bermuda. Enjoy!

Ron and Caryl Krannich
krannich@impactpublications.com

1

Welcome to Beautiful and Predictable Bermuda

WELCOME TO ONE OF the world's most beautiful, exclusive, and romantic places that often redefines the notions of "travel" and "vacation." If you like colorful, clean, lush green, sunny, friendly, sedate, efficient, civil, laid back, and service-oriented islands – centered around inviting beaches, lovely sunsets, distinctive architecture, and upscale shopping, fine dining, golfing, water sports, fishing, and tournaments – Bermuda may be the perfect place for you. It's a popular travel destination that has few of the tourist trappings found in most other islands around the world. Here you can just enjoy yourself in a hassle-free environment that exudes great service and sophisticated island ambience.

However romanticized and enthusiastically portrayed in cruise literature and travel brochures, Bermuda is not for everyone. It can be boring for some but the perfect paradise for others. For island lovers, it's a very special place for those who love to escape to a very pristine and beautiful world where they can be pampered and rejuvenated in style.

For those who fall in love with this place, Bermuda becomes their special little paradise where they enjoy returning to again

I

and again – because it is so **predictable**. Indeed, after a few days here, you'll know what to expect, and you'll seldom be surprised with the unexpected.

Tiny and Tidy Upscale Islands

Located only two hours by air from Toronto, Boston, New York, Baltimore/Washington, Atlanta, and Fort Lauderdale, Bermuda is easily accessible from eastern North America for an extended weekend adventure or a more lengthy vacation, honeymoon, or business trip. Cruise ships departing from Boston, New York, or Baltimore take less than two days to make the more or less 800-mile journey to the islands.

Bermuda often appears larger in prospective visitors' minds than the actual reality they encounter on the ground. This fishhook-shaped island chain, fused by landfill and bridges and running 21 miles in length and two miles at its widest point, occupies a 22-square-mile landmass that is only one-third the size of Washington, DC. The local population

> ❑ Bermuda redefines the notions of "travel" and "vacation."
>
> ❑ Expect to encounter a hassle-free environment along with sophisticated island ambience.
>
> ❑ While not for everyone, Bermuda is a very predictable place to visit.
>
> ❑ Bermuda often seems much larger than reality.

of fewer than 62,000 annually hosts 550,000 visitors (220,000 by cruise ship) who primarily come from the United States (85 percent), Canada (5 percent), and the United Kingdom (5 percent). The major city, the capital of Hamilton, has a population of only 1,100. Since Hamilton is the main cruise ship destination, with ships docking in the center of the town, its population can fluctuate considerably (2,500) on days when ships are in port. The second largest population center, the quaint historical town of St. George on the east end of the island chain, has a population of a few hundred. Cruise ships also stop here and at the Royal Naval Dockyard at the west tip of the island.

By most any standards, Bermuda is a very small place that can be leisurely covered in a day or two. Its many hills, winding two-lane roads, slow moving traffic, and pleasant and distracting scenery make Bermuda seem much larger than reality. Don't expect to just zip from one end of the island chain to the other within an hour. It takes some time, at least a lazy half day of island exploring – as well as a good attitude and a sense of leisure – to make this journey by road or water. Along the way you'll see Bermuda's unique architecture and colorful buildings and view lovely beaches, harbors, and resorts. You may even catch a beachfront wedding along the way.

Far Beyond the Caribbean

Some visitors mistakenly think Bermuda is either part of the Caribbean or merely an extension of the northern Caribbean islands. Nothing could be further from the truth. One of the world's most isolated island groups, Bermuda lies 950 miles north of Nassau, Bahamas, 650 miles east of Cape Hatteras, North Carolina, and 3,460 miles southwest of London. It's literally in the middle of nowhere in the Atlantic Ocean.

If you are used to visiting the Caribbean islands, you may be pleasantly surprised by the travel culture of Bermuda, especially the near absence of pestering touts, hustlers, beggars, and poverty. This is a very neat, clean, and well regulated island, with local businessmen wearing distinctive Bermuda shorts complemented with knee socks and a jacket and necktie. Given Bermuda's low crime rate and healthy economy, most visitors feel relatively safe and secure here. Like most of the local population, even the taxi drivers are a class operation – relatively well educated, extensively traveled, honest, and helpful.

> *A very friendly, civil, and upscale island, most visitors feel relatively safe and secure in Bermuda.*

This is a very friendly, civil, and upscale island that is primarily oriented toward business, families, beaches, shopping, golf, tennis, water sports, and international sporting events. Unlike most Caribbean islands where tourism is the number one industry and employer and where poverty is readily apparent, in Bermuda international business, especially the lucrative insurance and reinsurance industry, is the number one foreign exchange earner that has contributed to Bermuda's high cost of living – the second highest in the world. Accountants are in much demand! With near full employment, many individuals working in the travel and hospitality industry are actually seasonal "guest workers" from the United States, Canada, United Kingdom, Europe, and Asia.

Seductive and Hassle-Free

Bermuda's seductive natural beauty, from pink sand beaches and iridescent turquoise waters to beautiful gardens, romantic sunsets, and alfresco waterfront restaurants, captivates many visitors who enjoy being left alone to just enjoy their holiday without the many hassles attendant with visiting some foreign destinations. As a guest, you are treated well and with utmost

respect. Hire a taxi to tour the island and you'll quickly make a local friend who will impress you with his knowledge of Bermuda and other places he has traveled.

Swingers may be disappointed since in Bermuda they won't find much lively night time entertainment and decadent youth activities beyond dining in restaurants, visiting a pub, or taking in one of the island's few nightclubs and casinos. Like many visitors, you may come to enjoy quiet breezy evenings where only the loud chorus of tiny chirping tree frogs breaks the evening solace. Indeed, you may quickly fall in love with Bermuda's perfect evenings! Since most restaurants close by 10:30pm, early to bed may become your nightly routine here.

Whatever your travel interests or plans, Bermuda is definitely worth your consideration. But there are a few things you should know about this unique place as you plan your ideal Bermudian adventure. A little knowledge will help you enjoy the best of the best Bermuda has to offer its many visitors. Armed with this knowledge, you should be well prepared to make the most of your Bermudian holiday.

Not a Typical Tourist Destination

If you are used to traveling to places where you stand out as a tourist, often as an object of exploitation, you may be surprised how well you blend into the local landscape in Bermuda. In fact, this is one of the few places we have visited where we do not feel like a tourist. This is a very laid back, orderly, and civil place where visitors are treated as respected guests who normally reciprocate by observing local rules on dress and behavior. Indeed, you are expected to be on your best travel behavior – civil, respectful, polite, and observant of rules. Since good manners are very important in Bermuda, you should always mind your manners wherever you go!

With buildings painted in pastel colors and boasting a unique residential architectural style topped with limestone slate roofs, Bermuda is picture-postcard neat, clean, colorful, and orderly. If you are used to traveling to places that are relatively disorganized, chaotic, noisy, and unkempt, where annoying touts pester and exploit tourists, you'll find Bermuda to be in a different class altogether. It has none of such irritating nonsense. Boasting a full employment economy, with much of it geared toward upscale and discerning travelers, Bermuda has few idle hands to prey on tourists.

> ❑ Good manners are very important in Bermuda.
>
> ❑ Bermuda is geared toward upscale and discerning travelers.
>
> ❑ Bermuda is picture-postcard neat, clean, orderly, and colorful.

Bermuda is a unique oasis where tourists feel unusually safe, secure, stress-free, and pampered. Indeed, it's rare to learn of crimes committed against tourists. The major safety issues are driving a motor scooter, jogging along the narrow, winding roads, or being stung by a man–o–war.

A Very Special Upscale Place

Bermuda is a very special place that disproportionately appeals to upscale travelers in search of a relatively quiet and relaxing holiday, including thousands of honeymooners. While many visitors tend to return again and again to this appealing island, it's not for everyone, especially those in search of an active holiday complete with lots of glitzy nightlife. It's also not a good destination for the budget-minded who quickly discover this place can be very expensive and thus unforgiving of travelers in search of cheap places to eat and sleep. Budget travelers tend to arrive on cruise ships where their food and accommodations are already prepaid.

> ❑ Bermuda is a popular business meeting, honeymoon, golf, cruise, and shopping destination.
>
> ❑ Shopping is primarily found in Hamilton, St. George, and the Royal Naval Dockyard.
>
> ❑ Except for cruise ship passengers, Bermuda is not an attractive destination for budget travelers.

Bermuda is especially popular as a business meeting and wedding and honeymoon destination, and many cruise lines regularly stop here for two or three days of shopping and sightseeing. Independent travelers find the islands especially appealing for golf, fishing, boating, scuba diving, snorkeling, hiking, lying on the beach, or just relaxing at one of the island's many resorts.

Boasting a rather sedate nightlife, most of Bermuda's treasures and pleasures are found during the day, from 9am to 5pm. Nightlife tends to be centered on dining from 7 to 10pm at one of the many appealing restaurants or pubs.

If you live a very stressful life, you'll find Bermuda especially appealing. Once you arrive, there's not much you need to do or think about. Bermuda is so laid back and easygoing that your major decisions for the day may center on which beach or golf course to visit, where to go scuba diving or snorkeling, and where to have lunch and dinner. While Bermuda is a major business center for the offshore insurance and reinsurance industry, which is centered in the commercial buildings in downtown Hamilton and adjacent hotels that function as meeting centers, you would not know this from the leisure atmosphere of the city and island.

One thing most visitors have in common is shopping. Primarily centered in the town of Hamilton and to a lesser extent historic St. George and the Royal Naval Dockyard, shopping has a distinct resort character with clothing, watches, jewelry, china, and art taking center stage. You can easily spend a couple of days browsing through the island's many upscale boutiques, department stores, shops, and galleries.

Exclusive and Predictable

But this all comes at a price, which for some travelers is a major deterrent to visiting Bermuda. Simply put, Bermuda is not a cheap destination for independent budget travelers. You can easily travel to Asia or Latin America and spend less for your stay. Bermuda most likely appeals to individuals who do not like to travel to unpredictable places, preferring a familiar place where they can relax without the hassles, bright lights, and noise of many travel destinations. And they pay for this exclusive and predictable playground.

While not as expensive as London and Paris, nonetheless, Bermuda is pricy. Backpackers are conspicuously absent in Bermuda, and for good reason. Indeed, one senses the high cost of visiting Bermuda guarantees that the well-heeled continue to visit this pristine playground. Except for cruise ships that visit this place at bargain prices, Bermuda is definitely not a good destination for budget travelers, although you can definitely minimize your costs in Bermuda, as we note at the end of Chapter 2.

A Prosperous Economy

Many American and European corporations operate lucrative insurance and reinsurance businesses from Bermuda. In fact, over 10,000 international businesses are registered here, and over 300 maintain offices in and around downtown Hamilton. A relatively unobtrusive industry for most tourists, nonetheless, at the western end of Hamilton you will see the many office complexes and banks that house this industry. The nearby Fairmont Princess Hotel, which hosts many workshops, seminars, and conferences for this industry, is the island's major business hotel and resort.

Tourism constitutes Bermuda's second largest industry. Most business and leisure travelers find a very well developed first-class tourist infrastructure centered on hotels, resorts, restaurants, golf courses, beaches, and water sports.

Getting to Know You

Located 650 miles east of the North Carolina coast and 774 miles southeast of New York City, Bermuda consists of 138 limestone islands, of which only a few are inhabitable. The main island, Great Bermuda Island, is home to the capital city of Hamilton. Several adjacent islands are connected by bridges and landfill to make up a chain of islands or archipelago that resembles a fishhook and which is collectively known by most visitors as Bermuda. Taken together, these islands form a narrow landmass of 22 square miles that stretches for 21 miles from one end to the other.

Bermuda's mild sub-tropical climate makes it an attractive destination most of the year. However, since it is too cold for swimming in the winter and most airlines do not regularly service Bermuda during the low season winter months, many resorts close during that period. The best times to visit Bermuda are during the spring, summer, and fall.

As we noted earlier, Bermuda is not part of the Caribbean, which lies much farther south. Nor does it have the look and feel of a Caribbean island. Bermuda is unique, with its own personality and attractions – beautiful pink sand beaches, lovely flora, pastel colored buildings, a friendly and courteous population, and one of the highest standards of living in the world.

One of the major attractions of Bermuda is its people, who trace their heritage from North America, England, Africa, the Azores, and the West Indies. This is a very friendly, well edu- cated, traveled, and accommo- dating population whose Bermuda's local language and culture has a strong British influ- ence. Indeed, you will sometimes feel you are on a British island. Approximately 60 percent of the population is black and 40 per- cent is white. Given the island's booming business and tourist economy, unemployment is vir- tually unheard of in Bermuda.

> ❏ Bermuda has a mild sub- tropical climate.
>
> ❏ The best times to visit are spring, summer, and fall.
>
> ❏ Bermuda's population of nearly 62,000 is very friendly, well educated, traveled, and accommo- dating.
>
> ❏ Most resorts are concen- trated along the southern shore.
>
> ❏ Tourists are prohibited from renting and driving cars.

For administrative purposes, the Great Bermuda Island is di- vided into a series of nine par- ishes (see map on page 63) that run from east to west:

- St. George's
- Hamilton
- Smith's
- Devonshire
- Pembroke
- Paget
- Warwick
- Southampton
- Sandys

Most resorts and cottage colonies are concentrated on the south- ern shore in the parishes of Southampton, Warwick, Paget, Devonshire, and Smith's. The main urban shopping centers are found in the parishes of Pembroke (Hamilton), St. George's (St. George), and Sandys (Royal Naval Dockyard). We examine each of these parishes and towns in Chapter 3.

Getting around Bermuda is a combination of convenience and inconvenience. Since tourists are prohibited both from renting and driving cars, their transportation options are limited to taxis, buses, motorbikes, bicycles, and boats. While permitted, renting a motorbike also can be dangerous given the winding and nar- row two-lane roads. Many inexperienced tourists have motor- bike accidents. Taxis are the most convenient means of transpor- tation, but they are expensive. Buses are somewhat inconvenient and less expensive, but they are by no means cheap. A boat service regularly runs from the Royal Naval Dockyard on the northwestern tip of the island to Hamilton in the center of the island – one of the most convenient and pleasurable ways to

Primary Focus on Treasures

The Treasures and Pleasures of Bermuda is a different kind of travel book for a very special type of traveler – lifestyle travel-shoppers. It doesn't present the typical smorgasbord of history, culture, popular sites, and sightseeing tours, nor does it promote cheap travel or the latest travel fads. You'll find plenty of excellent travel guides that already cover such popular travel preferences. We, on the other hand, primarily focus on quality shopping (treasures) as well as dining, accommodations, sightseeing, and entertainment (pleasures).

Like we did, we want you to experience the best of the best Bermuda has to offer discriminating travelers. Accordingly, we uncover a different slice of travel reality – shopping for local treasures and experiencing the best in local pleasures. When, for example, most tourists spend four hours sightseeing, we may spend only one hour sightseeing and three hours sleuthing through Bermuda's many quality shops. We leave with lots of photos of both the sights and vendors, a few choice purchases, and a wider range of experiences than the other sightseers. We mine destinations for **both** treasures and pleasures.

The book is designed to provide you with the necessary knowledge and skills to enjoy Bermuda's many wonderful treasures and pleasures. Going beyond the typical tourist attractions, we focus in part II on how you can acquire Bermuda's many treasures by becoming a savvy shopper. We especially designed the book with three major considerations in mind:

- Learn a great deal about Bermuda's society and culture by meeting its many talented artists, craftspeople, and shopkeepers and exploring major studios, shops, and shopping centers.

- Do quality shopping for items having good value.

- Discover unique items that can be integrated into your home and/or wardrobe.

As you will quickly discover, this is not a book on how to find great bargains in Bermuda, although we do show you how to find good deals in Chapter 4. Nor are we preoccupied with shopping for expensive brand-name luxury goods – imported from the United Kingdom, Europe, or North America – which appear in many shops of Hamilton. Many of these items tend to be overpriced and reflect an "imported" shopping culture.

> ❏ We primarily focus on shopping for local treasures and experiencing the best of local pleasures.
>
> ❏ The number one pleasure is the Bermudian people themselves.
>
> ❏ Bermuda boasts the world's largest number of golf courses per square mile!

While you will find some bargains in Bermuda, this book focuses on quality shopping for unique items that will retain their value. As such, we are less concerned with shopping to save money and to get great bargains than with shopping for local and unique products that can be taken home, integrated into one's wardrobe and home decor, and appreciated for years to come. Rather than purchase an inexpensive piece of jewelry or art, we prefer finding the best of what there is available and selectively choosing those items we both enjoy and can afford. If, for example, you buy a single piece of exquisite jewelry or a special work of art that fits nicely into your wardrobe or home, chances are these purchases will last much longer, and you will appreciate them for many more years to come than if you purchased several cheap pieces of jewelry or tourist kitsch that quickly lose their value and your interest.

Our general shopping rule is this: *A "good buy" is one that results in acquiring something that has good value; when in doubt, go for quality because quality items will hold their value and you will enjoy them much more in the long run.*

Indeed, some of our most prized possessions from our shopping sojourns around the world are those we felt we could not afford at the time, but we purchased them nonetheless because we knew they represented excellent quality and thus we would continue to value them. In retrospect our decision to buy quality items was a wise one because we still love these items today.

We have learned one other important lesson from shopping abroad: good craftsmanship everywhere in the world is declining due to the increased labor costs, lack of interest among young people in pursuing traditional craft skills, and erosion of traditional cultures. Therefore, any items requiring extensive hand labor and traditional craft skills – such as woodcarvings, textiles, silver and bronze work, ceramics, furniture, basketry, and handcrafted jewelry – are outstanding values today, because many of these items are disappearing as fewer craftspeople are trained in producing quality products.

Throughout this book we attempt to identify the best quality shopping in Bermuda. This does not mean we have discovered the cheapest shopping nor the best bargains. Our search for unique shopping and quality items that retain their value in the long run means many of our recommended shops may initially appear expensive. But they offer top value or unique items that you may not find in other shops.

Many Appealing Pleasures

The second half of our travel equation consists of Bermuda's pleasures, which are outlined in Part IV. And Bermuda has many unforgettable pleasures that will remind you of this delightful place for many years to come. The number one pleasure is the Bermudian people themselves, an exceptionally friendly, cultured, well mannered, and accommodating people. You will especially like Bermuda because of its people. Bermuda's other pleasures include its many lovely beaches, landscapes, sightseeing attractions, sunsets, golf courses, water sports (snorkeling, scuba diving, fishing, parasailing, sailing, water-skiing), hiking, biking, hotels, and restaurants. If you are a golfer, Bermuda will not disappoint you with its many fine golf courses. Indeed, it boasts the world's largest number of golf courses per square mile!

Perhaps you just want to come to Bermuda and take it easy –

do nothing other than be pampered at a lovely resort or spa or spend part of your day golfing or sport fishing. You could get bored here if you don't plan to sample enough of Bermuda's travel pleasures. Indeed, there's plenty to see and do in Bermuda to occupy at least four to six days. Spending more than a week in Bermuda may be too much time for many visitors who seem to run out of things to see and do.

Bermuda has several fine properties to sample, from the two huge Fairmont Princess resort hotels (the Fairmont Hamilton Princess on the edge of downtown Hamilton and the Fairmont Southampton in Southampton Parish) to Elbow Beach Bermuda in Paget Parish and the Pink Beach Club and Cottages in Smith's Parish.

If you judge a place by its food, you'll be pleasantly surprised by the many good restaurants serving everything from local seafood to fine French, Italian, Mediterranean, and international cuisine. In the absence of many nightclubs, discos, and casinos, Bermuda's evening entertainment tends to center on dining – picking a good restaurant and lingering for two or three hours. Some of Bermuda's best restaurants are also found in its best hotels. If where you stay and what you eat are major travel concerns, then you should enjoy our many "best of the best" hotel and restaurant recommendations in Chapters 8 and 9.

Selecting the Right Place to Stay

While Bermuda is a relatively small island, where you decide to stay can make a difference in how well you enjoy your visit. It also will impact on your local transportation budget and determine whether or not you will experience many of Bermuda's fine restaurants. If, for example, you primarily want to enjoy the beaches and take in some golf, consider staying at one of the major resorts on the southern coast, such as the Fairmont Southampton, Elbow Beach Bermuda, The Reefs, or Pink Beach Club and Cottages. These properties also have good restaurants, spas, and other activities to keep you active while staying at their resorts. The map on page 63 includes these properties.

If you are more interested in shopping and dining, you may want to stay closer to the city of Hamilton where you will find most of the island's shops and major restaurants. Here, the waterfront Fairmont Hamilton Princess resort hotel is a good choice. It also provides a complementary shuttle service to its sister property in Southampton, which has a golf course, beach, a spa, family programs, and fine dining restaurants. Alternatively, try the smaller Rosedon or Waterloo House properties in Hamilton.

If you arrive by cruise ship and your ship docks in Hamilton, you're all set for shopping and sampling the town's many cafes and restaurants. If you dock in St. George or the Royal Naval Dockyard – the island's two alternative ports – your shopping and dining alternatives will be limited because of the small size of these communities. If time permits, try to visit Hamilton, where you will find the most shopping and dining opportunities.

Wherever you do stay, you can easily arrange to get around the island by taxi through the front desk of your hotel or resort. While expensive ($10 to $25 a ride and/or $30 an hour with a three-hour minimum), especially when you must take them at night when buses do not run, taxis are the most convenient way to get around the island. Renting a motorbike is neither cheap (expect to pay $65 to $75 a day) nor safe, but they are convenient for getting around on your own. Buses and ferries cost $4.00 to $4.50 a ride, although you can purchase unlimited one-, three-, four-, and seven-day bus and ferry passes that will reduce your pre-ride costs. The most popular pass is a three-day pass for $28.00. We detail these alternatives in Chapter 2.

Products and Prices

Bermuda has a reputation for being an expensive travel destination, which is generally true. Given the high cost of living in Bermuda, everything from food and hotels to transportation and shopping is costly. Despite what you may be told in Bermuda, shoppers from the United States can usually do better on prices back home than in Bermuda. Also, Bermuda is not a duty-free destination. However, many treasures you discover in Bermuda are not available back home, because they are either made in Bermuda or imported from the United Kingdom and Europe. Consequently, you will find many unique items in the shops of Bermuda, especially in case of jewelry, watches, art, and clothing.

At the same time, cruise ship passengers are often avid shoppers who quickly deplete the inventories of some shops, especially those that offer unique items. While you may be able to do some comparative shopping in Bermuda, be aware that something you may fall in love with may quickly disappear when so many other shoppers are around.

Our general rule for doing comparative shopping in places with many other foreign shoppers is this: *If you see something you love, buy it now; if you wait to find it elsewhere, chances are you won't find a comparable item, and the one you left behind may be gone when you return!* Indeed, too much comparative shopping can lead to disappointments.

Organize for Bermuda

The chapters that follow primarily take you into Bermuda's best shops, hotels, restaurants, and attractions. In so doing, we've attempted to construct a completely user-friendly book that first focuses on the shopping process but also includes the best of Bermuda's many other treasures and pleasures.

The chapters are organized as one would organize and implement a travel and shopping adventure to Bermuda. Each chapter incorporates basic details, including names and addresses, to get your adventure started in the islands.

Indexes and a table of contents are especially important to us and others who believe a travel book is first and foremost a guide to unfamiliar places. Therefore, our index includes both subjects and shops: the shops are printed in bold for ease of reference; the table of contents is elaborated in detail so it, too, can be used as another handy reference index for subjects and products. By using the table of contents and index together, you can access most any information from this book.

The remainder of this book is divided into three parts and nine additional chapters. The two chapters in Part I – **"Smart Travel-Shopping"** – assist you in preparing for your shopping adventure by focusing on the "how-to's" of traveling. Chapter 2, "Know Before You Go," takes you through the basics of getting to and enjoying your stay in Bermuda, including transportation, customs, immigration, money, tours, cruise ships, safety, costs, and budgeting. Chapter 3, "Getting to Know You," introduces you to the highlights of Bermuda's nine parishes and three communities.

The three chapters in Part II – **"In Search of Treasures"** – introduce Bermuda's shopping world by examining critical "what" and "how" questions. Chapter 4, "Shopping Smart," prepares you for Bermuda's distinct shopping culture where knowing important shopping rules, including tips on buying jewelry, observations on cruise ship shoppers, and commission games, are keys to becoming an effective shopper. Chapter 5, "Where to Shop" outlines Bermuda's major shopping areas along with maps of each location. Chapter 6, "What to Buy," surveys the major products you will encounter in your Bermuda shopping adventure as well as identifies the best shops for quality and value. Chapter 8 "Best Quality Shopping," identifies 90 shops we have found to be some of Bermuda's best as well as 14 special shopping experiences.

The three chapters in Part III – **"In Pursuit of Pleasures"** – examine Bermuda's best hotels, restaurants, sightseeing, sports activities, and entertainment.

Beware of Recommended Shops

Throughout this book we concentrate on providing you with the necessary **knowledge and skills** to become an effective shopper in Bermuda. We would prefer not recommending and listing specific shops and services – even though we have favorite shops we use when shopping in Bermuda. We know the pitfalls of doing so. Shops that offered excellent products and service during one of our visits, for example, may change ownership, personnel, and policies from one year to another. In addition, our shopping preferences may not be the same as yours. We believe it is much more important for you to **know how to shop** than to be told where to shop.

Our major concern is to outline your shopping options in Bermuda, show you where to locate the best shopping areas, and share some useful shopping strategies and tips that you can use anywhere, regardless of particular shops we or others may suggest. Armed with this knowledge and some basic shopping skills, you will be better prepared to locate your own shops and determine which ones offer the best products and service in relation to your own shopping needs and travel goals.

However, we also recognize the "need to know" when shopping on limited time in Bermuda. While this is a small island chain that you can cover in a few days, you should benefit from reliable advice on the what, where, and how of quickly shopping in Bermuda. Indeed, we hope to save you a great deal of time and money by cutting through Bermuda's shopping maze and focusing on the really good shops and buys. Therefore, throughout this book, we list the names and locations of various shops we have found to offer good quality or unique products. In some cases we have purchased items in these shops and can also recommend them for service and reliability. But in most cases we surveyed shops to determine the type and quality of products offered without making purchases. To buy in every shop would be beyond our budget, as well as our home storage capabilities! When we do list specific shops, we do so only as reference points from which to start your shopping.

We do not guarantee the quality of products or service. In many cases our recommended shops offer exceptional quality, honesty, and service. While we believe you should have the advantage of this information, we also caution you to again evaluate the business by asking the necessary questions. Like any hotel or restaurant, quality, service, value, and personnel do change from time to time. You need to read the signs and make your own decisions accordingly. Most shopping problems our readers encounter are usually outlined as cautionary rules in this book, especially in Chapter 4. Failure to read and adhere to these rules can result in some unpleasant "*I told you so!*" shopping and travel experiences.

If you rely solely on our listings, you will miss out on one of the great adventures of shopping in Bermuda – discovering your own special shops that offer unique items, exceptional value, and excellent service.

Should you encounter any problem with our recommended shops, we would appreciate hearing about your experience. We also welcome readers' recommendations and success stories! We can be contacted through the publisher:

Ron and Caryl Krannich
IMPACT PUBLICATIONS
9104 Manassas Drive, Suite N
Manassas Park, VA 20111-5211
Fax 703-335-9486
E-mail: krannich@impactpublications.com

While we cannot solve your problems, future editions of this book will reflect the experiences of our readers.

You also may want to stay in contact with the publisher's two travel websites:

www.ishoparoundtheworld.com
www.travel-smarter.com

The *i*ShopAroundTheWorld site is designed to complement the Impact Guides with numerous additional resources and advice. The site includes travel and shopping tips, updates, profiles of shops, a travel reservation system, recommended resources, and an online travel bookstore. If you have questions or comments, you may want to address them to us at this site.

The **Travel-Smarter** site includes some of the world's best deals on hotels, car rentals, travel insurance, cruises, airlines, travel packages, and golf tours around the world. Be sure to check out the "Hot Rates" and "Hot Deals" sections for great travel buys.

Expect a Rewarding Adventure

Whatever you do, enjoy your travel-shopping adventure to Bermuda. This is a very special place that offers many unique items for discerning travel-shoppers.

So arrange your flights and accommodations, pack your credit cards, ATM card, and traveler's checks, take your sense of humor, wear a smile, and head for one of the world's delightful shopping and travel destinations. You should return home with much more than a set of photos and travel brochures and a weight gain attendant with new eating habits. You will acquire some wonderful products and accumulate many interesting travel tales that can be enjoyed and relived for a lifetime.

Experiencing the treasures and pleasures of Bermuda only takes time, money, a sense of adventure, and the references found in this book and on www.ishoparoundtheworld.com. Take the time, be willing to part with some of your money, and open yourself to a whole new travel-shopping world. If you are like us, you will encounter an exciting new travel world of quality products, friendly people, and interesting places that you might have otherwise missed had you passed through these places as a typical tourist or traveler who came here to only eat, sleep, see sights, be entertained, and take pictures. When you travel and shop in Bermuda, you learn about a wonderful place by way of the people, products, sights, and activities that define its many treasures and pleasures.

P A R T I

Smart Travel-Shopping

Know Before You Go

AS YOU PREPARE FOR YOUR Bermuda adventure, be sure to acquaint yourself with the many facts, observations, tips, and strategies revealed in this chapter. They can save you time, money, and headaches as well as ensure a relatively trouble-free trip to Bermuda.

A Short Story of Bermuda

The story of Bermuda began in the 16th century. Spaniard Juan de Bermudez is usually credited with discovering the islands. He visited there in 1503, but failed to claim them for Spain. More than 100 years later, in July 1609, the British Admiral Sir George Somers wrecked his flagship, the Sea Venture, on the reefs less than one mile off the shore of what is now St. Catherine's Point. They were on their way from England to assist the struggling new colony of Jamestown, Virginia. While he and his crew managed to build two small sailing ships, the Patience and Deliverance, to complete their journey to Jamestown in May 1610, two of his crew, who were deserters, stayed behind and became the first colonists.

Word spread in England about the island's temperate climate and fertile soil, not to mention the birds, skinks, and wild hogs the recent visitors encountered. In 1612 the ship called the Plough left England to colonize Bermuda. The island became part of the Virginia Company, and 60 Englishmen settled St. George on the eastern end of the island chain. In 1620 Bermuda officially became a British colony with the convening of the first parliament.

In 1684 its status was elevated to that of a Crown Colony, and it received its first appointed governor.

> □ Bermuda's fortunes have gone up and down in such ventures as whaling, shipbuilding, pirateering, and farming.
>
> □ Bermuda remains the oldest, largest, and most prosperous British colony.
>
> □ Bermuda has become the Hong Kong of the Atlantic Ocean, albeit on a much smaller and less aggressive scale.

The people of Bermuda have had an adventuresome past. Their fortunes have gone up and down in such ventures as whaling, shipbuilding, pirateering, and, until the early 20th century, farming. In the last quarter of the 19th century, farming flourished in the islands. The colony's soil and climate produced excellent vegetables, including onions for export to the U.S. market. Trade was so brisk that the capital of Hamilton was often called Onion Town. The onion market collapsed, however, when Texas farmers discovered how to simulate Bermuda's growing conditions.

Today Bermuda exports no agricultural products. Also, it has no heavy industry. However, soft drink concentrates, perfumes, and pharmaceutical drugs are some of the island's exports from the light industrial companies operating as a free port in the former Royal Naval Dockyard at the western end of the island.

Bermuda's expanding tourist economy began with the arrival of steamships in the early 1900s. In the latter half of the 20th century, Bermuda's tourist trade grew by leaps and bounds, accounting for 70 percent of the nation's economy. Within the last few years, the financial sector has become Bermuda's dominant economic force.

Today Bermuda remains the oldest, largest, and most prosperous British colony thanks to recent changes elsewhere in the fading British Empire. In some respects, Bermuda has become the Hong Kong of the Atlantic Ocean, although on a much smaller and less visible and aggressive scale. When Britain turned over sovereignty of Hong Kong to China in 1997, hundreds of British and Chinese banking, insurance, and holding companies registered and relocated some of their operations to Bermuda.

While Bermuda today is ostensibly a British Overseas Territory, many locals prefer referring to themselves as a "self-governing colony." Today, Bermuda is all about business, especially financial, real estate, and tourism.

Climate and When to Go

Any time of year is a good time to visit Bermuda, although many visitors have definite seasonal preferences. Since this is a semi-tropical and sunny island where the temperature is relatively mild, Bermuda is seldom too hot or too cold for visitors. The Gulf Stream, which flows between Bermuda and continental North America, regulates much of its climate.

Bermuda's **high season** runs from April through October. As might be expected, this is the time of year for large crowds at beaches and in shops, high prices at hotels and resorts, long lines at restaurants and bars, and numerous special events. This also is the warmest time of the year. An occasional tropical storm or hurricane, which also plague the Caribbean and the U.S. eastern coast, may threaten the island in September or October. Hurricane season officially runs from June to November.

The island's **low season** is from November to March. The weather tends to be spring-like during the day and cool in the evening. While it is often too cool to swim at this time of year, this is otherwise a perfect time to visit Bermuda because of bargain prices at hotels, resorts, restaurants, and shops. Indeed, many properties offer very attractive rates during this time of the year. You'll also find the island relatively uncrowded, and you'll experience great weather for golf, tennis, hiking, and other outdoor activities. However, some properties close during this time of the year, and fewer flights come to Bermuda.

Bermuda basically has two seasons – summer and spring. It does not have a rainy or real cold season. No time during the year will you encounter excessive rain, unless the islands get hit with a tropical storm or hurricane, or extreme temperatures.

Showers may be heavy at times, but the skies usually clear quickly. In fact, the Bermuda Department of Tourism, in cooperation with many hotels, shops, museums, and attractions, has come up with programs to promote Bermuda that guarantee visitors good weather during the low season. If the temperature during the day fails to reach 68°F, properties participating in the Temperature Guarantee program will give guests a 10 percent refund, buses and ferries will give free transportation passes for the next day, and guests will receive free admissions to participating museums and other attractions.

- ❑ Bermuda's high season runs from April through October.

- ❑ Bermuda's temperature rarely gets above 85°F during the day.

- ❑ Expect cool evenings from December through March.

- ❑ As a rule, you should dress conservatively.

The weather seldom interferes with outdoor activities. Summer temperatures prevail from May to mid-November, with the warmest weather in July, August, and September.

Except in August, when temperatures can climb to 90°F, Bermuda's temperature rarely gets above 85°F during the day, and cool sea breezes constantly fan the island – perfect for shopping, sunning, swimming, or touring the islands. Expect cool breezes at night. Temperatures average from 75°F to 85°F between May and October. Spring-like weather provides cooler temperatures from mid-December to late March with average daytime temperatures of 60°F to 70°F; evenings are generally cool at this time of year. The months of December and January are often warm enough for some people, especially hardy Europeans, to sun and swim. The change of seasons comes during mid-November through December and from late March through April. Either spring or summer weather may occur during the change of seasons, and visitors should be prepared for both.

What to Pack and Wear

Pack as if you were to visit a resort island – swimwear, sun screen, sunglasses, hat or cap, umbrella, shorts, comfortable walking shoes, sportswear, and any sports equipment you might need, such as golf clubs and tennis rackets. Since you may encounter cool evenings, especially in the off season, you may want to pack a lightweight sweater and/or jacket. At the same time, you need to be prepared for Bermuda's rather formal and proper dress requirements.

Be sure to bring a camera since Bermuda offers many nice colors and scenery shots you'll probably want to capture on film or disk.

Bermuda exudes a certain element of British reserve and dig-nified formality in many of its hotels, resorts, guest houses, and restaurants. As a rule, you should dress conservatively. Bathing suits, abbreviated tops, and short shorts are not acceptable ex-cept at beaches and pools. In public, including public areas of hotels, beachwear should be covered. Bare feet are not accept-able in public. It is an offense to ride cycles or appear in public without a shirt or just wearing a bathing suit. Joggers, how-ever, may wear standard run-ning shorts and shirts. Casual sportswear is acceptable in res-taurants at lunchtime, but many of the larger restaurants and nightclubs in and out of hotels  request gentlemen to wear a jacket, and preferrably a tie, in the evenings. A blue blazer, white cotton shirt, and khakis will be appropriate for just about any occasion requiring formal attire.

It is best to check on dress requirements when making dinner or nightclub reservations, since some places do have evenings when a jacket is not required.

During the warmer months of May to mid-November, women should plan to wear summer-weight sports clothes, cotton dresses, swimsuits, casuals of lightweight travel fabrics, a light dressy sweater or wrap for evenings, cocktail-type outfits for evenings, and a raincoat or light-weight windbreaker. Men should consider summer-weight sports clothes, swimsuits, a lightweight suit or sport jacket, a tie for evenings, and also a raincoat or a light-weight windbreaker. During the cooler months of Decem-ber through late March, women should plan to wear light-weight woolen or fall-weight casual attire, sweaters, skirts, slacks, dressier sweater or wrap, and cocktail-type outfits for the eve-nings, and a raincoat or lightweight windbreaker. Appropriate dress for men would include light-weight woolens or fall-weight casuals, sports jacket, slacks, sweaters, suit or sports jacket, a tie for evenings, and a raincoat or winter jacket.

During the change of seasons from mid-November to Decem-ber and late March through April, either spring or summer weather may occur, so a combination of clothing is normally ideal.

Bermuda shorts are acceptable year round. However, you will find that the famous Bermuda shorts, which stop just above the knee, are normally worn with long socks. It is not uncommon to see many businessmen wearing Bermuda shorts with shirts and ties year round and occasionally as an evening dress in the sum-mer.

Required Documents

While it's always best to travel abroad with a passport, and Bermuda prefers visitors with passports, Bermuda Immigration does not require a passport of U.S. and Canadian citizens. Instead, they can enter Bermuda on one of the following alternative documents:

- Original birth certificate or a certified copy with a photo ID
- U.S. naturalization certificate
- U.S. Alien Registration card
- Canadian certificate of citizenship

A driver's license is not acceptable as proof of citizenship. It's only good for renting a motorbike. Visitors from the United Kingdom and Europe must arrive with a passport. All visitors also must have a return or onward ticket. Individuals arriving without return tickets or Bermuda Immigration authorization to land on a one-ticket basis, will not be admitted unless they have prior authorization from Bermuda Immigration authorities.

If you plan to stay in Bermuda for more than three weeks, you will need to complete an Immigration Application for an extended stay by contacting the Chief Immigration Officer at the Government Administration Building, 30 Parliament Street, Hamilton, Tel. 441-295-5151.

Arrival, Departure, and Customs

Arrival in Bermuda is seemingly well organized at the airport and cruise ship terminals. At the airport, you normally will be met by a local musical group playing touristy Caribbean music as you enter the terminal. If you're lucky, the immigration process will go well and you'll be out of the airport within 10 minutes. However, many people at times report long lines, with waits of more than an hour while they unhappily stand in line having to listen to the cheesy welcoming music! Just before you enter the baggage area, look for the Information booth, which may or may not be manned by personnel, and lots of free literature on all aspects of visiting Bermuda. The baggage carts are free for visitors to use within the terminal and taxi pick-up areas. You will find several international long distance calling card machines located in the baggage area.

> *Taxis from the airport will cost from $15 to $45, depending on your destination.*

Bermuda Customs allows visitors to bring in duty-free all wearing apparel and articles for personal use, such as sports equipment, cameras, 200 cigarettes, one quart of liquor, one quart of wine, and approximately 20 pounds of meat. You can also bring in $30 of gifts duty-free. Fruits, vegetables, plants, and animals are prohibited from entering Bermuda. All imports may be inspected upon arrival.

As soon as you exit the terminal, you'll see several taxis lined up to assist you with your luggage and transportation to your next destination. Since the taxis have fixed prices, there is no need to haggle over fares, which will be expensive. The taxi fare from the airport to the eastern side of the island (St. George) is around $15.00. If you're going to Hamilton, which is a 30-minute drive, expect to pay around $25.00. The average fare to the South Shore hotels is $30.00. If you must travel to the western side of the island (Royal Naval Dockyard), expect to pay nearly $45.00 for this one-hour drive.

All visitors leaving the island must pay a Passenger Tax. If you leave by air, this tax is collected at the airport and runs $20 for adults and children (those under two years of age are exempt). If you leave by ship, a $60 per person tax (children under two exempt), which you've already prepaid as part of your transportation package, is paid to the government by your cruise ship company.

Language and Culture

British English with some Bermudian modifications is the language of Bermuda. However, you may find some words and meanings unusual. For example, expect to hear a few of these words:

Local terms		English equivalent
Burr	=	Beer
Crucial	=	Excellent
Get hot	=	Get drunk
Greeze	=	Food
Eez-me-up	=	Give me a break

The local culture tends to value individuals who are conservative, polite, civil, proper, reserved, hospitable, patient, and nice. Rules and regulations govern proper behavior, especially dress and decorum. Be sure to greet people by saying "*Good morning*" or "*Good afternoon*" – greetings that usually start every conversation. Most people you meet will be outwardly friendly and courteous. You are expected to reciprocate. Loud, unruly, impatient, rude, and frank in-your-face behavior is frowned upon.

Take, for example, the local taxi drivers. Many of them are well educated and traveled. But they sometimes complain that visitors from America treat them improperly – some think Bermudian taxi drivers might rob them! They point out that taxi drivers in Bermuda are very different from taxi drivers in the big cities of America. You can normally carry on an intelligent conversation with Bermudian taxi drivers who tend to be very polite, helpful, and honest. Take advantage of their goodwill by engaging them in conversations and fully using their services. Ask them about Bermuda – where to go, what to do, the best of Bermuda, life in Bermuda, their families, rules and regulations, local culture, tours, etc. You'll quickly discover that most Bermudian taxi drivers also double as very informative and reliable guides. Indeed, while they can be expensive for one or two passengers, nonetheless, you may want to hire a taxi driver as a guide during your stay.

When in doubt how to best behave in Bermuda, just try being **nice** in what you say, do, and wear. Nice people get along very well in Bermuda.

Time and Business Hours

Bermuda is one hour ahead of Eastern Standard Time in the U.S. and four hours behind London. When it's 9am in New York City, Boston, Atlanta, and Toronto, it's 10am in Bermuda. When it's 9am in London, it's 5am in Bermuda. A two-hour flight from the U.S. east coast will put you into Bermuda an hour later than your departure time.

Normal business hours for most shops are 9am to 5pm Monday through Saturday. Some shops may close for lunch, but most shops along the main shopping streets of Hamilton and St. George stay open. Some shops are open on Sunday, especially if there is a cruise ship in port in either St. George or Hamilton. Shops at the Naval Royal Dockyard stay open on Sunday. Most hotel shops have Sunday business hours.

Both Hamilton and St. George have special evening shopping and festival hours between April 28th and October 13th. Hamilton celebrates **Harbour Nights** every Wednesday from 7pm to 10pm during that period. St. George celebrates **Heritage Nights** every Tuesday from 7pm to 10pm. These special hours tend to coincide with cruise ship schedules.

Safety, Security, and Insurance

Bermuda is a relatively safe place to visit in terms of criminal activity directed toward tourists. However, some visitors do encounter pickpockets and thieves, daylight muggings have occurred, and some gang violence has been reported. Drug and alcohol abuse and gangs and hoodlums are normally associated with such criminal activities. Do take normal and sensible precautions with your valuables and don't assume Bermuda is crime-free.

The major safety issue in Bermuda relates to accidents because of roads, transportation, and sports activities. Be very careful when walking along Bermuda's narrow and winding roads. Since few roads have adequate shoulders for safety purposes, walking along roads can be very dangerous and deadly. The same is true for motor scooters and mopeds which many visitors rent. On more than one occasion we have seen tourists driving such vehicles seriously injured by cars and buses. The best evidence of this safety problem is what you may see in the airport departure lounge – injured tourists in wheelchairs and on crutches anxiously awaiting

> *The major safety issue relates to accidents because of roads, transportation, and sports activities.*

their departure from Bermuda! If you are not used to defensive motorbike riding, think twice about the convenience and fun of renting a motor scooter or moped. See our additional cautionary notes under "Local Transportation" later in this chapter.

You should consider taking out a special insurance policy when traveling, to cover situations not covered by your medical, home, auto, and personal insurance back home. For example, many insurance policies do not cover treatment for illnesses or accidents while traveling outside your home country. Check whether your medical insurance will cover treatment abroad, and consider acquiring evacuation insurance in case serious illness or injuries would require that you be evacuated for medical treatment in a nearby country or home through special transportation and health care arrangements. Many companies offer this insurance. One of the best kept travel secrets for acquiring inexpensive evacuation insurance is to join DAN (Divers Alert Network). In the U.S., call 1-800-446-2671 (The Peter B. Bennett Center, 6 West Colony Place, Durham, NC 27705; website: www.diversalertnetwork.org). Without such insurance, special evacuation arrangements could cost US$20,000 or more! DAN's yearly rates are the best we have encountered. American Express now offers yearly insurance coverage at special rates as an option to its card holders. Whether or not you are into adventure travel and plan to engage in physically challenging and risky activities, health and evacuation insurance should be on your "must do" list before departing for your international adventure.

When considering special travel insurance, first check your current insurance policies to see if you have any coverage when traveling abroad. Also contact a travel agent to find out what he or she recommends for special coverage. The following websites will connect you to several companies that offer special insurance for travelers:

- **WorldTravelCenter**   www.worldtravelcenter.com
- **TravelGuard**   www.travelguard.com
- **GlobalTravelInsurance**   www.globaltravelinsurance.com
- **MedexAssist**   www.medexassist.com
- **Travelex**   www.travelex.com
- **Wallach & Co.**   www.wallach.com
- **QuoteTravelInsurance**   www.quotetravelinsurance.com
- **InsureMyTrip**   www.insuremytrip.com
- **eTravelProtection**   www.etravelprotection.com
- **TravelSecure**   www.travelsecure.com
- **TravelProtect**   www.travelprotect.com
- **GlobalCover**   www.globalcover.com

Getting There

Bermuda is regularly serviced during the high season by airlines and cruise ships. Most originate from the east coast of the United States, especially Boston, New York, Newark, Philadelphia, Washington, Baltimore, and Atlanta, and to a lesser extent from Canada (Toronto) and the United Kingdom (London).

AIRLINES

The major airlines servicing Bermuda with nonstop flights from
North America include:

- **Air Canada**   www.aircanada.ca
  (Toronto, Halifax)
- **American Airlines** www.aa.com
  (New York City)
- **Continental Airlines** www.continental.com
  (Newark)
- **Delta Airlines**   www.delta.com
  (Boston, Atlanta)
- **USA3000**   www.USA3000.com
  (Baltimore, Philadelphia, Newark)
- **USAir**   www.usair.com
  (Boston, New York City,
  Philadelphia)

British Airways (www.britishairways.com) flies nonstop from
the United Kingdom (London's Gatwick Airport)to Bermuda
three times a week.

Most nonstop flights originating in North America take from
two to three hours to reach Bermuda. A flight from Baltimore to
Bermuda takes just over 2 hours, while a flight from Toronto
takes 2 hours and 50 minutes.

For many years round-trip air transportation to Bermuda was
ridiculously expensive – more than $800 for a short two-hour
flight during high season! Indeed, the high cost of transportation
to Bermuda has long been a deterrent to visiting Bermuda, and
such high costs added to Bermuda's image of exclusivity. However, times have changed as airlines have become more competitive, and Bermuda has encouraged more tourists to visit its
shores especially during the low season. But you can still pay a
premium price for airfare to Bermuda if you don't heed our
airfare shopping advice.

Round-trip economy airfares now range from US$300 to
US$800, depending on how well you shop around for discounted
rates and whether you travel during the high season or low
season. Some of the best rates are found with an excellent young
airline called USA3000: Tel. 1-877-USA-3000 (872-3000) or
www.USA3000.com. In business for nearly four years, this airline often offers inexpensive rates (less than US$250 round trip,
including taxes) even during the high season. It flies from Baltimore, Philadelphia, and Newark to Bermuda. We've taken this
airline to Bermuda and were very pleasantly surprised with its
roomy new equipment (Airbus A320), experienced pilots, and

excellent service – some of the best we have encountered from any airline! It's best to book your flight directly with this airline or use a travel agent. Many online booking services, such as Travelocity and Expedia, do not include this airline in their databases. In fact, if you use such online services to book your flight, you may foolishly pay a real premium for your airline ticket.

Most major airlines offer special promotional rates during the low season. Round-trip rates may drop to $400 to $450 during that time.

Many airlines also offer special vacation packages that include hotels. You may want to check directly with the airlines or contact a travel agent for these and other package deals. However, such packages may not be such a deal once you figure a discounted airfare separate from a discounted room rate. Again, shop around for the real deals. Not surprisingly, there are few good deals during high season when most visitors pay full retail. Excellent deals are reserved for the low season.

CRUISES

One of the most popular ways to travel to Bermuda is by cruise ship. Several cruise lines include Bermuda in their port schedules. During the high season you'll find from three to five cruise ships

 docked in Hamilton, St. George, and King's Wharf at the Royal Naval Dockyard. The largest ships dock at King's Wharf. Hamilton will usually have two to three ships in port.

Most cruises run for five to seven days and originate in Boston, New York, or Baltimore. They usually spend three to four days in Bermuda and one to two days cruising to and from their U.S. ports. Five major cruise lines currently run regular cruises to Bermuda:

- **Celebrity Cruise Lines**
  1-800-437-3111
  www.celebrity.com

- **Carnival Cruise Lines**
  1-800-866-299-5698
  www.carnival.com

- **Cunard Cruise Lines**
  1-800-528-6273
  www.cunard.com

- **Norwegian Cruise Lines**
  1-800-327-7030
  www.ncl.com

- **Radisson Seven Seas**
  1-877-505-5370
  www.rssc.com

- **Royal Caribbean Cruise Lines**
  1-800-327-6700
  www.royalcaribbean.com

Several companies also specialize in discounted cruises, including last-minute deep discounted rates. Check out these companies for special cruising deals to Bermuda:

- **America's Vacation Center**
  1-800-646-4320
  www.americasvacationcenter.com

- **The Cruise Company**
  1-800-854-0500
  www.thecruisecompany.com

- **Cruise Dealerships**
  1-800-604-0279
  www.cruisedealership.com

- **Cruise Shopping**
  1-800-650-SAIL
  www.cruisehshopping.com

- **Cruises.com**
  1-800-288-6006
  www.cruises.com

- **Cruises, Inc.**
  1-800-854-0500
  www.cruisesinc.com

- **Cruises Only**
  1-800-278-4737
  www.cruisesonly.com

- **CruiseWeb**
  1-800-377-9383
  www.cruiseweb.com

- **Cruises of Distinction**
  1-800-634-3445
  www.cruisesofdistinction.com

- **Cruise Ship Centers**
  1-800-707-7327
  www.cruiseshipcenters.com

- **Hartford Holidays**
  1-800-828-4813
  www.hartfordholidays.com

- **OurCruise**
  1-800-578-5760
  www.ourcruisecom.com

- **TravelZoo**
  www.travelzoo.com

- **Vacations To Go**
  1-800-338-4962
  www.vacationstogo.com

Considering the high cost of air transportation and hotels in Bermuda during high season, cruising to Bermuda can be a good deal. Most cruises start around $800, although some deep discounted rates start as low as $499. In addition, you'll spend another $200 on departure taxes and tips. So for less than $1,000, you may get your international transportation, meals, and accommodations by taking a cruise to Bermuda. Comparable costs for air and local accommodations and meals could run much more per person for a six-day trip to Bermuda. The math is very simple. If you want to visit Bermuda and save a great deal of money on your vacation, consider taking a five- to seven-day cruise. It's the best deal money can buy.

However, cruising is not for everyone. Shipboard visitors miss a lot of the romance, leisure, service, and activities of Bermuda by taking a crowded cruise. After all, your ship doesn't have a nice beach, a golf course, or many leisure activities associated with local hotels, resorts, and tour companies. If you think you'll be entertained while in port, think again. While docked in Bermuda, local rules prohibit cruise ships from operating onboard entertainment programs.

Tour Groups and Packages

While your best tour group deals will be with a cruise line, several travel packages are available to Bermuda through airlines, travel agents, and online travel sites. Most of these packages include special airfare and hotel rates. However, don't expect any great deals since most packages still put you into hotels and resorts that run $300 to $400 a night during the high season. The best deals will be during the off season when hotels and resorts slash prices in anticipation of few visitors. You will find some specialty tours that focus on golf and water sports. Bermuda is especially known as a popular wedding and honeymoon destination complete with wedding consultants and wedding and/or honeymoon packages (see separate section below).

The following airlines offer combination air and hotel packages to Bermuda:

- **American Airline Vacations**
  1-800-321-2121
  http://aav1.aavacations

- **Continental Airlines Vacations**
  1-800-301-3800
  www.coolvacations.com

- **Delta Vacations**
  1-800-221-6666
  www.deltavacations.com

- **United Vacations**
  1-888-554-3899
  www.unitedvacations.com

- **US Airways Vacations**
  1-800-422-3761
  www.usairwaysvacations.com

The following websites offer tour packages to Bermuda:

- **American Express**
  www.americanexpress.com/vacations

- **Infohub.com**
  www.infohub.com

- **Island Resort Tours**
  1-800-351-5656
  www.islandresorttours.com

- **Specialty Travel Index**
  www.specialtytravel.com

- **Sunburst Vacations**
  www.sunburstvacations.com/Bermuda

- **TravelAdvisor.com**
  www.Traveladvisor.com

- **Vacation Outlet**
  www.vacationoutlet.com

Several major travel websites also offer special travel packages. Check these three for any specials on Bermuda:

- **Expedia.com**
  www.expedia.com

- **Hotel.com**
  www.hotel.com

- **Travelocity.com**
  www.travelocity.com

We also operate a travel website which may at times include cruises, golf, and travel packages on Bermuda:

- **Travel-Smarter.com**
  www.travel-smarter.com

Golf Holidays

Since golf is one of Bermuda's major draws, including annual tournaments, both cruise lines and travel agencies offer specialty  golf tours and packages. Every summer, for example, Celebrity Cruises sails to Bermuda from New York (Zenith) and Philadelphia and Norfolk, VA (Horizon) with golf pros on board who operate an enhanced golf program involving state-of-the-art video and computers that compare passengers' swings to those of over 100 PGA professionals. Elite Golf Cruises also promotes golf cruises to Bermuda. It's an exclusive provider of Golf Academies at Sea which provide onboard instruction, equipment, simulation, and excursions through various cruise lines:

- **Elite Golf Cruises, LLC**
  Tel. 800-324-1106

Fax 954-382-5398
www.elitegolfcruises.com
E-mail: info@elitegolfcruises.com

Tour operators specializing in golf tours include:

- **Sophisticated Golfer**
  1-877-288-9799
  www.sophisticatedgolferbermuda.com
  E-mail: info@sophisticatedgolfer.com

- **Ultimate Golf Vacations** (Canada)
  1-800-465-3034
  www.ugv.net/ultimategolf/bermuda.html
  E-mail: info@ugv.ne

Weddings and Honeymoons

Bermuda and romance are often synonymous. Its pink sand beaches, secluded coves, lush tropical gardens, quaint churches, ideal weather, gorgeous sunsets, horse-drawn carriages in Hamilton and St. George, romantic candlelight dinners, evening sea breezes and distinctive sounds, and impeccable service distinguish it as the perfect place for weddings and honeymoons. Indeed, Bermuda remains a very popular wedding and honeymoon destination for visitors from North America. In fact, nearly 23,000 honeymooners (first and second-time) come to Bermuda each year. Hundreds of other couples decide to get married in Bermuda. You will often see weddings taking place along the shores

of Bermuda, at the Botanical Gardens, in churches, or on yachts.

Many hotels and resorts offer attractive wedding packages or can help you arrange a wedding, complete with ceremony, photographer, band, flowers, wedding cake, and reception. Four hotels are especially noted for arranging wedding and honeymoons: Fairmont Hamilton Princess, Fairmont Southampton, Elbow Beach Bermuda, Grotto Bay Beach Hotel, Harmony Club, and the Sonesta Beach Resort.

If you need a local wedding consultant, contact the following companies:

- **The Bridal Salon**
  Tel. 441-292-2025
  www.bridalsuitebermudaweddings.com

- **The Bridal Suite**
  Tel. 441-292-2025
  888-253-5585 (Canada)
  www.bridalsuitebermudaweddings.com

- **Bermuda Bride**
  Tel. 441-232-2344
  www.bermudabridge.com

- **The Wedding Salon**
  Tel. 919-217-4395
  www.bermudaweddingsalon.com

Most travel agents can advise you on honeymoon packages and how to make special wedding arrangements in Bermuda. You also may want to check with a local wedding travel specialist:

- **Bermuda Travel**
  Tel. 781-662-1953
  www.bermudatravel.bm
  Email: info@bermudatravel.bm

If you plan to get married in Bermuda, you will need to file a "Notice of Intended Marriage" with the Bermuda Registrar General's Office. It costs $210 plus $10 for a certificate or license which is good for three months. You can get the necessary form mailed to you by calling the Bermuda Tourist Office (800-BER-MUDA), contacting the Bermuda Department of Tourism office nearest you, or by downloading the form from the Bermuda Tourism website: www.bermudatourism.com (go to the "Wedding/Honeymoon" section found on the left navigation bar). However, be sure to print this form on legal-size paper – 8½" x 14" – a legal requirement for submitting your application. The Bermuda Tourism website also includes useful information on other aspects of weddings and honeymoons in Bermuda – bands for hire, video services, and photographers.

Bermuda Tourist Offices Abroad

The Bermuda Department of Tourism (www.bermudatourism.com) operates a few offices in North America and Europe:

UNITED STATES

- 675 Third Avenue, 20th Floor
  New York, NY 10017
  1-800-225-6106

- 124 Peachtree Centre Avenue NE
  Suite 803
  Atlanta, GA 30303
  Tel. 404-524-1541

- 184 High Street, 4th Floor
  Boston, MA 02110-3001
  Tel. 617-422-5892

- 1420 New York Avenue NW
  Washington, DC 20005
  Tel. 202-628-9899

CANADA

- 1200 Bay Street, Suite 1004
  Toronto, Ontario
  Canada M5R 2A5
  Tel. 416-925-9600

EUROPE

- **Bermuda Tourism**
  1 Battersea Church Road
  London SW11 3LY
  England, UK
  Tel. 44-0-207-771-7001

Holiday packages in UK/Europe:

- **Austria and Switzerland:** Tel. 06131-627-7491
  Germany: Tel. 06131-627-7491
  Italy: Tel. +39 02 -820-5466
  UK: Tel. 020-8410-8188
  Elsewhere in Europe: Tel. +44 20-8410-8188

In Bermuda the Department of Tourism is found at this location:

- **Bermuda Department of Tourism**
  Global House
  45 Church Street
  Hamilton HM 12
  Tel. 441-292- 0025

Local Travel Assistance

Bermuda is well organized for tourists. Once you arrive in Bermuda, look for the helpful Visitors' Service Bureaus in Hamilton, St. George, and the Royal Naval Dockyard as well as boxes of tourist information at the airport and in hotels and resorts (near reception desks). Visitors' Service Bureaus are found in the following locations:

- **City of Hamilton**
  8 Front Street (next to the Ferry Terminal)
  Tel. 441-295-1480

- **Royal Naval Dockyard**
  The Cooperage Building
  Tel. 441-254-3824

- **Town of St. George**
  7 King's Square
  (on the waterfront)
  Tel. 441-297-1642

- **Bermuda International Airport**
  Tel. 441-299-4857

When visiting these information centers, be sure to pick up copies of the following free maps, brochures, and guidebooks produced by the Bermuda Department of Tourism, KeyGuide Publications, and Bermuda Directories Limited:

- *Bermuda: East to West*
- *Bermuda: Handy Reference Map*
- *Bermuda: Where to Stay*
- *Destination Bermuda*
- *Discover Your Bermuda*
- *Experience Bermuda: Dining and Menu Guide*
- *Experience Bermuda: Royal Naval Dockyard*
- *Experience Bermuda: Sights and Sports*
- *Experience Bermuda: Town of St. George*
- *Key to Attractions*
- *Key to the City*
- *Key to Restaurants*
- *Preview Bermuda*
- *This Week in Bermuda*

Some of this information can be accessed online by visiting the publishers' websites:

- **Bermuda Department of Tourism**
  www.bermudatourism.com

- **Bermuda Directories Ltd.**
  www.thisweekinbermuda.com

- **Preview Bermuda Ltd.**
  www.previewbermuda.com

For information on upcoming events, be sure to check "The Bermuda Calendar" that appears in the local newspaper, *The Royal Gazette*. The free local guidebook *This Week in Bermuda* includes an extensive list of special events for the month. The magazines *The Bermudian* and *Bermuda Business Visitor* include many informative articles on various aspects of Bermudian culture and business.

Local Transportation

Transportation is a major issue in Bermuda for both locals and tourists. Bermuda has very strict car ownership and driving rules because of environmental concerns and limited capacity of Bermuda's narrow two-lane road system.

In fact, locals are prohibited from owning more than one car and visitors are prohibited from driving a car altogether. A typical local family has one car, a motor scooter or moped, and one or more bicycles. The wife usually takes the car, and the husband and children take the family motor scooter, moped, and/or bicycle.

Since visitors are prohibited from driving cars in Bermuda, your local transportation alternatives are:

- motorbike/motor scooter rental
- bicycle rental
- buses
- mini-buses
- taxis
- ferries and boats
- horse-drawn carriages

By most any standard, local transportation in Bermuda is expensive. For example, most taxis cost between $10 and $25 a ride or $30 per hour with a three-hour minimum.

Renting a taxi by the hour becomes cost-effective for parties of four or more that split costs. Several companies rent motorbikes or motor scooters at the rate of $65 to $75 a day. The general transportation rule in Bermuda is the same as elsewhere in the world: the more expensive the alternative, the safer and more convenient the transportation. The least expensive transportation (buses), while safe, is also the least convenient (long waits and limited operating hours) for getting around the island. The most dangerous transportation modes (motor scooters, mopeds, and bicycles) are relatively convenient.

Many visitors prefer renting a **motor scooter** to get around the island. You can rent one upon arrival at the Bermuda International Airport by using the **Bermuda Fly 'N Ride** service – you pick up the scooter upon arrival at the airport while your luggage is delivered directly to your hotel. You must make reservations 24 hours in advance of arrival to have your luggage picked up:

- **Bermuda Fly 'N Ride**
  Tel. 441-293-6188
  E-mail: evecycle@ibl.bm

Several companies rent motor scooters and mopeds. Many will deliver them free to your hotel, resort, or guest house:

- **Concord Cycle Shop**
  Tel. 441-238-3336

- **Eve's Cycle Livery**
  Tel. 441-236-6247

- **Oleander Cycles**
  Tel. 441-236-5235

- **Wheels**
  Tel. 441-292-2245

While the image of happy and free-spirited tourists and loving couples motorbiking around Bermuda on a clear blue day is enticing, all is not well with this transportation alternative, especially if you visit the local hospital or come across accidents, which are frequent with self-drive tourists. Or just look around the departure lounge of the airport, where you will often see tourists leaving with broken limbs and bandaged because of a bad case of "Bermuda road rash." Indeed, we caution you on renting a motor scooter or moped for some very good safety reasons. These are literally death machines. The realities of driving in

Bermuda are quite different. For example, the roads in Bermuda are narrow and winding, shoulders are nearly nonexistent, cars and buses dominate the roads, and when it rains, roads can be very slippery. Always avoid driving at night when you will be most vulnerable to getting hit by a car. Unfortunately, but little publicized, the fact is that many tourists are involved in accidents with motor scooters and mopeds. Unless you are an experienced and defensive biker, you should consider safer transportation alternatives. There's nothing worse to ruin a holiday than to end up in an accident or have to pay $25,000 to be evacuated by air because of injuries. If you decide to rent a motor scooter or moped, be sure you have adequate international medical and evacuation insurance. Also, remember that in Bermuda you must drive on the left-hand side of the road, the speed limit is 35 kilometers (22 miles) per hour, and gas stations are normally open from 7am to 7pm, although some are open until 11pm or later.

Buses and ferries are the most popular ways to get around Bermuda. Most bus and ferry rides cost $4.00 (token) to $4.50 (cash) per ride. You need exact change, tokens, or a Transportation Pass to board buses and ferries. The best way to minimize your transportation costs is to purchase bus and ferry tokens and Transportation Passes at the Central Terminal www.Bermu daBuses.com) in Hamilton (adjacent to City Hall on Washington Street), Visitors' Service Bureaus, and at some hotels and guest houses at the following rates:

- $12   1 day
- $28   3 days
- $35   4 days
- $45   7 days
- $55   1 month
- $135   3 months

Keep in mind that buses stop running around 6:30pm during the week and have limited hours on Sundays and holidays. If you've been traveling around the island by bus and fail to catch the last buses by 5:30 or 6pm, you may have to call an expensive taxi to get back to your hotel – a high cost that will far outweigh the advantage of using economical Transportation Pass!

Most visitors learn to use the island's **bus system**, which is relatively convenient and inexpensive if you purchase a Transportation Pass. All buses depart from the Central Bus Terminal in Hamilton and stop at bus shelters or by pink and blue poles along the road. Buses stopping at **pink poles** are inbound to Hamilton. Those stopping at **blue poles** are outbound from Hamilton. You can download information on bus and schedules at www.bermudabuses.com.

Ferries are wonderful and convenient ways to get around various parts of Bermuda, especially between Hamilton and the Royal Naval Dockyard. Ferry schedules are posted at each dock. Ferries follow three routes throughout the year:

- Pink Route   Hamilton-Paget-Warwick
- Green Route   Hamilton-Rockaway
- Blue Route   Hamilton-West End (Somerset) Dockyard

From mid-April to mid-November a seasonal Orange Route service operates between the Dockyard and St. George. Two high-speed catamarans operate between the Dockyard and Hamilton and between the Dockyard and St. George during the summer months. The ferries on the Dockyard, Rockaway, Somerset, and St. George's routes permit cycles on board. You can purchase ferry tokens and tickets at the Ferry Terminal on Front Street in Hamilton. For information on ferries, visit the Sea Express website: www.seaexpress.bm.

Horse-drawn carriages, which are found along Front Street in Hamilton, cost $30 for a 30-minute ride. They also are available along the main street in St. George.

You can rent **bicycles** for $15 to $20 a day. Several companies (Dowlings Cycles, Eve's Cycle Livery, Georgiana Cycles, and Smatts Cycle Livery) also have special two- ($25.00) and three-day ($35.00) rates. Bicycling along the roads of Bermuda faces similar safety challenges as driving a motor scooter or moped. Be very careful of cars and buses that dominate the narrow and winding roads.

Three companies operate **mini-buses** (St. George's Mini-Bus Service, 441-297-8199; Suburban Transit Mini-Bus, 441-235-5299; West End Mini-Bus, 441-295-5298) along different areas of the island. Mini-buses can be called or flagged down along the road.

As noted earlier, **taxis** are very expensive, but they are the most convenient way of getting around Bermuda at all hours. All taxis are metered and rates are established by the government: $4.80 for the first mile and $1.68 for each additional mile. Rates are higher after midnight and on Sundays and public holidays. Taxi drivers also tend to be very friendly and informative, with many doubling as tour guides and available for sightseeing on an hourly basis. You'll most likely encounter your first nice taxi driver at the airport who will take you to your hotel or resort in a roomy vehicle. This is a good time to engage in a conversation about island transportation, tours, and sightseeing. You may like your taxi driver so much that you arrange to have him take you around the island during your stay. Remember, most taxis charge $30 an hour with a three-hour minimum for such sightseeing services.

If you need a taxi, your hotel, resort, or guest house front desk or concierge can call one for you. Several taxi companies also offer tour services. Bermuda's major taxi operators are:

- **B.I.U. Taxi Co-op Transportation**
  40 Union Street, Hamilton
  Tel. 441-292-4476

- **Bermuda Taxi Radio Cabs Ltd.**
  Trott Road, Hamilton
  Tel. 441-295-4141

- **Bermuda Taxi Operators Company Ltd.**
  P.O. Box HM 1433, Hamilton HM FX
  Tel. 441-292-4175

- **Bermuda Taxi Services Ltd.**
  P.O. Box HM 2252, Hamilton HM JX
  Tel. 441-295-8294

- **Trott Travel Ltd.**
  P.O. Box HM 721, Hamilton HM CX
  Tel. 441-295-0041

Physically challenged visitors can get assistance by contacting Keith Simmons at:

- **Access Bermuda**
  1 Loyal Hill
  Devonshire FL 03
  Tel. 441-295-9016
  www.access.bm
  E-mail: keithsimmons@ibl.bm

Touts, Hustlers, and Greedy Guides

One of the pleasant surprises of Bermuda is the near absence of annoying touts, hustlers, and greedy guides that are real negatives for tourism in many other parts of the world. Although you may occasionally be approached by a town drunk, drug user loitering near a liquor store or shop, or even a mugger, Bermuda is largely free of these elements. The absence of ubiquitous touts, hustlers, commission-greedy tour guides, and beggars in a heavily touristed area is somewhat remarkable. But after all, Bermuda is not a poor Third World country nor a major metropolitan area where such individuals tend to plague the tourist industry and raise major questions about safety and security. Tourists in Bermuda are largely left alone, and helpful assistance is readily offered to those who seek it. You won't feel like a tourist target in Bermuda. After all, you're paying top dollar to be left alone!

Money Matters

The Bermudian dollar is on par with the U.S. dollar – US$1 = BD$1 and is divided into 100 cents. However, there is no need to exchange U.S. dollars into local currency since the U.S. dollar is interchangeable with the Bermudian dollar. Since you will often receive Bermudian coins and bills as change, be sure to unload local bills and coins before you leave Bermuda. Better still, ask for change in U.S. currency in order to avoid having to exchange money before leaving Bermuda.

While MasterCard and Visa are widely accepted throughout Bermuda, most shops prefer cash because of high credit card fees. American Express and Diners Cards are accepted by some establishments. If you have a Discover card, leave it at home since no one accepts it in Bermuda.

If you use an ATM card when traveling, you'll find many 24-hour ATM machines in Bermuda. Traveler's checks also are widely accepted in Bermuda.

Tipping

Tipping is widely expected, accepted, and appreciated in Bermuda. Tips at hotels, resorts, and restaurants are already included in the "gratuity" section (15%) of your bill. There's no need to leave extra or tip the bellman. However, if a gratuity is not included in the bill, plan to tip 15%.

Taxis drivers like to receive 10-15% tips, but it's not necessary to tip since fares are already very high, especially on weekends.

Be sure to carry lots of small bills and coins for tips and exact change situations, such as payment for buses. You will not be allowed on buses unless you pay with exact change.

Taxes

All guest houses, hotels, and resorts are subject to a local government occupancy tax. This runs from 6% for guest houses to 7 ¼% for hotels and resorts.

The government also charges a Passenger Tax which is $20 (children under 2 are exempt) for those leaving by air (which may or may not be included in your ticket) and $60 for those leaving by ship (since it's included in your cruise ship tax payment, you don't directly pay this tax in Bermuda). The government also charges cruise ships $20 per day per passenger while docking in Bermuda. In fact, Bermuda is one of the most expensive ports for cruise ships!

Electricity and Water

Electricity in Bermuda is the same as in the U.S. and Canada – 110 volts, 60-cycle AC – and the plug configuration (flat two-pronged) is the same. Tap water is safe to drink, but bottled water is readily available in grocery stores and restaurants. Many restaurants give you the option of pouring free "regular water" or costly "bottled water." If you don't ask or indicate a preference, you may be charged for expensive bottled water.

Family-Oriented Travel

More and more properties in Bermuda are becoming very family-oriented with many organized activities for children. Indeed, many families now vacation in Bermuda. If you are traveling with children, be sure to ask about organized family activities. The Fairmont Southampton and Hamilton Princess, for example, are two of the most family-friendly hotel resorts in Bermuda with their well organized "Explorers Camp" which functions as a fun daycare center for children. Just drop your children off at "Explorers Camp" and you'll be free for the day while your children will be in good hands.

Bermuda also has many attractions and activities that appeal to kids. Several beaches also include playgrounds. Aquariums, horseback riding, forts, parks, caves, the lighthouse, zoo, and the Underwater Exploration Institute especially appeal to children.

Festivals, Tournaments, and Shows

There's always something going on in Bermuda, be it a golf, fishing, or rugby tournament or a race, show, parade, or festival. Check with the local Visitors' Tourist Bureaus for the specific dates (they vary each year) and details (costs, eligibility, schedules) for the following annual events:

JANUARY
- ADT Bermuda Race Weekend
- Annual Bridge Tournament
- The Bermuda Festival (theater, music, dance –
  runs through February)

FEBRUARY

- Bermuda Amateur Golf Festival
- Bermuda Chess Tournament
- Bermuda Rendezvous Bowling Tournament
- National Badminton Tournament
- Valentine's Mixed Golf Foursomes

MARCH

- All Breed Championship Dog Shows
- Annual Hamilton Street Festival
- Bermuda College Weeks
- Bermuda House and Pony Show
- Bermuda Men's Amateur Golf Championship
- Bermuda Youth Soccer Cup (runs through April)
- Easter Lily Ladies Golf Tournament
- Hasty Pudding Club Show

APRIL

- Agricultural Exhibition Show
- Easter Rugby Classic
- Open Houses and Gardens (runs through May)
- Palm Sunday Walk
- Peppercorn Ceremony

MAY

- Beating Retreat Ceremonies (through October)
- Bermuda Game Fishing Tournament (through November)
- Bermuda Heritage Month
- Invitational International Race Week
- Open Badminton Tournament

JUNE

- Bermuda Duathlon
- Bermuda Ocean Race
- Gibbons Ironkids Triathlon
- Men's Amateur Stroke Play Golf Championship
- Newport-Bermuda Race
- Queen's Birthday Parade

JULY

- American Independence Day
- Cup Match Cricket Festival (or August)
- Marine Science Day

AUGUST

- Bermuda Field Hockey Festival
- Bermuda Reggae Sunsplash Concert
- Non Mariners Race

SEPTEMBER

- American-Bermudian Friendship Festival
- Bermuda Triathlon
- Member's Flower Show

OCTOBER

- Bermuda Horse and Pony Show
- Columbus Day Weekend Regatta
- Convening of Parliament
- Ladies Amateur Golf Championship
- Men's Open Golf Championship
- Omega Gold Cup Match Race

NOVEMBER

- All Breed Championship Dog Shows
- Bermuda Equestrian Festival
- Guy Fawkes Night
- International Flower Show
- Lawn Tennis Club Invitational
- World Rugby Classic

DECEMBER

- Goodwill Golf Tournament
- Santa Claus Parades
- XL Tennis Classic

Useful Websites

You'll find lots of information about Bermuda on the Internet. In fact, this is a highly wired island where e-commerce plays an increasingly important role in the local economy. The following websites are well worth visiting before departing for Bermuda:

- General information   www.bermuda-online.org
                         www.ExperienceBermuda.com
                         www.bermuda.com
- Travel and tourism   www.bermudatourism.com
                         www.bermuda4u.com
                         www.bermudatravelnet.com
- Shopping   www.bermudaemporium.com
- Restaurants   www.bermudadining.com
                         www.diningbermuda.com
- Accommodations   www.bermudahotels.com
                         www.bermudarentals.com
- Entertainment   www.bermudamusic.com
- Business   www.bibn.com
- Flowers and gifts   www.bermuda-flowers.com
- News   www.bermuda-news.com
                         www.theroyalgazette.com
                         www.bermudasun.bm
- Sports   www.bermudatennis.com
- Books and magazines   www.bermudabookstore.com
- Nightclubs   www.oasisbermuda.com
- Cruises   www.bicbda.com
- Art and artists   www.bermuda-gallery.com
- Chamber of Commerce   www.bermudacommerce.com
- Key contacts   www.whoiswho.bm
- Yellow pages   www.bermudayp.com
- Airport   www.bermudaairport.com
- Government   www.gov.bm

One of the best sources for linkages to Bermuda's tourism complex – including accommodations, dining, horseback riding, shopping, watersports, and weddings – is the "Bermuda Links" section under "About Bermuda" on the Bermuda Tourism website: www.bermudatourism.com.

For interesting news and chatter from local expatriates, visit the Limey in Bermuda website: www.limeyinbermuda.com.

Recommended Reading

If you enjoy reading about a place before, during, and after your stay, you may want to get copies of these books:

- *Architecture Bermuda Style* (David R. Raine)
- *Atlantis: Bermuda Triangle* (Greg Donegan)
- *Bermuda: Houses and Gardens* (Sylvia Shorto)
- *Bermuda Antique Furniture and Silver* (Bermuda National Trust)
- *Bermuda Shipwrecks* (Aqua Explorers)

- *Bermuda Shorts: The Hidden Side to the Richest Place on Earth* (T. C. Sobey)
- *The Bermuda Triangle Mystery Solved* (Larry Kusche)
- *Images of Bermuda* (Roger A. LaBrucherie)
- *Into the Bermuda Triangle* (Gian Quasar)
- *The Mystery of the Bermuda Triangle* (Chris Oxlade)
- *Tea With Tracey* (Tracey Caswell)

However, you may want to skip the Bermuda Triangle books since they have little to do with Bermuda. While the triangle encompasses three locations – Miami, Puerto Rico, and Bermuda – most "incidents" take place near Miami and to a lesser extent Puerto Rico!

Alternative travel guides on Bermuda include:

- *Adventure Guide Bermuda* (Blair Howard)
- *Bermuda Pocket Guide* (Brian Bell)
- *Diving Bermuda* (Jesse Concelmo and Michael Strohofer)
- *Fodor's Bermuda* (Fodor's)
- *Frommer's Bermuda* (Darwin Porter)
- *Hiking Bermuda* (Keith Miles)
- *Insight Guide Bermuda* (Brian Bell)
- *Lonely Planet Bermuda* (Lonely Planet)
- *Maverick Guide to Bermuda* (Catherine Harriott)

Anticipated Costs

As we noted earlier, given the high cost of living, Bermuda can be a very expensive destination for independent travelers. Most everything here is expensive, especially hotels and resorts.

During the high season, many resorts and hotels start at $350 a night and go up, and you often don't get much for your money, especially if you are used to traveling in other parts of the world, such as Southeast Asia, where you may be used to staying at fabulous properties for under $200 a night.

For years airfares from the United States to Bermuda have been notoriously expensive, often costing more than flights from the United States to Europe. This is in part due to limited competition faced by major airlines. Paying $800 for a two-hour flight deterred many budget-conscious travelers from visiting Bermuda. However, this situation is now changing with the arrival of a new budget airline, USA3000, which offers round-trip flights from Baltimore, Philadelphia, and Newark for under $300 (taxes included) during the high season. Other airlines, such as JetBlue, are rumored to soon follow with similar discounted airfares. How long this will last is anyone's guess. Airfares from Canada and the United Kingdom still remain high.

The cost of food at restaurants tends to be on the high side, although not as high as one might expect for top restaurants in the United States or Canada. They are a bargain compared to restaurants in London or Paris. Food and beverages in grocery stores are high – nearly twice what one would pay in the United States.

The cost of local transportation, especially taxis, is extremely high, and it's even higher on Sundays and holidays when taxis add a surcharge to their already high rates. Expect to pay between $10 and $20 for most taxi rides. Even bus fares, which start at $4, are high.

Shopping seems to be a better value in Bermuda than other buys. Prices of jewelry, watches, crystal, clothing, and cosmetics are similar to U.S. prices. However, British-made goods such as woolens or china are less expensive than in the U.S. Many stores have occasional sales on clothes. The best shopping buys will be on unique items, such as locally designed jewelry and art. One unique gallery offers good buys on Shona stone sculptures from Zimbabwe!

Just expect to pay a lot in Bermuda for almost everything. Here's a sampling of what you can anticipate in terms of costs:

- Round-tip air from Boston,
  New York, Baltimore/Washington $250-$900
- Taxi from airport to Hamilton $25
- Short taxi ride $10
- Single one-way bus trip $4
- Hamburger $10
- Three-day bus and ferry pass $28
- Three-course lunch (basic) $25
- Dinner for two with wine $200
- High tea $29
- Pint of beer in a pub $5
- Cup of coffee $3
- 12-ounce Pepsi Cola at grocery store $1.25
- Mixed drink in a hotel or restaurant $7
- Golf green fees at Port Royal $95
- Daily motor scooter rental $65
- One week motor scooter rental $183
- Luxury hotel room per night $350
- Guest house room per night $140
- Half day fishing trip $90
- Snorkeling and glass bottom
  boat cruise (half day) $50
- Entrance fee to the Bermuda
  Aquarium Museum and Zoo $10
- Art and Architecture Tour (with lunch) $65

- Bermuda National Gallery   Free
- Botanical Gardens   Free
- Bermuda Cathedral Tower $3
- Bermuda Underwater Exploration Institute $10.50
- Crystal Caves $12
- Champagne Evening Sail $40
- Half-hour dolphin dip $150

Cutting Your Costs

While Bermuda can be a very expensive destination, you can easily cut some of the high costs and become more of a budget-oriented traveler by doing the following:

1. **Fly to Bermuda from the United States via USA3000 (www.usa3000.com).** You may be able to save over $500 on this flight compared to other carriers.

2. **Take a cruise**, which can run as low as $499 (plus $200 for taxes and tips), but probably will run from $900 to $2,000 for five to seven days. The cost of a cruise includes transportation, accommodations, and food. You simply can't match such prices as an independent traveler who pays $900 alone for transportation to and from Bermuda!

3. **Stay at guest houses, villas, cottages, or apartments** for under $150 a night rather than at expensive hotels or resorts, which can easily cost over $300 a night. Good choices include the Clairfont Apartments (6 Warwickshire Road, Warwick on South Shore, Tel. 441-238-0149, e-mail: clairfont@ibl.bm) or properties found through Bermuda Accommodations (Tel. 416-232-2243 or www.bermudaren tals.com).

5. **Shop around for special package deals** that include airfare and accommodations rather than book your accommodations at the full rack rate.

6. **Explore discounted accommodations** for Bermuda available through such websites as www.travel-smarter.com and www.hotels.com.

7. **Check on special off-season rates at hotels and resorts.** Bermuda's off-season can be very pleasant if your interests are other than swimming and the beaches (it gets a bit cool for swimming and water sports, although Canadians are known to frequently test the waters). The off-season for most properties runs from November to March. However, different properties define the off-season dif-

ferently, and some properties may close altogether during that period. Some properties may discount their rooms by as much as 60% during the off-season.

8. **Take buses and ferries using a one-, three-, four-, or seven-day or monthly discount pass** ($12, $28, $35, $45, or $55 respectively) rather than take expensive taxis. While you'll sacrifice convenience, you'll save a lot of money if you plan to travel a great deal around the islands. You can purchase this pass at the Visitors' Service Bureaus (Airport, St. George's, Hamilton, and Dockyard).

9. **If you rent a taxi to sightsee by the hour, do so with a group of people.** Taxi drivers who also serve as tour guides charge $30 an hour for 1-4 people or $42 an hour for 5-6 people. They usually require a minimum of three hours.

10. **Rent a motor scooter or moped for one week.** For a single rider, three hours usually costs $50; one day costs $65; three days cost $110; and seven days cost $183.

11. **If you plan to do much sightseeing, cut the cost of entrance fees by purchasing a Heritage Passport** for $25 (adults) or $15 (children ages 6-16), which gives you unlimited admission to eight cultural and historic attractions within a seven-day period: Aquarium, Museum and Zoo, Bermuda Maritime Museum, Bermuda National Gallery, Bermuda National Trust (Globe Hotel, Tucker and Verdmont Houses), Fort St. Catherine, and Bermuda Underwater Exploration Institute. You can purchase this pass at various branches of the Visitors' Service Bureaus (Airport, St. George's, Hamilton, and Dockyard).

12. **Book a hotel or resort that includes both breakfast and dinner** (Modified American Plan) in their rates.

13. **Skip lunch** since you'll probably have a heavy breakfast, which is usually included in the price of your accommodations. Alternatively, try a fast food restaurant or put together a picnic at a grocery store.

14. **For dinner, try the less expensive pubs or the many street vendors** that offer excellent foods at the Market Night (Wednesday evening in Hamilton) or Heritage Night (Tuesday evening in St. George). Many families with children find pubs to be good dining alternatives. Alternatively, eat your main meal of the day at a pub and organize an inexpensive picnic, including a bottle of wine (see #14), in the evening.

15. **Watch what you order, especially the tempting wine list,** which can easily start at $50 a bottle and go up to over $500 a bottle. Wine will quickly escalate your dinner bill. A good selection of relatively inexpensive (under $15) wines, including the popular Australian Yellow Tail brand (their Shiraz is probably the best and costs just under $11 in Bermuda), can be found in grocery stores and at Gosling's liquor stores. Enjoy wine from your room overlooking the ocean as the sun sets.

16. **When asked whether you want "regular water" or "bottled water" in a restaurant,** remember, the former is free and the latter is treated like any drink on the menu – it's costly.

Passing U.S. Customs

U.S. citizens returning home may or may not have to pay Customs duties on purchases from Bermuda, depending on the amount you have purchased. Always keep good records of your purchases, such as receipts and an itemized list of everything you purchased.

It's always good to know Customs regulations before leaving home. If, for example, you are a U.S. citizen planning to travel abroad, the Department of Homeland Security's Customs  and Border Protection (formerly the U.S. Customs Office) provides several helpful publications which are available through the agency's website: www.cbp.gov. Go to the "Travel" button at the top of the front page to access several useful online reports, including:

- *Know Before You Go! – Online Brochure*: Outlines facts about exemptions, mailing gifts, duty-free articles, as well as prohibited and restricted articles. Includes duty-free exemptions and duty rates.

- *International Mail Imports:* Answers many questions regarding mailing items from foreign countries back to the U.S. The U.S. Postal Service sends packages to Customs for examination and assessment of duty before they are delivered to the addressee. Some items are free of duty and some are dutiable. The rules have changed on mail imports, so do check on this before you leave the U.S.

- **GSP and the Traveler:** Explains the Generalized System of Preferences program and itemizes goods from particular countries that can enter the U.S. duty-free when they accompany you on your return home. GSP regulations, which are designed to promote the economic development of 140 developing countries, permit many products, especially arts and handicrafts, to enter the United States duty-free, but only if GSP is currently in effect. If not, U.S. citizens will need to pay duty as well as complete a form that would refund the duties once GSP goes into effect again and is made retroactive – one of the U.S. Congress's annual budgetary rituals that is inconvenient to travelers and costly for taxpayers.

U.S. citizens returning from Bermuda may bring back $800 worth of goods free of U.S. taxes every 30 days; the next $1,000 is subject to a flat 3-percent tax (effective as of January 1, 2002). Goods beyond $1,400 are assessed duty at varying rates applied to different classes of goods.

Items mailed home are exempt from duty if the value is US$200 or less. Antiques that are 100 years old (get a receipt documenting the age of the item) or more may enter duty-free, but folk art and handicrafts are dutiable.

The good news for U.S. citizens departing Bermuda by air is that they may clear U.S Customs at the Bermuda international airport before getting on their plane to go back home. However, this service is only available for certain flights departing for the U.S.

3

Getting to Know You

T HERE ARE CERTAIN THINGS you need to know about Bermuda to best orient yourself to this place. First, this is a very small island chain by any standards. Shaped like a fish-hook, this narrow archipelago of 138 limestone islands runs 21 miles in length, covers a land area of 22 square miles, and is 259 feet above sea level at its highest point. It is home to nearly 62,000 local residents. Its largest city, Hamilton, has a population of only 1,100. However, approximately 14,000 people, or 40 percent of the island's employed population, work in Hamilton.

The second thing you'll likely remember is that this small island is an economic powerhouse unlike any you may ever encounter outside of Hong Kong or Singapore. Surprising to many first-time visitors, despite the many cruise ships that frequent this island, it's not tourism that powers this idyllic place. A quick visit to a few choice streets in Hamilton and the super rich enclave of Tucker's Town, tell a very different story about a supercharged economy and the high cost of living in Bermuda. Here's an island where two-bedroom apartments start at $3,000 a month and an average three-bedroom home sells for nearly $1 million.

Median household income is $72,000 a year. Many of these high costs spill over into Bermuda's tourist infrastructure of costly hotels, restaurants, transportation, and sightseeing.

Location and Geography

Found on a map of the Atlantic Ocean, Bermuda seems to be located in the middle of nowhere – 774 miles southeast of New York City, 650 miles east of Cape Hatteras, North Carolina, 950 miles north of Nassau, Bahamas, and 3,460 miles southwest of London. Indeed, Bermuda is the second most isolated inhabited island in the world. It's literally a tiny dot in the middle of the Atlantic Ocean.

Bermuda's seven largest islands make up Bermuda proper. Connected by bridges and causeways, these islands stretch from east to west for a total length of 21 miles, with a maximum width of nearly two miles.

Geological surveys indicate Bermuda is perched on the summit of a submarine mountain that rises about 15,000 feet from the bottom of the sea. Created nearly 100 million years ago by a volcano, the limestone islands consist of fertile land, with pink sand, blue water, and a varied and colorful plant life. In contrast to the tropical islands of the West Indies, which are located more than 1,000 miles south, Bermuda is a sub-tropical island where palm trees and other tropical plants thrive. While small, the islands do have a diverse landscape that is somewhat hilly and rocky in places. Lacking rivers or streams, Bermuda is largely dependent upon rainfall for its water supply, which is caught on the white roofs of homes and stored in underground tanks.

Early residents long ago discovered the excellent building property of the limestone which lies beneath the sandy soil. Cut from hillside quarries, the stone is soft and porous and easily sawed into building blocks. Exposed to the weather, the limestone of

Limestone Construction

Bermuda's houses harden, and there are hundreds of homes on the island today that are more than a century old. Thin slabs of the limestone are laid in overlapping layers to form the distinctive terraced roofs on which rainwater is collected and directed to storage tanks beneath or beside every home. The roof of every Bermuda building is lime-washed or painted white.

Wealthy Waters

Since the 1980s, tourism has played an important yet secondary role in the Bermudian economy. While noted for its excess of sun, sand, and surf, Bermuda is also about serious international business rather than just a tax haven for greedy and unpatriotic

businesses (there are exceptions, including the infamous efforts of Stanley Works and Ingersoll-Rand to locate offshore). Today Bermuda boasts the largest per capita number of lawyers, accountants, and bankers in the world who operate Bermuda's burgeoning international insurance, reinsurance, and financial empires. Indeed, Bermuda is the world's largest captive insurance center, and it ranks as the world's third largest reinsurance center, after New York and London. Nearly 1,600 insurers handle more than $49 billion in insurance premiums each year. That's an impressive global business achievement given the relatively isolated location of Bermuda in the Atlantic Ocean. But then Bermuda has also become a leader in e-commerce, which has quickly redefined the traditional notions of geographic isolation.

Hamilton is a very deceptive-looking harbor-front city. The initial impression is that this is a very small, laidback community lined with trees, flowers, pretty buildings, shops, and restaurants just waiting for the next cruise ship to unload its passengers along Front Street. But dig a little deeper and you find a sophisticated money machine operating at a very low-key level. Front

Street, between Queen Street and Parliament Street, is primarily tourist territory. But the rest of the city is oriented to much bigger players who fuel the local economy.

Covering less than 200 acres, on an average workday this city of 1,100 permanent residents expands after morning rush hour to 14,000 people, many of whom operate the city's business and financial institutions headquartered in the city and concentrated along four major streets and roads – Front Street, Reid Street, Par-La-Ville Road, and Pitts Bay Road. Here you'll find such major and highly respected insurance giants as XL Capital ($10.6 billion) and ACE Insurance ($9.7 billion) and financial powerhouses such as Jardine Matheson Holdings ($4.5 billion) and Ocean Wilsons Holdings ($4.3 billion) as well as some infamous companies such as Tyco International ($40.1 billion). Nearly half of the Fortune 500 companies are represented here. Nearby, along Pitts Bay Road, is the stately, old, but always first-class and elegant Fairmont Princess Hotel that serves as a major center for this thriving business community and its many meetings and conferences. Just stroll through this hotel's lobby, bar, restaurants, or the Fairmont Gold Wing lounge area and you'll see the lawyers, accountants, bankers, and consultants gathering to conduct the business of Bermuda. Altogether, the city of Hamilton contributes nearly $2 billion a year to Bermuda's gross domestic product, an impressive accomplishment for a small town of only 1,100 people!

A Statistical Profile

Bermuda's population is well educated and skilled. Indeed, 19 percent of the people possess a university degree – a higher rate than Canada and the United Kingdom. Nearly 73% of Bermuda's population are born in Bermuda. Its population is predominantly black (61%). The total workforce of nearly 38,000 consists of 77% Bermudians and 23% expatriates. The majority of expats come from the United Kingdom, the United States, and Canada. Since many hotels and resorts either downsize or close during the winter months (December through February), some of Bermuda's workforce is seasonal. Average employment income is $44,000 a year, and median household income is $72,000 a year. While the unemployment rate is estimated to be 2.6%, employment is readily available and many jobs pay very well. Nearly 30% of Bermuda's population is classified by the government as poor or nearly poor (compared to 32% in the United States). Another 46% are classified as middle-class and another 24% are considered well-to-do. Most visitors see few visible signs of poverty in a country that prides itself in being visually neat, clean, green, flowering, and tidy.

Bermuda's narrow winding roads are often crowded and congested, especially near Hamilton during rush hour. To control the excess of cars, the government mandates only one private car per household, and most of these cars are small economy-sized European or Japanese models, such as Peugeot, Renault, Volkswagen, Honda, and Toyota. This translates into 22,000 private cars and over 24,000 motorcycles and mopeds, along with nearly 5,100 buses, trucks, and other vehicles.

Bermuda's Nine Parishes

Bermuda is divided into nine parishes, each with its own distinct character and set of attractions. It's important to orient yourself to this grid of parishes, since much of Bermuda's travel and shopping attractions are defined in terms of parish locations. Running from east to west, the parishes include:

ST. GEORGE'S PARISH

This is Bermuda's most historic parish – where the settlement of the islands began in 1609. Located at the eastern end of the island, St. George's Parish includes the town of St. George, the Bermuda International Airport, St. George's Golf Course, and Fort St. Catherine. Most visitors focus attention on the town of St. George, which includes a cruise ship terminal and several shops, restaurants, local attractions (Bermuda National Trust Museum, St. George's Historical Society Museum, Tucker House Museum, Carter House, Deliverance, Old Rectory, Old State House, St. Peter's Church, Somers Garden, Unfinished Church, and Town Hall). St. George's parish also includes two public beaches good for swimming and snorkeling (Tobacco Bay and St. Catherine's Beach). Several cruise ships dock just off the town square at the Ordnance Island cruise ship terminal.

HAMILTON PARISH

One of two eastern parishes (the other is Smith's Parish to the south), Hamilton Parish is located on the north side of the island, immediately west of St. George's Parish. Primarily a residential area, this parish is home to the Grotto Bay Beach Resort and Tennis Club and boasts scenic walks, beautiful beaches, several parks, the famous Crystal Caves found at Walsingham Estate, Bermuda Perfumery, Bermuda Railway Museum, and the Bermuda Aquarium, Museum, and Zoo (BAMZ). The attractions in this parish are very kid-friendly, especially the caves, aquarium, museums, and zoo.

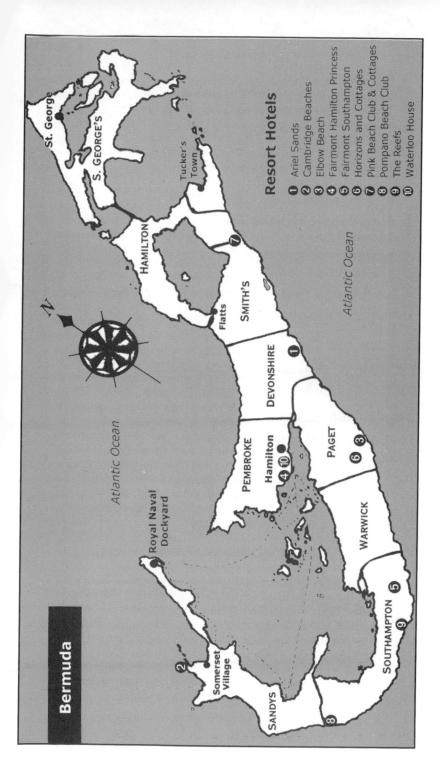

SMITH'S PARISH

Located immediately south of Hamilton Parish along a spectacular coastline, this residential area is the site of the upscale Tuckers Town, two golf clubs, the island's largest wildlife sanctuary (great for birdwatching), John Smith's Bay Park, Devil's Hole Aquarium, and the historic Spanish Rock and Jeffrey's Cave. It's also home to one of Bermuda's top cottage resort and condo complexes – Pink Beach Club and Cottages.

PEMBROKE PARISH

Located in the center of the island chain, on the north shore, and immediately west of Devonshire Parish, this is Bermuda's most important parish. It's home to the city of Hamilton, the island's center for employment, commerce, finance, and government. It's also the island's major center for shopping, dining, accommodations, and cruise ships. Many visitors prefer staying here because of the convenience and attractions of this community. Outside the city center Pembroke Parish is noted for the Bermuda Underwater Exploration Institute, Admiralty House Park, Clarence Cove, and Pembroke Marsh and Parson's Road Playground. The most famous resort complex here is the classic pink Fairmont Hamilton Princess, which is located along the water on the western edge of the city. Several other popular properties, such as the Rosedon and Waterloo House, also are located nearby.

> *Pembroke Parish is home to the city of Hamilton – the island's center for employment, commerce, finance, and government.*

DEVONSHIRE PARISH

Located between Pembroke Parish on the west and Smith's Parish on the east, Devonshire stretches the full width of the island and thus has both a northern and southern coastline. Devonshire Parish is noted for its Arboretum, Palm Grove Garden, Devonshire Marsh (popular for birdwatching), Ocean View Golf Course, Palmetto Park (popular for picnicking and water views) Devonshire Bay Park (great hilltop coastal views and a small beach), and hiking trails. This also is home to the popular Ariel Sands resort which is located on its southern shore.

PAGET PARISH

Located southwest of Devonshire Parish and immediately east of Warwick Parish, Paget Parish is noted for is popular Elbow Beach Park (great beach), Waterville (National Trust Headquarters and elegant home of the famous Trimingham family of the 1700s), Botanical Gardens and Camden, Paget Marsh, and the Railway Trail (a historical 2¼ mile, or 2 hour, hiking trail with terrific view of the island that begins in Paget Parish and ends in Southampton Parish). This is also home to one of Bermuda's most exclusive top quality resorts – the Elbow Beach Bermuda.

WARWICK PARISH

Located between Paget Parish on the east and Southampton Parish on the west, Warwick Parish is noted for its resorts, beaches, and golf courses. Here you'll find the Riddells Bay Golf Club and Belmont Hills Golf Club on the northern shore, the continuation of the Railway Trail (many new points of interest), Astwood Park (popular for cliff or beach weddings), South Shore Park (stretches for a half mile from Warwick Parish to the popular Horseshoe Bay in Southampton Parish), Warwick Long Bay Park (good and less crowded beach). You'll also find the very reasonably priced Clairfont Apartments located in this parish.

SOUTHAMPTON PARISH

Sandwiched between Warwick Parish on the east and Sandys Parish on the north, here you'll find the huge Fairmont Southampton resort complex and its adjacent Fairmont Southampton Golf Club. It also includes the Bermuda Golf Academy, and Port Royal Golf Course. Other noteworthy resorts and hotels in this area include the Wyndham Bermuda Resort and Spa (formerly the Sonesta Beach Resort), Pompano Beach Club, and The Reefs (its Coconuts Restaurant offers a unique barefoot candlelight dining experience on the beach). You'll also find the historic Gibbs' Hill Lighthouse Park (climb the 562 feet above sea level lighthouse for a great view of the island), South Shore Park (famous beaches, including Horseshoe Bay), Church Bay Park (great for snorkeling), and Whale Bay Battery and West Bay Fort (interesting history and great views).

SANDYS PARISH

This is Bermuda's westernmost parish that lies immediately north of Southampton Parish. Connected to Pembroke Parish and the City of Hamilton by public ferry (will save you lots of road time).

Sandys Parish is home to Somerset Village and the famous Royal Naval Dockyard where the largest cruise ships dock and where a few noted artisans practice their trades and offer unique shopping opportunities. Sandys Parish also is noted for its Hog Bay Park, Somerset Long Bay Park and Nature Reserve, Heydon Trust Estate, Springfield and Gilbert Nature Reserve, Lagoon Park (Ireland Island South), Scaur Hill Fort and Park, Somerset Bridge, and St. James' Church, and several attractions at the Dockyard complex (see our separate section below on the Royal Naval Dockyard).

Bermuda's Three Major Communities

Most visitors to Bermuda spend a disproportionate amount of time in the island chain's three major communities: Hamilton, St. George, and the Royal Naval Dockyard. These communities also have cruise ship terminals and several shops and restaurants.

HAMILTON

Chances are you will spend a great deal of time shopping, sightseeing, and dining in the city of Hamilton, Bermuda's capital since 1815. If you're looking for action, Hamilton is the place to be. Easily navigated on foot, this quaint town of 1,100 residents and nearly 14,000 weekday workers is noted for its many colorful and historic buildings, interesting architecture, churches, museums, galleries, shops, parks and gardens, attractive accommodations, and two cruise ship terminals that serve as disembarkation points for hundreds of tourists who crowd the main streets of Hamilton.

Picturesque **Front Street**, which runs east to west along the harbor, is the town's busiest street that is packed with shops, department stores, and restaurants, especially between Queen Street in the west and Parliament Street in the east. Its small

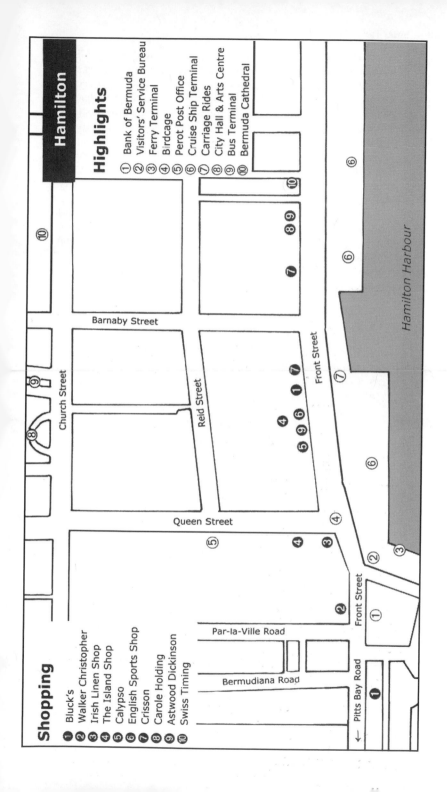

Hamilton

Highlights

1. Bank of Bermuda
2. Visitors' Service Bureau
3. Ferry Terminal
4. Birdcage
5. Perot Post Office
6. Cruise Ship Terminal
7. Carriage Rides
8. City Hall & Arts Centre
9. Bus Terminal
10. Bermuda Cathedral

Shopping

1. Bluck's
2. Walker Christopher
3. Irish Linen Shop
4. The Island Shop
5. Calypso
6. English Sports Shop
7. Crisson
8. Carole Holding
9. Astwood Dickinson
10. Swiss Timing

Hamilton Harbour

Barnaby Street

Church Street

Reid Street

Front Street

Queen Street

Par-la-Ville Road

Bermudiana Road

Pitts Bay Road

Front Street

lanes, balcony restaurants, and shops offering "original" Bermuda products (pepper sauces, perfumes, black rum cakes, and Gosling's Black Seal Rum) give this area a very unique character. Along this 1,500-foot stretch of road you'll find two adjacent cruise ship passenger terminals, the ferry terminal, the Visitors' Service Bureau, and Bird Cage (traffic policeman directing traffic at the intersection of Front Street and Queen Street.

Two parallel streets immediately to the north of Front Street – **Reed Street** and **Church Street** – are home to many of Hamilton's shops, business offices, Government House, Post Office, City Hall, central bus terminal, and churches.

Front Street continues west as **Pitts Bay Road**. Here you'll find more shops and restaurants, the Royal Bermuda Yacht, and the stately pink Fairmont Hamilton Princess Resort as well as the Waterloo House and Rosedon Hotel.

Visitors to Hamilton can easily find a full day of sightseeing attractions. The most popular places to visit include:

- Bermuda Cathedral (Cathedral of the Most Holy Trinity)
- Bermuda National Public Library and Historical Society Museum
- Bermuda Underwater Exploration Institute
- Cabinet Building and Senate Chamber
- Ferry Terminal
- Fort Hamilton
- Government House
- Hamilton City Hall and Arts Centre (includes the Bermuda National Gallery and the Bermuda Society of Arts Gallery)
- No. 1 Passenger Terminal
- Par-la-Ville Park
- Perot Post Office
- St. Andrew's Presbyterian Church
- St. Theresa's Cathedral
- Sessions House and Jubilee Clock Tower
- Victoria Park
- Visitors' Service Bureau

In addition to shopping and walking the streets of Hamilton, many visitors enjoy taking the regularly scheduled (Monday to Saturday, 10am - 4pm) **Art and Architectural Tours** of the town, which is sponsored through the Bermuda National Gallery (Tel. 295-9428, www.bng.bm). Chapter 7 includes information on each of these attractions.

ST. GEORGE

Located at the far eastern end of Bermuda, St. George is a sleepy, charming, and seductive little historical town that especially comes alive when cruise ships dock at the Ordance Island cruise ship terminal just south of King's Square. The oldest continually inhabited town of English origin in the New World, in 2000 St. George became a UNESCO World Heritage Site. Named for the legendary dragon slayer and patron saint of England, St. George was Bermuda's original settlement (1609), which also served as the island's capital for 200 years. Its long history is tied to colonial Jamestown in Virginia, the American Revolution, and the American Civil War. For example, the old Globe Hotel served as the headquarters for arms agents of the Confederacy during the American Civil War when Bermuda played an important role in supplying arms to both sides.

If you're looking for action, you won't need to spend much time here since St. George has limited attractions and staying power. But if you enjoy quiet and lazy days, strolling along quaint lanes and alleyways, dining and drinking in charming restaurants and pubs, viewing picturesque buildings, and examining unique military, civic, and religious architecture, St. George may be the perfect place to spend some time.

The center of St. George is **King's Square**. Here you will find the historic town hall, stocks, and Visitors' Service Bureau. **Water Street** begins on the western side of the square and runs nearly 1,500 feet until it intersects with the town's main street, **Duke of York Street**. Both streets are lined with shops and restaurants. The areas north and east of Duke of York Street include many of the town's attractions.

In addition to shopping and dining, visitors to St. George normally spend their time visiting the following sites in and around the town:

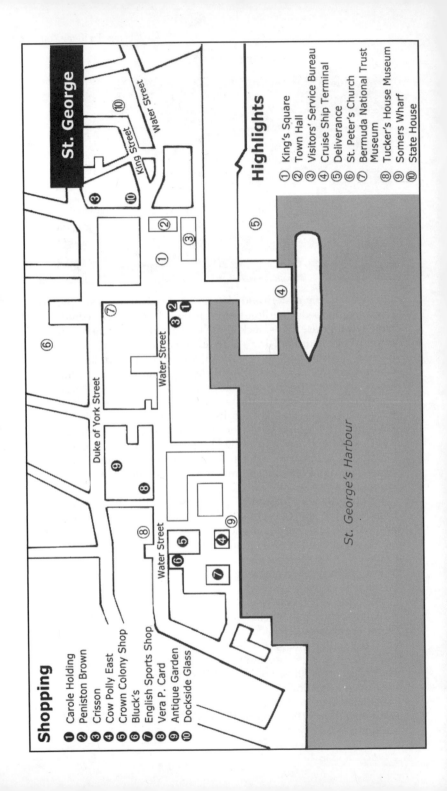

St. George

Shopping
1. Carole Holding
2. Peniston Brown
3. Crisson
4. Cow Polly East
5. Crown Colony Shop
6. Bluck's
7. English Sports Shop
8. Vera P. Card
9. Antique Garden
10. Dockside Glass

Highlights
1. King's Square
2. Town Hall
3. Visitors' Service Bureau
4. Cruise Ship Terminal
5. Deliverance
6. St. Peter's Church
7. Bermuda National Trust Museum
8. Tucker's House Museum
9. Somers Wharf
10. State House

St. George's Harbour

Duke of York Street

Water Street

King Street

Water Street

- Art Gallery (Bridge House)
- Barber's Alley
- Bermuda National Trust Museum (Globe Hotel)
- Bermudian Heritage Museum
- *Deliverance* (replica ship)
- Ducking Stool
- Fort St. Catherine
- Gates Bay (St. Catherine's Beach)
- Old Rectory
- Somers' Garden
- St. George's Golf Course
- St. George's Historical Society Museum, Printery, and Garden
- St. Peter's Church
- State House
- Tobacco Bay
- Town Hall
- Tucker House Museum
- Unfinished Church
- White Horse Pub

During cruise ship season, every Tuesday evening in St. George is a festive Heritage Night.

ROYAL NAVAL DOCKYARD

Located on the far northwestern end of Bermuda, at the tip of Ireland Island, the historic Royal Naval Dockyard once served as the largest British naval facility outside the United Kingdom and a symbol of British naval power in the western Atlantic for nearly 150 years. In fact, all forts built in Bermuda during the 1800s were designed to protect this strategic installation.

Construction on the Dockyard began in 1809, and it functioned until its closing in 1951. It was from here that the British Royal Navy sailed to the United States in the War of 1812 and attacked Washington, DC, which included burning the White House.

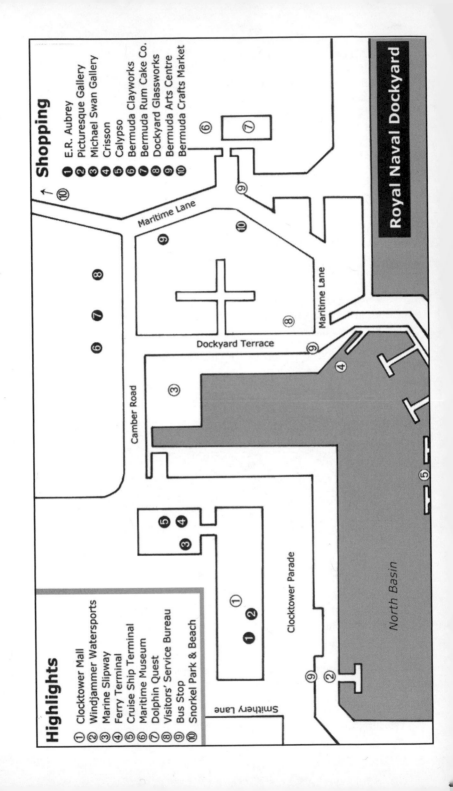

Highlights

1. Clocktower Mall
2. Windjammer Watersports
3. Marine Slipway
4. Ferry Terminal
5. Cruise Ship Terminal
6. Maritime Museum
7. Dolphin Quest
8. Visitors' Service Bureau
9. Bus Stop
10. Snorkel Park & Beach

Shopping

1. E.R. Aubrey
2. Picturesque Gallery
3. Michael Swan Gallery
4. Crisson
5. Calypso
6. Bermuda Clayworks
7. Bermuda Rum Cake Co.
8. Dockyard Glassworks
9. Bermuda Arts Centre
10. Bermuda Crafts Market

Royal Naval Dockyard

Maritime Lane

Maritime Lane

Dockyard Terrace

Camber Road

North Basin

Clocktower Parade

Smithery Lane

Today the attractive gray stone Royal Naval Dockyard complex has been converted into a shopping mall, arts center, craft market, and restaurants. Major attractions here include:

- Bermuda Arts Centre
- Bermuda Clayworks
- Bermuda Craft Market
- Bermuda Maritime Museum
- Clocktower Building (shopping mall and restaurants)
- Dockyard Glassworks and Bermuda Rum Cake Factory

The Bermuda Maritime Museum is the island's most popular tourist destination.

The largest cruise ships that visit Bermuda dock just across the bay from the Royal Naval Dockyard complex. The fastest and most pleasant way to get from this area to Hamilton is by public ferry, a trip that costs $4.00 and takes about 20 minutes when the high-speed catamaran is in service during the high season. Reaching this area by bus from Hamilton takes nearly one hour.

PART II

In Search of Treasures

4

Shopping Smart

BERMUDA HAS A WELL-DESERVED reputation as an upscale shopping destination, which also caters to middle-class locals and travelers. Visitors quickly discover one of the major activities here is shopping. Primarily centered near the cruise ship docks among the picturesque store fronts along Front Street in Hamilton and Water Street in St. George and within a complex of imposing limestone buildings at the Royal Naval Dockyard, shopping in Bermuda can well become a good two- to three-day lifestyle activity interspersed with dining, sightseeing, and relaxing bus and ferry rides.

Most shops offer imported luxury goods from the United Kingdom, Europe, and the United States, such as jewelry, watches, crystal, china, table ware, linens, clothes, beachwear, perfumes, cosmetics, leather goods, and liquor, which are found in most cruise ship ports worldwide. However, there is a decided British flavor to the mix of goods. A few shops also offer locally produced items, such as uniquely designed jewelry, ceramics, linens, fine art, crafts, souvenirs, T-shirts, liquor, perfumes, and foods.

Whatever your shopping preferences and budget, you're bound to find some treasures to take home as a momento of your visit to Bermuda.

Two Shopping Classes

Given the upmarket profile of Bermuda's visitors, one would expect most shops to primarily offer expensive imported name-brand products. However, shops in Bermuda tend to cater to two markets simultaneously. On the one hand, many visitors who fly into Bermuda and stay at expensive hotels and resorts and dine in local restaurants are relatively upscale travelers and discerning shoppers who expect quality. Accordingly, many shops offer expensive name-brand and exclusive lines of imported jewelry, watches, crystal, china, perfumes, clothes, and gift items from Europe for this well-heeled group of visitors.

On the other hand, Bermuda receives thousands of less affluent cruise ship passengers each week during the April to October cruise season. While some of these visitors are big spenders, other cruise ship passengers tend to shop for bargains, including inexpensive jewelry, art, souvenirs, T-shirts, and other gift items. They won't be disappointed, since many shops near the cruise ship docks, such as **Carole Holding**, **The Island Shop**, **Calypso**, **E.R. Aubrey**, and **A.S. Cooper & Sons** in Hamilton, are jampacked with a wide assortment of goods that appeal to all types of shoppers. In fact, one of the basic rules of shopping in Bermuda is this:

> Shops closest to the cruise ships tend to offer less expensive products and advertise sales on selected goods; shops farther away from the cruise ships, as well as those in hotels and resorts, offer better quality goods and few sales.

Therefore, if you are looking for bargains and sales as well as souvenirs, hang around the shops that cater to the cruise ship passengers. But if you're seeking quality products, venture a block or two beyond the central cruise ship shopping area as well as head for the shops found in Bermuda's major hotels and resorts, such as the Fairmont Hamilton Princess, Fairmont Southampton, Elbow Beach Bermuda, and the Wyndham Bermuda Resort and Spa (formerly the Sonesta Beach Resort). Here, you'll notice a considerable difference in the quality and cost of goods. A few top shops, such as Crisson and The Island Shop, manage to successfully cater to both shopping audiences.

Whatever your shopping preferences, you should find some excellent shopping opportunities in Bermuda. While prices may at times seem high, they probably aren't when compared to similar items at full retail price back home. Some shops claim 20% to 40% savings on jewelry, watches, perfumes, and clothing compared to retail prices in the United States. However, we're suspicious of such claims, since many of the same items can be purchased at similar, if not better, discounts in the United States. For example, Ron found the same Polo Ralph Lauren shirt he purchased on sale for $19 at a department store in Virginia a week before he visited Bermuda selling for the full retail price of $75 at A.S. Cooper in Hamilton. The U.S. store was moving summer items out in anticipation of the incoming fall merchandise. The Hamilton shop was still selling the summer season's clothing at full retail price, an issue you may encounter in other shops.

The Local Shopping Culture

There are certain things you need to know about the local shopping culture and scene that will help you become a smart and savvy shopper in Bermuda. Keep the following shopping information and tips in mind when you shop in Bermuda.

1. **Shopping hours vary, depending on cruise ship schedules and shopping areas.** Most shops in Hamilton and St. George are open Monday through Saturday from 9am to 5:30pm. However, many stores have extended hours when cruise ships are in town, including Sunday hours. Shopping is a seven-day-a-week affair at the Royal Naval Dockyard:

    Clocktower Mall
    (May-November)
    Monday - Friday, 9:30am - 6pm
    Saturday, 10am - 6pm
    Sunday, 10am - 5pm

    Clocktower Mall
    (November - March)
    Monday - Saturday, 10am - 5pm
    Sunday, 11am - 5pm

    Bermuda Arts Center
    Daily, 10am - 5pm

    Bermuda Craft Market
    Daily, 10am - 5pm

2. **Sunday is a good time to head to the far western tip of Bermuda (Ireland Island North) and shop at the Royal Naval Dockyard.** Since shops in downtown Hamilton and St. George are usually closed on Sunday, plan to do Sunday shopping at the Royal Naval Dockyard. You may want to

plan to spend several hours in this area combining shopping with dining and sightseeing.

3. **Look for special evening shopping in Hamilton and St. George.** During the cruise ship season (starting April 28th) Hamilton hosts "Harbour Night" along Front Street and adjacent to the cruise passenger terminal. The street becomes a pedestrian-only zone filled with arts and crafts vendors, food stalls, and live music. Many shops in this area stay open nightly until 9pm. St. George has a similar Tuesday evening festival called "Heritage Night."

4. **Don't expect to encounter much price competition, nor should you waste time doing comparative shopping in Bermuda.** While you might assume there is competition among shops, in reality such competition is not reflected in the prices of the same or similar goods. In fact, there is no advantage in comparing prices of hotel shops to shops in town. One reason for the "same prices" is that many of the shops in the hotels and resorts are owned by the same shops in town. Consequently, prices in Bermuda tend to be "fixed" – the same wherever you shop. Savvy shoppers do their comparative shopping back home **before** they arrive in Bermuda to see if indeed they are getting price advantages when shopping in Bermuda.

5. **Be leery of claims that prices are lower in Bermuda than in the United States.** Such claims may be true if you usually pay full retail back home. However, savvy shoppers in the U.S. look for sales, shop at discount warehouses and factory outlets, and shop online where they can often save 10 to 70 percent off of retail prices. Except on duty-free items, few shops in countries around the world can beat the prices offered by U.S. retailers and wholesalers. Like many tourist centers, there's a certain psychological dimension to shopping that is frequently observed among travelers who normally do not do much shopping back home. Many visitors enjoy shopping because they often (1) have free "shopping time" when traveling; (2) engage in impulsive activities they might not otherwise do back home; (3) like the selections and colors (often tropical); (4) find something unique to Bermuda; (5) shop for things imported from Britian, which are less than in the U.S., with china and woolen items predominating; (6) need gift and souvenir items for friends and relatives; and (7) don't know if they will find the same item back home. Indeed, shopping becomes a fun activity where they can meet merchants and artisans, acquire some unique items

and interesting stories, and bring back home souvenirs, gifts, and special items for their friends, relatives, homes and wardrobes. Whether or not they got "good deals" in the process is another question altogether.

6. **Shop prices and product quality tend to be high in Bermuda.** Despite the fact that Bermuda is a popular shopping center, don't expect to find many bargains in Bermuda. The cost of doing business in Bermuda tends to be very high – duties, rents, and labor costs. The shopping focus in Bermuda is on **quality** items, many of British and European origin, that cost even more in North America. Look for Irish linens, Scottish woolens, Shetland and cashmere sweaters, British and French clothing and accessories, Wedgwood and Royal Copenhagen fine tableware, unique Swiss timepieces, and top quality china and crystal. When shopping in Bermuda, Americans should think Neiman-Marcus, Saks Fifth Avenue, Bloomingdale's, and Tiffany's rather than Wal-Mart, Costco, Kay Jewelers, and a middle-class shopping mall.

7. **Shopping in Bermuda is almost tax free.** The only visible add-on taxes you will need to pay in Bermuda are the Passenger Tax (differs for air and cruise passengers) and accommodation tax (varies from 6 to 7¼ percent, depending on the type of accommodations. There is no sales tax in Bermuda. At the same time, Bermuda is not a duty-free port, but you can buy imported goods at very low dutied prices. Import duties have already been paid on most items that appear in various shops. Imported jewelry, for example, is assessed a 6-percent duty. Also, you will be responsible for paying any duties on purchases made in Bermuda when you return to your home country. See Chapter 3 for details on taxes and duties.

8. **You will find a few bargains in Bermuda.** Most good buys are found on locally produced items, such as jewelry, art, perfume, liquor, and cedar products, and any low-duty imported items, such as liquor, watches, china, crystal, linens, and other items not produced in your country of origin for which you may pay little or no duty when you return home. Several places claim Americans can save up to 40 percent on some imported goods, such as French perfumes, English bone china, crystal, porcelain, Swiss watches, Danish silver and jewelry, Irish linens, Scottish tweeds, Italian silks, and cashmere sweaters, because of special relationships Bermuda shops have with producers and wholesalers in the United Kingdom and Europe. However, that depends on where

you shop back home and whether or not you pay full retail prices for such items. At the same time, some items, such as Irish tablecloths, may have little appeal to Americans who generally do not use tablecloths. Since there is such a large mark-up and then major discounting on jewelry in North America, it's difficult to advise on whether or not jewelry purchases in Bermuda are a bargain. You need to know jewelry, especially different quality stones and craftsmanship, before you can determine whether or not you are getting a good deal. Jewelry is one of those unique items that people tend to fall in love with and thus may pay the asking price, less a negotiated discount if they can bargain.

9. **Look for sales, but be careful.** Jewelry stores near cruise ship terminals often put up sale signs primarily for cruise ship passengers whom they know are looking for a bargain. Department stores also place sale signs – 25-50 percent – on different tables. However, be careful and don't assume what you pick up is part of the sale grouping. Many sale signs in department stores are confusing. Be sure to carefully check prices before making a purchase. An item you thought was on sale may not be because of how stores handle their signage. Some locals claim this is an old department store trick!

10. **Look for 10-percent discount coupons.** Several of the free flyers and brochures for tourists include special 10- percent discount coupons. Look carefully through the free literature before you go shopping, to see if stores have such coupons. You can always ask a store if they have any special coupons or discounts, just in case you missed their advertising literature.

11. **The retail business in Bermuda is very incestuous and less than fully competitive.** The word in Bermuda commercial circles is "consolidation" – many shops and department stores have undergone a great deal of consolidation during the past 10 years. Indeed, it's increasingly difficult to find small independent mom-and-pop shops in Bermuda these days. Most shops are owned by large companies that have numerous branches. Such companies often use different names to distinguish one shop from another and thus give the false impression of competition. **Crisson's** jewelry and watch stores now have 10 branches throughout Bermuda. **A.S. Cooper**, **E.R. Aubrey**, **The English Sports Shop**, and

Carole Holding also have several branch shops, including The Bermuda Shop at the Fairmont Southampton Resort. Calypso also owns Voilá and United Colors of Benetton. Even the Dockyard Glassworks at the Royal Naval Dockyard calls itself Dockside Glass in St. George. The names may be different, but the ownership is the same. Such consolidation is clearly one of the reasons why there is little or no price competition in Bermuda. Indeed, you will quickly begin recognizing familiar names wherever you shop in Bermuda, especially the ubiquitous Crisson, Cooper, E.R. Aubrey, and The English Sports Club. However, consolidation also has its limitations. For example, the venerable yet increasingly troubled Trimingham's department store consolidated with Smith's department store in early 2004. But in July 2005, Trimingham's closed its doors for good, after 163 years in Bermuda. Not only did this closure shock the local community and lay off 275 workers, it also left a big hole along Front Street in Hamilton, directly across from the cruise ship terminals.

12. **Cruise ship passengers tend to be steered toward particular "recommended" shops.** Like elsewhere in cruise ship ports, in Bermuda many cruise ship personnel have special deals with shops – shops pay them a fee or commission for sending them passengers. These are not necessarily the best shops and prices are often inflated in order to pay back their commissioned clients. If you arrive by cruise ship and onboard personnel recommend particular shops, be careful in following their recommendations for "good deals." Chances are these people have a conflict of interest – they may make more money on shore from their shopping recommendations than on board from their ship duties! Savvy shoppers use their own judgment in finding the best shops and are usually suspicious of anyone in the travel business who claims to be a shopping expert, which often translates into someone who gets 10 to 20 percent commissions on everything you purchase!

13. **Art lovers should be prepared to travel around the island for their shopping treasures and make appointments.** Bermuda's art scene tends to be dispersed throughout the island, with galleries and studios in Hamilton, the Royal Naval Dockyard, and private home studios. You are well advised to call ahead for appointments in the case of private studios, such as The Birdsey Studio and the Lisa Quinn Studio, and even the studios in the Bermuda Art Centre at the Royal Naval Dockyard which often keep irregular "artist/island hours."

14. **Look for attractive locally produced items.** Many shops offer items produced by local manufacturers and artists. A few quality jewelry shops design an exclusive line of their own jewelry. Several local artists pro-  duce attractive paintings, sculptures, and drawings. Look for cedar wood products, including works of master carvers. Many artists and craftspeople produce a wide range of arts and crafts. You'll also find a few surprising Bermudiana and gift shops, such as the popular Carole Holding and The Island Shop. Also look for locally produced liquors as well as many antiques and collectibles.

15. **Merchants prefer cash but most will accept credit cards.** Since credit card commissions tend to be high, with American Express being the most costly to handle, many merchants prefer dealing with cash. However, most places will accept credit cards, preferably Visa or MasterCard. Leave your Discover card at home.

16. **Prices are generally fixed in Bermuda.** Wherever you shop, you are expected to pay the marked price. Most shops do not bargain, and many shops periodically run sales. However, there are a few exceptions to this pricing rule that can lead to bargains. If you buy several items, purchase large quantities, or consider a high-ticket item, such as jewelry, art, or antiques, you can ask for a discount, which you may or may not receive. In the case of china and crystal, you may want to inquire about old or discontinued collections or editions or any items that may be on consignment. Some shops, such as Coopers, may have last season's Wedgwood holiday collection still in stock and thus will offer a good discount on such items – but only if you ask. Our general rule is to ask for a discount if we feel a price is too high. The worst thing that can happen is to be told "no." We have no problem being rejected for such price trimming efforts!

17. **Watch out for last season's collections selling at full retail price.** Some shops sell last season's clothing and accessories as if they were current season's collections. Such items would normally be on sale back home. Don't assume you are always looking at current merchandise.

5

Where to Shop

W hile shopping opportunities can be found throughout Bermuda, most shopping is concentrated in three communities that frequently receive cruise ships: Hamilton, St. George, and the Royal Naval Dockyard. The largest concentration of shopping is found in the town of Hamilton. Many shops in St. George are essentially branches of shops based in Hamilton. While some shops at the Royal Naval Dockyard also are branch shops, several other shops are operated by local artists and craftspeople, giving the Royal Naval Dockyard its own special shopping character. Indeed, if you are looking for unique local products, spend some time exploring the galleries, studios, and markets at the Royal Naval Dockyard.

Hamilton

Most quality shopping in Bermuda is concentrated in a three-block area along picturesque Front Street lined with candy-colored two- and three-story shops and department stores. Here you will find the best jewelry, watch, clothing, china, crystal, art,

and souvenir shops facing the docks where two ocean liners can berth. Since two ships usually come in here on Wednesday during the cruise season, many shops along Front Street, between Burnaby and Parliament streets, stay open until 9 or 9:30pm on that day. This section of the street also is turned into a festive pedestrian-only night market (Harbour Night) complete with live music, children's activities, and street vendors selling arts, crafts, foods, and drinks.

Front Street also houses many main branches of Bermuda's major shops, such as **Crisson, Cécile, The English Sports Shop, E.R. Aubrey, Smith's, Ashwood Dickinson Jewellery, Bluck's,** and **A.S. Cooper & Sons.** It's also home to a few of Bermuda's very special one-of-a-kind shops and galleries, such as **Walker Christopher, Vera P. Card, Irish Linen Shop, Kirk's Jewelry, Desmond Fountain Gallery, Crisson and Hind Fine Art Gallery, Carole Holding, Masterworks Foundation,** and Barbara Finsness's **The Island Shop.** Two blocks north along Church Street (between Queen and Burnaby streets and adjacent to the central bus terminal) are two "must visit" art galleries, the **Heritage Gallery** and **City Hall and Arts Centre.** A very compact shopping area, Hamilton can be easily covered on foot within an hour. To shop it well, you will need more than one day in Hamilton.

St. George

Located at the very eastern end of the archipelago, this old, quaint, and picturesque small town, with its narrow cobblestone streets, tidy row buildings, and bay front location, is filled with historical significance and great colonial character. Designated a World Heritage Site by UNESCO, St. George was initially settled in 1609. It subsequently served as Bermuda's first capital from 1612 until 1815. Thereafter the capital was moved to Hamilton, and St. George became a sort of museum along the water, attempting to preserve its historical character. It is the oldest continually inhabited town of English origin in the New World.

Just wander St. George's two major parallel streets, Water and Duke of York, and explore Kings Square for a few minutes – it doesn't take long to cover this town on foot – and you'll take in most of this town's historical, architectural, and shopping treasures. Picture-postcard red, pink, yellow, green, beige, and white buildings trimmed in white or black define the unique architectural character of St. George. Museums, shops, restaurants, the post office, and public restrooms are housed in attractive historical buildings. When a cruise ship comes into port, shops and restaurants here come alive. As soon as they leave, the town regains its sleepy character. Tuesday night during the summer cruise season (May 4th to September 28th, 7-9:30pm) is designated the festive Heritage Night. Centered on Kings Square, visitors enjoy street markets, late-night shopping, and entertainment. You can easily shop this town in two hours. A half day trip here should be sufficient to shop, see the sights, and stop for lunch or dinner.

Many visitors head for **Somers Wharf**, a small shopping complex just off of Water Street. Here you will find branch shops of several Hamilton-based shops. Some of the best shops here include **A.S. Cooper & Sons**, **Cow Polly East**, **Crown Colony Shop**, and **English Sports Shop**. Other popular shops in St. George are **Crisson**, **Dockside Glass**, **Antique Garden**, **Carole Holding**, and **Peniston Brown**.

The Royal Naval Dockyard

Located at the western tip of this island chain, the Royal Naval Dockyard was initially built in the late 1700s after Britain lost its naval bases in American as a result of their defeat in the American Revolution. It was intended to be the largest British naval facility outside the United Kingdom. Today it serves as another cruise ship dock area and interesting restored historical site. The docks can accommodate the largest ships that come into Bermuda. This impressive fortress-like six-acre limestone complex is an up-and-coming one-stop tourist development area for shopping, dining, entertainment, sightseeing, culture, and sports. Full of character, this historical area includes art galleries, a craft market, a rum cake and glass factory, museums, restaurants, an authentic naval pub, a shopping center, and water sports. This area is especially known for its unique Bermudian character, with many shops and galleries offering products made in Bermuda. Here you can sample some of the island's best painters and photographers, such as

Michael Swan (**Michael Swan Gallery** at Clocktower Mall) and Roland Skinner (**Picturesque** at Clocktower Mall). Shoppers can easily cover this area in a couple of hours, visiting several small shops and galleries in the Clocktower Mall, **Bermuda Clayworks** pottery factory, **Rum Cake Factory**, **Dockyard Glassworks**, and several galleries and vendor stalls in the **Bermuda Arts Centre** and the **Bermuda Craft Market**. Showcasing Bermuda's maritime history, the Bermuda Maritime Museum is well worth a visit. A delightful ferry ride, which takes only 20 minutes, connects the Royal Naval Dockyard with downtown Hamilton via the Hamilton Harbour and docking at Albuoy's Point.

Hotel/Resort Shopping Arcades

The major resorts have shopping arcades or a few shops that cater to their guests:

- Fairmont Hamilton Princess Hotel
- Fairmont Southampton Hotel
- Elbow Beach Bermuda
- Wyndham Bermuda Resort (formerly the Sonesta)
- Coral Beach Club

You'll quickly discover that most tenants are branch shops of major shops found in downtown Hamilton – **Crisson, A.S. Cooper, English Sports Shop, Calypso, Vera P. Card, Carole Holding (The Bermuda Shop)**, and **Cécile**. The shops also maintain the same prices in the hotels and resorts as in their other main and branch shops found in St. George and the Royal Naval Dockyard. Consequently, if you see something you love in one of the hotel shopping arcades, buy it now rather than visit their other stores, or even their seeming competition, in anticipation of getting better prices. The selections and prices are usually the same wherever you shop. If you stay at one of these three properties, shopping in your hotel or resort arcade is simply more convenient than going into Hamilton.

Shopping Centers

Bermuda has few shopping centers since most stores are standalone shops occupying colorful row houses. Bermuda's main shopping center is the **Clocktower Mall** at the Royal Navy Dockyard. Small by most any standard, this shopping center includes the **Michael Swan Gallery, Picturesque Gallery, House of Stuart, E. R. Aubrey, The Reef Gift Shop, Swiss Connection, Dockyard Linens, A.S. Cooper, Crisson, Calypso**, and **Davison's of Bermuda**. Be sure to explore the section to the right and rear since you can easily miss it the way this shopping center is laid out. In fact, the best shops are to the right and rear.

You'll also find a few shopping arcades and alleys off of Front Street in Hamilton:

- **Walker Arcade:** Primarily consists of **Astwood Dickinson Jewellery** and a few restaurants upstairs.

- **Butterfield Place Shopping Concourse:** *67 Front Street.* An upscale shopping center with two top quality luggage and leather goods shops – **Voilé** and **Louis Vuitton** – and a small but very talented custom jeweler, **Kirk's Jewelry**.

- **The Emporium Building:** *69 Front Street.* Primarily occupied by fine art, crafts, and souvenir shops – **Desmond Fountain Gallery** (bronze sculptures), **The Gallery Ltd.** (arts, crafts, paintings, African emphasis – www.kalahariart.com), and **Desert Rose** (specializes in Egyptian rugs, boxes, lanterns, and crafts).

- **Washington Mall:** *Between Church and Reid streets.* Includes a few small shops such as **Harrington Jewellers** and **A & J Sports Cards**.

- **One Cellar Lane:** *47 Front Street.* Primarily occupied by a branch of Barbara Finsness's attractive **The Island Shop**.

In St. George, you'll find a small shopping center and dining complex called **Somers Wharf**, two blocks west of Kings Square and just off Water Street on the left. Here you'll find several branch shops, or familiar looking shops with different names, such as **A.S. Cooper and Sons**, **Bluck's**, **Crown Colony Shop**, **Cow Polly East**, and **The English Sports Shop**.

Department Stores

With the recent demise of Trimingham's and Smith, the department store scene is now dominated by **A.S. Cooper** on Front Street and **Marks & Spencer** at 7 Reid Street in Hamilton. These multi-story department stores are jam-packed with everything from clothing and accessories to perfumes, cosmetics, linens, crystal, tableware, jewelry, and home decorative items. These are very popular shopping centers for tourists. Marks & Spencer is part of the famous Brit-

ish department store chain that carries many of the same products found in the United Kingdom.

Markets

Bermuda basically has three markets that showcase many of the island's arts and crafts:

- **Harbour Nights in Hamilton:** Every Wednesday night during cruise season (April to September) the section of Front Street adjacent to the cruise ship terminal is closed to all traffic except pedestrians. The street becomes a lively night market with arts and crafts vendors, artists, children's activities (such as face painting), restaurants, and live music. Most shops in this area also stay open until 9pm.

- **Heritage Nights in St. George:** Every Tuesday night during cruise season the area around Kings Square becomes a night market, similar to Harbour Nights in Hamilton.

- **Bermuda Craft Market:** Open Monday through Saturday, 10am to 5pm, and Sunday, 11am to 5pm. Closed on Christmas Day and Good Friday. Located next to the Bermuda Arts Centre in the Royal Naval Dockyard (4 Freeport Road), this building is occupied by several craftspeople who showcase an eclectic combination of products – rum cakes, jams, pepper sauce, painted glass, dolls, jewelry, ceramics, T-shirts, cedar boxes, quilts, jewelry, Christmas ornaments, ceramics, small paintings, wearable art, and wickerwork.

Cruise Ship Shoppers

If you arrive in Bermuda by cruise ship, chances are your ship will dock in one or two of these locations – Hamilton, St. George, and/or the Royal Naval Dockyard. The largest ships will put in at the Royal Naval Dockyard while other ships will often visit the other two ports. In the case of Hamilton and St. George, most shopping is within 500 feet of the cruise ship terminals. In Hamilton, 80 percent of the shops are along a three block section of Front Street along Hamilton Harbour – between Bermudiana Road and Parliament Street, which also encompasses the ferry terminal and the Visitors' Service Bureau. If you turn left at Parliament Street, go one block north to Reid Street, turn left, and walk two blocks east along this street until you come to Queen Street. You've now covered over 90 percent of the shops in Hamilton. In St. George, most shops are clustered around King's Square and Water Street and Somers Wharf to the west and to a lesser extent along York Street to the north. In both places, passengers can easily cover most shops within a couple of hours.

If your cruise ship only docks at St. George or the Royal Naval Dockyard, you are well advised to take a taxi or ferry to Front Street in Hamilton. A taxi from St. George to Hamilton takes about 30 minutes. A ferry from the Royal Naval Dockyard takes less than 30 minutes while a bus or taxi can take one hour. Hamilton is where you will find most of the Island's major quality shopping. Most stores in St. George and the Royal Naval Dockyard are small branch shops of larger shops headquartered along Front Street in Hamilton. However, you will find a few specialty shops in St. George and the Royal Naval Dockyard.

If you only have an hour or two to shop in Hamilton, we strongly recommend heading to the major department stores (A.S. Cooper and Marks and Spencer) and a few of our highly recommended shops for top quality gifts, souvenirs, china, glassware, clothing, linens, and jewelry: The Island Shop, Carole Holding, Bluck's, Vera P. Card, Cécile, The English Sports Shop, Archie Brown, The Irish Linen Shop, Astwood Dickinson, Walker Christopher, or Crisson.

Most shops are experienced in packing and delivering goods to cruise ships. If you purchase something that is too large to take on board, most shops can easily arrange sea or air shipments to your final destination.

Depending on your time in port, try to see as much of the island as possible. While taxis tend to be expensive ($30 per hour), they are the most convenient way to see the island, and most taxi drivers will also serve as informative tour guides. You can cut your transportation costs by sharing a taxi with a few other people.

6

What to Buy

T he shops in Bermuda overflow with a wide selection of goods and a decided emphasis on top quality products. Expect to encounter the following products as you navigate the shops of Hamilton, St. George, the Royal Naval Dockyard, and elsewhere in Bermuda:

Jewelry

Jewelry is one of the favorite purchases of visitors to Bermuda. While many jewelry shops primarily import jewelry from Europe, Asia, and the United States, several shops have talented designers who produce unique one-of-a-kind jewelry pieces as well as special theme collections emphasizing Bermuda's flora, fauna, and traditions. Some shops will do custom work.

Quality, trust, and price go hand in hand when shopping for jewelry in Bermuda. Many of Bermuda's jewelry stores are family-owned operations that have been in business for decades. The oldest (Astwood Dickinson Jewellery) recently celebrated its 100th anniversary and the youngest has more than 15 years experience. Indeed, you'll often enjoy talking with the owners, observing their designers at work, and learning about their unique operations.

Since duties on imported jewelry and raw materials into Bermuda are relatively low at 6½ percent, the cost of jewelry in Bermuda is very competitive with the United States, especially since there are no sales taxes in Bermuda. While you will most likely find wider jewelry selec-tions further south in the Virgin Islands, many shops in Bermuda offer a wide range of jewelry in silver, gold, semi-precious stones, and pearls. Some shops, such as **Walker Christopher** (9 Front Street), **Solomon's Fine Jewelry** (17 Front Street), **Astwood Dickinson Jewellery** (Walker Arcade and 83-85 Front Street), and **Kirk's** (Butterfield

Place Shopping Concourse, 67 Front Street) in Hamilton offer their own unique designs and collections, many with Bermudian themes (flora, fauna, landmarks, culture) and old coins recovered from Spanish colonial shipwrecks incorporated in gold settings and made as pendants, bracelets, and cufflinks. Most of these jewelers also will do special designs for clients as well as repair jewelry. If you visit the **Bermuda Arts Centre** at the Royal Naval Dockyard, be sure to stop at artist **Lynn Morrell's** gallery shop, which includes nicely designed one-of-a-kind jewelry using silver and semi-precious stones.

However, most jewelry shops cater to cruise ship passengers with a mix of inexpensive jewelry and imported name-brand jewelry, such as Tiffany's, Cartier, Kaban, and Roberto Coin. Some of the best quality imported jewelry can be found at **Walker Christopher**, **Astwood Dickinson Jewellery**, and **Crisson** (55 and 71 Front Street). **E.R. Aubrey** (19 and 101 Front Street) and **Cooper's Cachet** (27 Front Street) are especially popular with cruise ship passengers. Both Crisson and E.R. Aubrey have numerous branch shops, which are much smaller than their Front Street operations, in major hotels as well as in St. George and the Royal Naval Dockyard.

Watches

Watches are ostensibly a good buy in Bermuda, although we are unable to substantiate this local claim. Before making a watch purchase, you may want to have a particular model watch in mind with information on comparative pricing back home. In fact, since most hotels or resorts in Bermuda have Internet access, you can quickly check on watch prices by browsing several websites specializing in watches. Use one of the search engines,

such as Google or Yahoo, to find prices on the Internet for the watch that interests you. If the watch is a big ticket item, you can always ask for a discount, which you may or may not get. For the widest selection of top quality watches, be sure to visit the jeweler **Crisson** at both 55 and 71 Front Street in Hamilton. They carry such name brands as David Yurman, Longines, Seiko, Ebel, Citizen, Rolex, Raymond Weil, Tissot, Corum, Omega, TagHeuer, Swiss Army, and Movado.

Astwood Dickinson Jewellery at 83-85 Front Street also carries a good selection of name-brand watches, including Chopard, Cartier, Patek Philippe, TagHeuer, Tissot, Citizen, and Omega. **Swiss Timing** at 95 Front Street in Hamilton offers a unique collection of Swiss-made watches. While you may not recognize some of the names, most are top quality timepieces, such as Zenith, Concord, Michel Herbélin (Paris but with Swiss movements), Jean Perret, Certina Alfex, and Jean d'Eve.

Perfumes and Fragrances

Shops and department stores carry a combination of imported and locally produced perfumes and fragrancies. One of the largest selections of perfumes is found at **Peniston Brown and Company Ltd.** (23 Front Street, Hamilton, and 6 Water Street, St. George). The locally produced fragrance Royall Lyme can be found at **A.S. Cooper & Son Ltd.**, **English Sport Shop**, and **Peniston Brown & Company Ltd.** The **Bermuda Perfumery** (212 North Shore Road, Bailey's Bay) creates Bermuda's signature fragrance 'Paradis'. You can visit their factory and gardens and shop at the **Calabash Gift Shop** (Tel. 441-293-0627, Fax 441-293-8810, or e-mail: cmcurtis@ibl.bm. Admission: $1.50 with children under 13 free).

Clothing and Accessories

Several shops and department stores are jam-packed with fashionable men's and women's imported clothes and accessories from the United Kingdom, Europe, and the United States, as well as colorful resort wear. A wide selection of European designer fashion and accessories for women can be found in one of Bermuda's most attractive boutiques, **Cécile** (15 Front Street,

Hamilton). **Calypso** (23-24 Front Street, Hamilton) offers European designer wear and a large selection of swimwear by U.S.-based Ralph Lauren, Calvin Klein, and Jansen on its second floor. The **Crown Colony Shop** and **Cow Polly East** (Somers Wharf shopping complex, St. George) offers a good selection of women's clothing and accessories. Trendy and youthful fashions are available at **Stefanel** (12 Red Street, Hamilton) and **27ᵗʰ Century Boutique** (4 Burnaby Street, Hamilton). Fashionable men's clothes are found at **Aston & Gunn** (2 Reid Street, Hamilton), **English Sports Shop** (Front Street,

Hamilton, and Somers Wharf, St. George), **Archie Brown** (Front Street, Hamilton), and **A.S. Cooper Man** (Front Street, Hamilton).

China, Crystal, Tableware, and Glassware

Bermuda is well known for its excellent selection of fine imported china, crystal, tableware, and glassware. All the major European name brands are well represented here: Royal Doulton, Wedgwood, Royal Copenhagen, Minton, Herend, Chase, Hermes, Aynsley, Royal Worcester, Belleek, Waterford, Daum, Baccarat, Lalique, Orrefors, Royal Brierley, and Lladró, One of the largest collections of china and glassware is found at one of Bermuda's oldest (since 1897) department stores, **A.S. Cooper & Sons** (59 Front Street, Hamilton). Look for exclusive Wedgwood designs and Belleek Darian china here. **Bluck's** (4 Front Street and second contemporary shop next to Marks & Spencer, two blocks east along Front Street, Hamilton), another long established (since 1844) company, is noted for its

fine collection of china, porcelain, crystal, and antiques. Bluck's is especially known for its fine line of Herend china from Hungary, Daum crystal from Germany, and gorgeous contemporary glassware. The expansive two-level **Vera P. Card** shop (11 Front Street, Hamilton) specializes in Lladró figurines, china, Czech crystal, Goebel plates and figurines, and Swarovski glass. **Cooper's Cachet** (27 Front Street, Hamilton) specializes in Waterford crystal.

Calypso (23-24 Front Street, Hamilton) offers uniquely designed colorful and fun ceramic plates and bowls.

Paintings, Sculptures, and Photography

Bermuda offers a good selection of quality art and photography produced by local artists and professional photographers. Some of Bermuda's most popular artists with visitors include Michael Swan (**Michael Swan Galleries**), Carole Holding (**Carole Hold-**

ing Studios), Desmond Fountain (**Desmond Fountain Gallery**), Jo Birdsey Lindberg (**The Birdsey Studio**), and Lisa Quinn (**Lisa Quinn Studio**) – all of whom have shops or galleries. Bermuda has many talented contemporary artists, including Charles Anderson, Dana Cooper, Frank Dublin, Vaughan Evans, Graham Foster, Jason Jones, Heather Macdonald, Rebecca Payne, Bruce Stuart, William West, and Charles Zuill. You can findtheir works exhibited at the Bermuda National Gallery (Hamilton), the Bermuda Arts Centre (Royal Naval Dockyard), and in several private galleries, including corporate galleries (these are special art galleries sponsored by major corporations that support the local art scene).

Most galleries are found in Hamilton and several studios are located at the Royal Naval Dockyard. For a good overview of Bermuda's art scene, be sure to visit the **Bermuda National Gallery** (City Hall & Arts Centre, 17 Church Street, Hamilton, www.bng.bm) and take the **Art and Architectural Tour**, which includes visits to public, commercial, and corporate galleries in Hamilton. Sponsored by the Bermuda National Gallery and conducted by local art expert Laura Gorham, the tour starts at 10am every Tuesday. It costs $65 per person and includes lunch at the Waterloo House. For information and reservations, call 441-295-9428.

If you are interested in meeting some of Bermuda's top artists, we recommend visiting the **Bermuda National Gallery** (see displays and ask for contact info), **Bermuda Society of Arts** (City Hall & Art Centre at 17 Church Street – can purchase from biweekly contemporary art exhibits), **Bermuda Arts Centre** at the Royal Naval Dockyard, and local galleries, such as **Heritage House** and **New Heritage House Gallery** (26 Church Street – across from City Hall), **Michael Swan Galleries** (Butterfield Place, Front Street, Hamilton, and Clocktower Mall, Royal Naval Dockyard),

Carole Holding (81 Front Street, Hamilton), **Desmond Fountain Gallery** (The Emporium Building, 69 Front Street, Hamilton), **The Birdsey Studio** (5 Stowe Hill, Paget, Tel. 236-6658), **Lisa Quinn Studio** (9 Tribe Road #3, Southampton, Tel. 238-1438), and **Masterworks Foundation Gallery** (Bermuda House Lane, 97 Front Street, Hamilton, and at the Botanical Gardens – Arrow Root Factory). Also check out corporate galleries, such as ACE Gallery at the ACE global headquarters (17 Woodbourne Avenue, Pembroke, Monday to Friday, 1am to 5pm, Tel. 295-5200 for information and appointments). This one includes the works of Graham Foster, one of our favorite local artists.

For excellent photography of Bermuda, be sure to see the fine works of Roland Skinner, which are available through his two galleries, **Picturesque** (Clocktower Mall, Royal Naval Dockyard, and The Design Centre, 129 Front Street East, Hamilton – www.picturesquebermuda.com), and the outstanding photography of Ian MacDonald-Smith at his **Just Clicked Gallery** (Bermuda House, 95 Front Street, Hamilton – www.imacsmith.com)

For a unique collection of Shona stone sculptures from Zimbabwe in Africa, visit the **Crisson & Hind Fine Art Gallery**, which is located on the second floor of the Crisson jewelry store and watch emporium at 71 Front Street, Hamilton.

Crafts, Gift Items, and Bermudiana

Bermudian artisans produce numerous arts and crafts that make nice gift items and souvenirs. The emphasis here again is on quality – you'll find very little tourist kitsch in the shops of Bermuda. Local products range from inexpensive prints, T-shirts, shell items, coasters, napkin rings, candles, and cards to more expensive handmade dolls, cedar purses, carvings, ceramics, and pillow covers. One of the best places to acquire such items is at **Carole Holding** (18 Front Street, Hamilton, and the Fairmont Southampton Hotel),

Bermuda's one-stop shop for an excellent range of quality gifts and souvenirs, including the very reasonably priced prints (both framed and unframed) by artist and entrepreneur Carole Holding. This shop gives new meaning to cruise ship marketing – the perfect mix of souvenirs and gift items to satisfy just about any visitor to Bermuda and located directly across the street from the cruise ship terminal in Hamilton! **The Island Shop** (3 Queen Street, and Old Cellar Lane, 47 Front Street, Hamilton) is a "must visit" shop for anyone interested in excellent quality gift and home decorative items, including hand-painted ceramics from Italy and Barbara Finsness's signature collection of pillows, candles, trays, cedar purses, scarves, napkins, and coasters. Indeed, this is **the** favorite shop of many visitors to Bermuda. **Vera**

P. Card (11 Front Street, Hamilton) has good selections of china, crystal, glass, figurines, and jewelry that are popular with gift-givers. **Ronnie Chameau** produces unique Bermuda banana leaf dolls crafted from local flora – popular collector's items – as well as Bermuda cottage doorstops, key holders, and watercolor prints. **Pulp & Circumstance Gifts** (corner of Reid and Queen streets) has a good selection of greeting cards, wrapping papers, ceramics, and glass gift items.

If you enjoy shopping for Christmas decorations, many produced in Bermuda by local artisan Heidi Augustinovic, be sure to stop at **Cooper's Cachet** (27 Front Street, Hamilton), which is an unusual three-in-one shop specializing in fine jewelry and Waterford crystal at the front of the shop and displaying a separate year-round Christmas shop in the second half of the shop – complete with Christmas trees, ornaments, and decorations. If you fall in love with the picture-postcard Bermuda store fronts, you can purchase decorative souvenir plaques of store fronts, buildings, and attractions (Cat's Meow) at the **A. S. Cooper** stores in Hamilton, Royal Naval Dockyard, and St. George's (www.coopersbermuda.com).

Several shops and artisans at the Royal Naval Dockyard offer a good range of arts, crafts, and Bermudiana. In the Clocktower Mall you'll find several shops offering gift and souvenir items, including the **Reef Gift Shop** and **Wadsons** (good selection of inexpensive t-shirts and souvenirs). Immediately northeast of the Clocktower Mall is the **Bermuda Clayworks** (Tel. 234-3136, www.bermudaclayworks.com), a combination factory and shop that produces colorful ceramics. You also can produce your own ceramics here – a great treat for kids and others who enjoy hands-on arts and crafts. Nearby is the **Dockyard Glassworks** (1 Maritime Lane) for an interesting range of colorful glass creations, **Bermuda Arts Centre** (Museum Row, FreeportRoad) for art exhibitions and galleries/studios, **Bermuda Craft Market** (adjacent to the Bermuda Arts Centre) for a unique collection of arts, crafts, and Bermudiana (candles, cedar, ceramics, Christmas ornaments, decorative paintings, dolls, gems, glass, jewelry, miniature furniture, needlework, quilts, wearable art, wickerwork). Master wood sculptor **Chesley Trott**, who works in cedar (you may have noticed his six-foot carving in the baggage retrieval area at the airport), can be found carving in his studio at the Bermuda Arts Centre.

St. George includes a few shops offering good quality arts, crafts, and Bermudiana. Most are branches of shops in Hamilton or the Royal Naval Dockyard. Look for **Carole Holding**, **Bermuda Shop**, **Ceramica Bermuda**, **Paradise Gift Shop**, and **Dockside Glass** – all within a few minutes walk north and west of Kings Square.

Antiques and Collectibles

If you enjoy hunting for unique antiques and collectibles, you're in luck in Bermuda. Here you will find old books, unframed pictures, maps, porcelain, silver, brassware, copperware, and furniture. Shops will handle the appropriate certificates so that antiques can be imported into the U.S. free of duty. Most shops will arrange shipping if necessary.

However, don't expect to find many shops specializing in antiques and collectibles. For years **Bluck's** (4 Front Street, Hamilton) offered high-end antique furniture, but it no longer deals in antiques. **Heritage House** at 26 Church Street includes some antique furniture and old paintings. But the ultimate antique and collectible center is the **Antique Garden** (20 West Duke of York Street, St. George). This two-story house is jam-packed with antiques and collectibles from England and local estates

– china, glassware, mugs, pictures, lamps, books, and furniture. Be prepared for a disorienting experience – it may take you some time for your eyes to get focused on what is definitely a unique collection of varying quality treasures and trash! For old Bermuda maps, books, ephemera, prints, and paintings, make an appointment to see **Anthony Pettit** (Tel. 292-2482, www.anthonypettit.com). **A & J Sports Cards** (upper level, Washington Mall, between Church and Reid Streets, Hamilton) includes several collectibles for sports enthusiasts – mini-helmets, posters, albums, NASCAR cars, shirts, mugs, and stickers – "Magic" starter, booster packs, and Beanie Babies.

Linens

Fine linens from the United Kingdom and Europe are available in several shops and department stores. However, the stand-out shop for top quality linens is **The Irish Linen Shop** (Heyl's Corner, 31 Front Street, Hamilton). From tablecloths and napkins to bedding, bath items, sleepwear, children's clothing, cedar bags, and unique gift items, this two-story shop with nice displays is noted for its outstanding quality and pricey items. For different quality and selections of linens, especially embroidered pillows and hand towels, be sure to visit Barbara Finsness's **The Island Shop** (#3 Queen Street and Old Cellar Lane, 47 Front Street, Hamilton – www.islandexports.com).

Luggage and Leather Goods

A few shops offer excellent quality luggage and leather goods. Leather goods from Columbia and Italy are available at **The**

Harbourmaster (Washington Mall and Reid and Queen Streets, Hamilton). Top quality imported leather goods also are available at **Longchamp** (Fairmont Southampton Hotel shopping arcade), **Voilé** (Butterfield Place Shopping Concourse, 67 Front Street, Hamilton), and **Louis Vuitton** (also in the Butterfield Place Shopping Concourse).

Foods and Gourmet Products

Several companies produce foods unique to Bermuda and which are popular with visitors. One of the largest operations, the **Bermuda Rum Cake Company** (1 Maritime Lane, Royal Naval Dockyard – www.bermudarumcakes.com), bakes popular rum cakes in a variety of flavors – traditional chocolate, rum and ginger,

rum swizzle, banana, coconut, classic coffee, Bermuda gold, and fruit cake). You can sample the differnet cakes and buy directly from the bakery at the Royal Naval Dockyard. You also can purchase these cakes at Dockside Glass (St. George), Goslings Duty Free (airport), airport gift shops, Hamilton Princess Lobby Shop, and A.S. Coopers (Hamilton). **Onion Jacks Trading Post** (77 Front

Street, Hamilton – www.onionjacks.com) also produces its own signature rum and chocolate rum cakes. **Outerbridge Sherry Peppers** (www.outerbridge.com) produces the award-winning Outerbridge Sherry Pepper Sauces and a complete line of gourmet products for enhancing both food and drinks. Their sauces, as well as a related cookbook, are available in most department stores and grocery stores throughout the island. Both **Carole Holding** (81 Front Street) and the **Bermuda Craft Market** (Royal Naval Dockyard) have good selections of locally produced jams, rum cakes, and pepper sauces.

Liquor and Liqueurs

Bermuda is well known for its unique liquors and liqueurs. The most famous is Gosling's Black Seal dark rum. You can purchase this rum through the **Gosling Brothers, Ltd.** (Front and Queen streets, Hamilton – www.blackseal.com) or at the airport. If you purchase it in Hamilton, you may want to do so as an "in-bond" purchase that will be exported and thus not subject to local taxes. Gosling Brothers will deliver purchases to ships. If you are leaving by air, you must make your liquor purchases at the airport. **Burrows, Lightbourn Ltd.** (57 Front Street, Hamilton) also offers a large range of liquors and liqueurs. They also have  stores in St. George and the Royal Naval Dockyard and will deliver to ships. Most liquor stores have good prices on imported wines – one of the better buys in Bermuda.

7

Best Quality Shopping

BERMUDA'S BEST SHOPS are disproportionately found in Hamilton. However, you'll also find many other good quality shops and shopping experiences in various parts of Bermuda. We urge you to include all of Bermuda in your shopping adventure.

This chapter identifies what we consider to be the best shops in Bermuda. While not everyone will agree with our selections, and some people may feel we have overlooked other outstanding shops, nonetheless, this listing should enrich your shopping experience by pointing you in the right direction for identifying your own quality shops.

Hamilton's Best Shops

Hamilton's best shopping is concentrated along Front, Reid, and Church Streets. Front Street, which faces the harbor and cruise ship terminals, is Bermuda's premier shopping center and its prime commercial retail estate section. Starting at the Fairmont Hamilton Princess Hotel's upscale shopping arcade on Pitts Bay Road, which is the western extension of Front Street, and then skipping to the western end of Front Street at Bermudiana Road and continuing east along Front Street until the intersection with Parliament Street, numerous shops and department stores offer a dazzling array of quality jewelry, watches, china, crystal, glassware, clothing, perfumes, cosmetics, linens, art, gifts, crafts, housewares, souvenirs, and liquors for all types of treasure hunters. Reid Street, which parallels Front Street, includes a few clothing stores. Church Street is known for a few art shops and galleries.

JEWELRY AND WATCHES

❑ **Walker Christopher:** *9 Front Street, Hamilton. Tel. 441-2995-1466, Fax 441-292-6656, or e-mail: walkerchris@cwbda.bm.* Located three blocks west of the cruise ship terminals and across

from the Bank of Bermuda and ferry terminal, this high-end shop especially appeals to well-heeled locals, who constitute nearly 50 percent of their business, and discerning visitors from nearby hotels (Waterloo House, Fairmont Hamilton Princess, and Rosedon) rather than passengers from the cruise ships who tend to shop at the other end of Front Street. Indeed, Walker Christopher gets our vote as the best jewelry shop in Bermuda, especially because of its top quality, unique designs, and personalized service. In business for over 20 years, it offers a good range of locally designed and crafted jewelry along with imported jewelry. In fact, about 50 percent of their offerings are produced locally. The shop is especially noted for crafting authentic treasure coins, such as gold doubloons and the silver "pieces of eight," recovered from Spanish shipwrecks around the world and ancient Greek and Roman artifacts spanning more than 2,300 years, into attractive wearable artwork (gold pendants, necklaces, earrings, and cufflinks). Walker Christopher is also known for its quality Tahitian black pearls, attractive Italian gold jewelry (good selection of gold chains), and unusual combinations of strung pearls. Look for design originals by Michael Good and Carrera y Carrera along with some art deco, art nouveau, and antique jewelry. If you have a few days in Bermuda, consider having a piece of jewelry designed and fabricated here to your specifications. The shop also does jewelry repairs. Its four talented designers do wonderful custom work. Try to make this one of your first jewelry stops in Hamilton since you may decide to have some jewelry made here and thus you'll need some time to have such work done before you leave Bermuda.

❑ **Crisson Jewellers:** *55 & 71 Front Street and 16 Queen Streets (Hamilton); Water and York Streets (St. George); The Clocktower Mall (Royal Naval Dockyard); and at all major hotels (10 locationsaltogether). Tel. 441-295-2351 or Fax 441-292-9153. Website: www.crisson.com.* Ubiquitous throughout Bermuda in terms of both shops and advertising, the Crisson jewelry stores are jam-packed with good quality name-brand watches and jewelry that especially cater to tourists from both cruise ships and hotels. The two main shops along Front Street appeal to cruise ship passengers. The shop at 71 Front Street includes the Crisson and Hind Fine Art Gallery on the second floor, which features African stone sculptures by master Shona artists from Zimbabwe. Quality shops with a mass marketing orientation designed to handle large crowds of cruise ship passengers, the emporium-style Crisson shops here are organized around each brand name so you can easily shop by manufacturer. Its two main shops on Front Street in Hamilton include these major watch manufacturers: David Yurman, Ebel, Cyma, Gucci, Citizen, Rolex, Raymond Weil, Tissot, Corum, Longines, Omega, Tag Heuer, Rado, Seiko, Swiss Army, and Movado. Its jewelry line includes the beautiful creations of Kabana and Roberto Coin. If you are looking for name-brand watches and jewelry, Crisson is well worth browsing. The smaller Crisson shops at the hotels and resorts have a more exclusive feel to them.

❑ **Solomon's Fine Jewelry:** *17 Front Street, Tel 441-292-4742 or Fax 441-295-9008.* Located across from the cruise ship terminal, this small and somewhat exclusive shop offers a nice selection of necklaces, earrings, and pearls along with some antique coins. Unlike its nearby mass-market jewelers, Solomon's has the look and feel of a fine jewelry shop, including excellent service. It offers a few unique pieces that are manufactured in its Canadian workshop.

❑ **Astwood Dickinson Jewellery:** *Walker Arcade and 83-85 Front Street, Tel. 441-292-5805.* This is one of Bermuda's oldest (since 1904) family-operated and very special theme jewelers. The Walker Arcade shop is a long, narrow, and at times very crowded jewelry shop. The 83-85 Front Street shop is the largest and most inviting. Astwood Dickinson produces its  own line of limited edition Bermuda theme jewelry (pins, pendants, brooches, bangles, earrings, cufflinks, tie tacks), the Original Bermuda Collection, with floral, faunal, landmark, and cultural themes – birds, ships, fish, lobsters, shells, kites, whales, palmetto trees, land crabs, dinghies, hog shillings, passion flowers, green turtles, lighthouses, lizards, Bermuda onions, tropical moons, whistling tree frogs, Gombey dancers, angel fish, and queen conchs. Its catalog includes photos of its many elegant creations. Astwood Dickinson also includes fine gemstones, pearls, coral, and gold jewelry from all over the world. The 83-85 Front Street shop also offers name-brand jewelry and time pieces from Patek Philippe, Chopard, Mont Blanc, Baccarat, Tiffany, Tissot, Citizen, Omega, Cartier, and Tag Heuer. If you're looking for jewelry with definite local themes, check out the selections at these delightful shops.

❑ **Kirk's Jewelry:** *Butterfield Place Shopping Concourse, 67 Front Street, Tel. 441-2967-9428. Open daily until 10pm.* This very small jewelry shop and personable custom jeweler produces beautiful designs, one-of-a-kind pieces, and a limited edition Bermuda Collection. Since 85 percent of their work is custom, you'll find unique jewelry pieces here. Be sure to ask to see their photo album of representative work since the shop is too small to display their creations. If you have time, you may want to have them design something for you. You can watch the owner and designer, who  started with Walker Christopher, at this workbench developing his latest creations.

❑ **E.R. Aubrey:** *19 Front Street, Tel. 441-295-3826, and 101 Front Street, Tel. 441-297-3171 (Hamilton); Clocktower Shopping Mall,*

Tel. 441-234-4577 (Royal Naval Dockyard); and 20 East York Street, Tel. 441-297-5059 (St. George). This is Bermuda's mass market jeweler who appeals to tourists in search of bargain jewelry and free gifts and prizes. It includes a very large selection of jewelry, especially rings and necklaces, along with inexpensive watches and some shipwreck coin jewelry. Most of the jewelry is stamped jewelry. This is the closest you may come to some sort of price competition in Bermuda. They advertise a price guarantee – they will not be undersold! Indeed, the shops always seem to have a special 20 to 60 percent sale going on along with offers of a free tanzanite stone with any purchase and special weekly drawings for a 14K gold sapphire and diamond ladies' ring. Heavily advertized as Bermuda's bargain jeweler, E.R. Aubrey – and pointedly critiqued in some ads about the pitfalls of buying questionable discount jewelers – is well positioned to attract visitors. Discerning shoppers need to examine this jewelry for quality. It's not the same quality as that in most other jewelry shops you'll encounter in Hamilton. You'll need to judge for yourself if this is the type of jewelry you want, especially after visiting a few of Bermuda's quality jewelry shops.

❑ **Swiss Timing:** *95 Front Street, Hamilton, Tel. 441-295-1376, Fax 441-295-2088, or e-mail:* swisstiming@ibl.bm. *Website:* www.swisstimingbermuda.com. This small shop offers several lines of quality Swiss-made watches: Zenith, Concord, Michel Herbélin, Jean Peret, Certina, Alfex, and Jean d'Eve. It also includes clocks and some jewelry, which are found on the left side of this shop. This is a good place to familiarize yourself with top quality Swiss timepieces that are less well known than heavily advertised major watch brands.

❑ **Herrington Jewellers:** *1 Washington Mall, between Church and Reid streets, Tel. 441-292-6527.* This shop offers exclusive Claude Thibaudeau and Bellari jewelry collections, uniquely faceted Lucere diamonds, cultured pearl jewelry, Masami mother of pearl jewelry, and watches from Bulova, Accutron, and Zodiac.

❑ **Lynn Morrell:** *Bermuda Art Centre, Royal Naval Dockyard. Tel. 441-236-7138, Fax 441-236-6118, or e-mail:* morrell@ibl.bm. *Website:* www.lynnmorrell.com. This gallery shop includes nicely designed one-of-a-kind jewelry, especially necklaces and earrings, using silver and semi-precious stones. Local artist Lynn Morrell also produces textiles and mixed media which are on display in this shop.

❑ **Cooper's Cachet:** *27 Front Street, Tel. 441-292-9872, Fax 441-295-2961, or e-mail: customerservice@ascooper.bm. Website: www.coopersbermuda.com.* This combination jewelry, Waterford crystal, and Christmas shop includes several show cases of jewelry at the front of the shop. It includes a good selection of Baltic amber, pearls, and turquoise.

LINENS

❑ **The Irish Linen Shop:** *Hely's Corner, 31 Front Street, Tel. 441-295-4089, Fax 441-295-6552, or e-mail: irishlinen@ibl.bm.* Located across the street from the police box ("bird cage"), this is one of the city's most popular shops which is often packed with shoppers. The first floor is filled with goregous tablecloths and napkin sets ($440.00). table wear, embroidered napkins, and handmade tablecloths ($750.00). The second floor includes a bed and bath section, children's clothing and accessories, sleep wear, infant goods, and unique gift items such as cedar handbags. Excellent quality. Everything is nicely displayed.

ART

❑ **Bermuda National Gallery:** *East wing of City Hall and Arts Centre, 17 Church Street, Tel. 441-295-9428 or Fax 441-295-2055. Website: www.bng.bm. Open Monday to Saturday, 10am to 4pm but closed on public holidays.* This is much more than a historical art museum. Opened in 1992, the Bermuda National Gallery houses Bermuda's national art collection as well as functions as the center for the island's art community. In addition to displaying a permanent collection of renowned local and international artists, the museum hosts three major temporary exhibits each year and the popular juried *Bacardi Limited Biennial* exhibition (usually May through August of even-numbered years – 2006, 2008, 2010, etc.), which showcases Bermuda's best contemporary artists. If you are interested in meeting local artists and acquiring the works of Bermuda's best contemporary artists, be sure to purchase a copy of the wonderful *Barcardi Limited Biennial* catalog, which is available at the entrance to the museum. This catalog provides extensive information on each artist (bio, exhibitions, commissions, awards) along with photos of their representative works. Museum personnel can provide you with contact information on the various artists. One of favorite artists, Graham

Foster (Tel. 441-232-1808 or www.grahamfoster.com), who works in steel, glass, and cowrie shells with African and nautical themes, has exhibited here. You also may want to take the Museum's **Art and Architectural Tour**, which takes you to 12 art centers – primarily public, commercial, and corporate galleries – in Hamilton. The director of the Bermuda National Gallery, Laura Gorham, conducts this popular and informative tour at 10am every Tuesday. It costs $65 per person and includes lunch at the Waterloo House. For information and reservations, call 441-295-9428.

❑ **Bermuda Society of Arts:** *West wing of City Hall and Arts Centre, 17 Church Street, Tel. 441-292-3824 or Fax 441-296-0699. Open Monday to Saturday, 10am to 4pm.* Founded in the 1950s, this is Bermuda's oldest arts organization. This small gallery with a children's section exhibits the works of local contemporary visual artists. The exhibits change every two weeks. All of the art is for sale. If you wish to contact local artists who are members of the Bermuda Society of Arts, be sure to visit the director's office which is within the gallery (open Monday to Friday, 9am to 5pm).

❑ **Desmond Fountain Gallery:** *Emporium Building, 69 Front Street, Tel. 441-296-3518, Fax 441-296-5147, or e-mail: sculpture @ibl.bm. Website: www.desmondfountain.com. Open Monday to Saturday, 10am to 6pm.* Desmond Fountain is one of Bermuda's most famous artists who is noted for his large and small

bronze sculptures (children, nudes, dog breeds, and creatures) and etchings. His bronzes are cast in limited editions of nine and thus are expensive and tend to sell quickly. Much of his work has the look and feel of the many bronze sculpture galleries found in Santa Fe, New Mexico. Several of his sculptures are on public display throughout the islands, such as "Johnny Barnes" and "Sir George Somers." You can pick up a map at this gallery that includes locations of his public sculptures. The gallery also showcases paintings of a few artists from around the world.

❑ **Masterworks Foundation:** *Bermuda House Lane, Front Street(in alley next to Tuscany Restaurant and Swiss Timing), Tel. 441-295-5580, Fax 441-292-5363, or e-mail: mworks@ibl.bm. Website: www.masterworksbermuda.com. Open Monday through Saturday, 10am to 4pm. Its main office is the Arrow Root Factory gallery* *at the Botanical Gardens.* This is one of Bermuda's largest and most respected art galleries that represents several local artists. The downtown location is a combination art gallery and shop that presents shows of local artists every two weeks and sells paintings, cards, posters, prints, and books. It includes a large inventory of paintings which are largely in storage at the Botanical Gardens location. Masterworks Foundation is much more than just an art gallery. It includes master paintings of Winslow Homer, Georgia O'Keeffe, and Jack Buss and others that make up The Collection of over 700 works. Masterworks Foundation also sponsors educational programs, workshops, lectures, and an Artist-In-Residence program in St. George.

❑ **Heritage House/New Heritage House Gallery:** *26 Church Street, Tel. 441-295-2615, Fax 441-295-1902, or e-mail: hhouse@ibl.bm.* Located across the street from the City Hall and Arts Centre, this gallery consists of two sections – an upstairs and downstairs gallery separated by three buildings

in between. The street level New Heritage House Gallery includes paintings, old silver flatware, antique furniture, accessory pieces, Persian carpets, and prints. This shop also does framing and regularly hosts art exhibitions of leading artists. You may want to ask when they plan to have  another exhibition and request an invitation card to attend their private opening, which usually takes place from 5:30pm to 8pm. Three doors to the right is the downstairs gallery, a very eclectic art and home decorative center. Its larger space includes more paintings and prints as well as numerous home decorative items – lamps, carpets, Asian furniture and decorative pieces, lampshades, and imitation flowers. It also offers framing services.

❑ **Carole Holding:** *81 Front Street, Hamilton; St. George's Town Square; and The Fairmont Southampton. Tel. 1-800-880-8570 from the U.S. or 441-297-1373. E-mail: carole@caroleholding.bm. Website: www.caroleholding.com.* Born in Morecombe, England and moved to Bermuda in 1968, Carole Holding produces a large line of paintings in various sizes depicting Bermuda scenes in soft colors that complement Bermuda's light. Popular with tourists, most of her paintings are produced as inex-

pensive ($30-$140) unlimited or limited editions (495) of various sizes. She also produces a line of T-shirts. She complements her work with many interesting gift and craft items produced by some of the best local artisans and craftspeople. The shop offers free delivery of framed artwork within the continental United States. Carole is often found on location painting or discussing her work in her shops. The main shop in Hamilton in Hamilton, which is located directly across the street from the cruise ship terminal, draws the largest traffic and includes a very innovative and eclectic mix of art, souvenirs, and Bermudiana.

❑ **Crisson & Hind Fine Art Gallery:** *2ⁿᵈ Floor, Crisson Building, 71 Front Street, Tel. 441-295-1117, Fax 441-295-1125, or e-mail: dusty@northrock.bm.* Website: www.CrissonAndHind.com. This is one of Bermuda's most unusual art shops – specializes in stone sculptures (primarily head figures and animals, such as wart hogs, kudus, elephants, rhinos, giraffes, and baboons) produced by the Shona in Zimbabwe, and located on the second floor of the popular Crisson jewelry store. The shop and selections represent the passions of the very personable

and knowledgeable owner, Colin M. (Dusty) Hind, who regularly travels to Zimbabwe, where he works with various Shona sculptors who he promotes in this unique gallery. He buys directly from a group of 40 talented sculptors as well as  visits several mines and quarries from which he personally selects the stones for his artists. Since these are stone sculptures, they require heavy lifting, good packing, and shipping services – all of which Dusty provides for his many clients around the world. If you purchase a sculpture weighing under 25 pounds, you want to take it with you as accompanying baggage. The gallery also includes a few wood African stools, Ethiopian silver crosses, jewelry pieces, textiles, and wood carvings. Be careful in buying what appear to be original wood carvings. The two we purchased here turned out to be pricey airport art. You may want to focus on the stone sculptures, which Dusty knows well since he is closely involved in the whole stone selection and sculpting process.

PHOTOGRAPHY

❑ **Picturesque Gallery:** *The Design Centre, 129 Front Street East, Tel. 441-292-1452, Fax 441-295-1326, or e-mail: rskinner@ibl.bm. Website: www.picturesquebermuda.com. Also has a branch gallery at the Clocktower Mall, Royal Naval Dockyard, Tel. 441-234-3342.* This photographic gal-

lery showcases the beautiful color photography of Roland Skinner, who has photographed many unique scenes of Bermuda for more than 40 years. Unframed photographs are available in five sizes, which range in price from $97 to $795. You'll also find many of Roland Skinner's best photos compiled in a coffee table book that is available in several stores in Bermuda.

❑ **Just Clicked Gallery:** *Bermuda House, 95 Front Street, Tel. 441-292-3295, Fax 441-292-8336, or e-mail: ian@imacsmith.com. Website: www.imacsmith.com.* Ian MacDonald-Smith, one of Bermuda's finest professional photographers, showcases his work in this gallery. Specializing in abstract and graphic photography, he represents some of the best photography of the unique architecture and sights of Bermuda. He also is the author of four photo books: *A Scape to Bermuda, Bermuda Homes and Gardens, Bermuda Triangle,* and *Setting Sail for the New Millennium.*

CHINA, CRYSTAL, AND GLASSWARE

❑ **Bluck's/William Bluck & Co.:** *4 Front Street, Tel. 441-295-5367. Also has a second location at 53 Front Street, in front of the cruise ship terminal. Website: www.blucksbermuda.com.* Commonly known as "Bluck's," this is our favorite shop for both

traditional and contemporary china, crystal, and glassware. Bluck's two locations offer different collections of these products. The two-story 4 Front Street shop, which is the older and located near the Fairmont Princess Hotel, is noted for its fine collection of imported porcelain, china, crystal, glassware, and ceramics as well as some prints. It no longer handles antiques. The second floor includes Bluck's extensive collection of exclusively designed Hungarian Herend plates. Other noted manufacturers represented here include Royal Copenhagen, Daum, Lalique, Orrefors, Villeroy and Boch, Waterford, Royal Crown Derby, Minton, Spode, Chase, and Ginori, You'll find many decorative vases and candle holders as well as a full range of table service, including wine glasses. The second shop in the heart of the cruise ship shopping area has a very contemporary home decorative and gift orientation, displaying gorgeous glassware and crystal (plates, bowls, vases, and art pieces) in dozens of niches. If you like colorful and artistic glassware and crystal, you'll quickly fall in love with this special shop. Bluck's extensive china collections are primarily found in the 4 Front Street shop.

❑ **Vera P. Card:** *11 Front Street (opposite Bank of Bermuda and Ferry Terminal), Hamilton, Tel. 441-295-1729, Fax 441-295-2833, or e-mail: vcard@ibl.bm. Also at Water Street in St. George and at the Wyndham Bermuda Resort.* Since 1949, Vera P Card has specialized in fine gifts from around the world with special emphasis on collecting figurines, crystal, clocks, watches, and jewelry.  Many of the designs are distinctively Bermudian and exclusive to Vera P. Card. This shop offers the largest collection of Lladro figurines in Bermuda, including Limited Edition pieces and larger Elite gallery pieces and pieces made exclusively for the store. It also showcases the German-manufactured Hummel figurines for collectors, which encompasses 350 figurines, including a unique Limited Edition "Caribbean Collection," the "Bermuda Collection" (only available in Bermuda), and many Closed Edition pieces. The shop also offers a special Bermuda Images Collection, a joint project to benefit the Bermuda Masterworks Foundation. The collection includes wall bowls and plates, framed porcelain pictures, service plates, and vases and trinket boxes. Specializes in beautiful bohemian Czech crystal and unusual find jewelry. This is the only place in Bermuda where you can buy Czech crystal with rich-cut, enameled, gilt, and colored overlay. Includes both hand-cut and hand-blown pieces in the form of elaborate plates, glasses, vases, jewelry boxes, and perfume bottles. The shop also offers a wide range of fine and unusual European designer jewelry, a large collection of Majorca pearls, and precious and semi-precious stones in unusual settings. Includes gold charms, necklaces, and bracelets. Includes Swarovski garnet jewelry, glass ships-in-a-bottle, and musical jewelry boxes.

❑ **A.S. Cooper & Sons, Ltd.:** *59 Front Street, Tel. 441-295-3961; Cooper's Cachet, 27 Front Street, Tel. 441-292-9872; Fairmont Hamilton Princess Hotel, Tel. 441-296-6401. E-mail: customer service@ascooper.bm. Website: www.coopersbermuda.com.* The

main five-story department store on Front Street, directly across from the cruise ship terminal, includes everything from perfumes to bridal gowns. However, the first floor offers an excellent selection of china and crystal with such brand names as Waterford, Wedgwood, Belleek Darian, Royal Doulton, Villeroy & Boch, Lladro, and Swarovski. During the month of June representatives from Wedgwood and Belleek Darian do demonstrations of their exclusive designs for A.S. Cooper & Sons. The Cooper's Cachet shop specializes in Waterford crystal. The shops claim visitors can save up to 40 percent on their china and crystal purchases. If you are from the United States, you may want to test such claims by pricing name brands before arriving in Bermuda.

CRAFTS, HOME PRODUCTS, AND GIFT ITEMS

❑ **The Island Shop:** *Old Cedar Lane, 47 Front Street, Tel. 441-292-6307; and 3 Queen Street, Tel. 441-292-5292. E-mail: www.kfins ness@ibl.bm. Website: www.islandexports.com.* These are two of Bermuda's most popular shops with visitors who quickly fall

in love with the more than 200 original items on display. Primarily quality gift and home products shops, the shops showcase the creative designs of owner Barbara Finsness, an American who has lived in Bermuda for nearly 25 years. The shops offer her exclusive signature collection of linens, embroidered cushion covers, and tableware depicting Bermuda cottages, reef fish, and other Bermudiana. The main shop on Queen Street offers a larger selection of items.

❑ **Carole Holding:** *81 Front Street, Hamilton; St. George's Town Square; and The Fairmont Southampton. Tel. 1-800-880-8570 from the U.S. or 441-297-1373. E-mail:* underline-carole@caroleholding.bm. *Website:* www.caroleholding.com. See above entry under "Art." Carole Holding includes a very appealing collection of reasonably priced gift items and souvenirs – from T-shirts to candles – which are popular with cruise ship passengers. The collection of charming banana leaf dolls and Gombey dancers is unique to Bermuda. The Front Street shop reflects the marketing acumen of Carole Holding – she knows what many visitors want – lots of inexpensive but decent quality souvenirs that can easily be carried home – and she offers a very good mix of such items.

❑ **Cooper's Cachet:** *27 Front Street, Tel. 441-292-9872 or e-mail:* customerserivce@ascooper.bm. *Website:* www.coopersbermuda.com While the front part of this shop specializes in jewelry and Waterford crystal, the rear of the store is primarily a Christmas shop with fully decorated trees and a good selection of Christmas ornaments. If you enjoy browsing through Christmas shops and discovering unique local products, Cooper's Cachet is the place to visit in Bermuda. The shop displays the unique Christmas ornaments of local artisan Heidi Augustinovic.

PERFUMES AND FRAGRANCES

❑ **Peniston Brown and Company Ltd.:** *23 Front Street, Tel. 441-295-0570.* Located opposite the Ferry Terminal, this popular shop carries a large selection of perfumes and fragrances from around the world, including Guerlain, Lauren, Calvin Klein, Yves St. Laurent, and Jean Patou.

❑ **A.S. Cooper & Sons Ltd.:** *59 Front Street, Tel. 441-295-3961; Cooper's Cachet, 27 Front Street, Tel. 441-292-9872; Fairmont Hamilton Princess Hotel, Tel. 441-296-6401. E-mail:* customer service@ascooper.bm. *Website:* www.coopersbermuda.com. Another good department store source for imported European perfumes.

ANTIQUES AND COLLECTIBLES

❑ **Heritage House/New Heritage House Gallery:** *26 Church Street, Tel. 441-295-2615, Fax 441-295-1902, or e-mail:* hhouse@ibl.bm. See the same entry on page 109. The street-level gallery includes some antique furniture, old silver flatware, and aging paintings and drawings.

❑ **Anthony Pettit:** *By appointment only, Tel. 441-292-2482, Fax 441-295-5416, or e-mail: apettit@northrock.bm. Website: www.anthonypettit.com.* This long-established expert on old Bermuda maps, books, ephemera, prints, and paintings is of special interest to collectors. Anthony Pettit's collection includes charts and guides, manuscripts, pamphlets, letters, documents, ships' logs, newspapers and magazines, albums and scrapbooks, incunabula, local imprints, almanacs, histories, railway effects, novels, descriptions, memoirs, parliamentary acts and bills, poetry, catalogues, bibliographies, genealogies, diaries, travel and cruising stories, works on flora and fauna, papers on geology, geography, race relations, reports and memoirs on the Dockyard, maritime and military publications. He also deals in engravings, lithographs, views, woodcuts, sketches, oils, watercolors, portraits and other art work. His ephemera includes postcards, posters, brochures, photographs, bookplates, tourist printings, hotel menus, programmes, theater promotions and stereographs. His sea collections encompasses old bottles, flasks, marine artifacts, bells, lights, anchors as well as coins, silver, medals and badges. He even has a collection of carvings from Boer War and German prisoners that includes picture frames, toys, cutlery, letter openers, napkin rings, pen holders, pipes, boots, walking sticks, and cedar boxes.

❑ **A & J Sports Cards:** *Upper level, Washington Mall, between Church and Reid Streets.* includes several collectibles for sports enthusiasts – mini-helmets, posters, albums, NASCAR cars, shirts, mugs, and stickers – "Magic" starter, booster packs, and Beanie Babies.

❑ **Perot Post Office:** *Queen Street at Par-la-Ville Park, Tel. 441-295-5151, ext. 1192.* Offers colorful postage stamps depicting Bermuda's flora, fauna, and historic highlights. A popular place for philatelists who collect unique postage stamps from around the world.

CLOTHING AND ACCESSORIES

❑ **Cécile:** *15 Front Street West, Tel. 441-295-1311 or Fax 441-292-0941.* If you are in the market for classy dresses, evening wear, and sportswear, it doesn't get any better than here. This is Bermuda's most exclusive shop for top name international fashion and accessories with a tropical flair. The shop is much larger than it initially appears, especially as you move toward the back and right side where it unfolds with additional rooms. Its three interior rooms are filled with various collections of nicely displayed casual wear, evening wear, beachwear, and hats, which are clearly labeled and neatly organized by designer. The front room, which is not really

representative of the interior rooms, offers a good selection of belts, buckles, handbags, neckties, shoes, ceramics, and linens. Most collections are produced by noted French, Italian, and German designers, such as Pucci, Armani Gerard, Tibi, Cacharel, and Basler. Lilly Pulitzer of Palm Beach is well represented here. A separate children's and infant section includes smocked dresses. Everything here is expensive but the quality and selections are outstanding. While there is only one Cécile shop in Bermuda, it does supply other shops with fashion and accessories.

❑ **The English Sports Shop:** *49 Front Street, Tel. 441-295-2672. Also several branch shops throughout Bermuda.* You can't miss this shop since it has so many branches and related shops (18) that come under The English Sports Shop umbrella. Most of these shops offer a good selection of colorful men's and women's clothing, most of which is imported from England. Look for shirts, sweaters, jackets, suits, Bermuda shorts, knee socks, scarves, hats,

neckties, and swimwear. The second floor includes a children's shop. Excellent selections and service.

❑ **Aston & Gunn:** *2 Reid Street (corner of Queen and Reed streets), Tel. 441-295-4866 or Fax 441-295-1824.* This is Bermuda's best quality men's shop specializing in shirts, suits, jackets, pants, sweaters, neckties, Bermuda shorts, jackets, and accessories under such well known brand names as Armani, Hugo Boss, Arnold Zimmer, and Pierre Balman from Germany, Holland, and Italy. Also includes some women's dresses and accessories.

❑ **Calypso:** *Front Street, Tel. 441-295-0954, ext. 109 or e-mail:* *service@calypso.bm.* This rather eclectic two-story shop combines unique and colorful ceramic plates and bowls with

swimwear, shoes, slippers, belts, hats, scarves, and handbags on the first floor, with women's dresses and sportswear on the second floor. Offers
European designer wear, including Solola, Rene Derhy, Eileen
Fisher, Terracotta, and Flax, and
swimwear by Ralph Lauren,
Calvin Klein, and Jensen. The shop
also owns nearby **Max Mara**
(clothing and accessories), **Violá**
(leather goods) at Butterfield Walk-
way, **United Colors of Benetton**
(trendy clothing) and **French Connection** on Reed Street.

❑ **Archie Brown:** *Front Street, Tel. 441-295-2928 or Fax 441-295-
4594.* Owned in part by The English Sports Shop, Archie
Brown offers a limited selection of swimwear, sweaters, and
shirts. Its **Pringle Shop** at the rear of the store includes a good
selection of cashmere sweaters from Scotland.

❑ **A. S. Cooper Man/A. S. Cooper & Sons:** *29 Front Street and 59
Front Street, Tel. 441-295-3961, or e-mail: customerservice@ascoo
per.bm. Website: www.coopersbermuda.com. Also has a shop in
the Fairmont Princess Shopping Arcade.* Offers a good selection
of men's casual and business attire and sportswear under
such brand names as Polo Ralph Lauren, Tommy Bahama,
Tommy Hilfiger, DKNY, Liz Claiborne, Jones New York,
Nipon, IZOD, Architect, and Helly Hanson. Includes a kids'
and bridal shop on the second floor and women's wear on
the fourth floor.

❑ **Crown Colony:** *1 Front Street, Tel. 441-295-3935.* Offers a good
selection of attractive women's wear.

❑ **French Connection:** *Reid Street, Tel. 441-295-2112.* Offers trendy
men's fashions. Operated by the owners of Calypso.

❑ **Stefanel:** *12 Reid Street, Tel. 441-297-1357.* A very trendy boutique for young people offering European men's and women's
fashions.

❑ **Marks & Spencer:** *17 Reid Street, Tel. 441-295-0031.* This famous British department store includes a good selection of
men's wear, including a house brand of briefs and boxers.

LUGGAGE AND LEATHER GOODS

❑ **The Harbourmaster:** *Washington Mall, Reid Street, Tel. 441-295-5333.* Specializes in quality imported leather and nylon luggage, briefcases, portfolios, laptop bags, handbags, and wallets. The best prices are on leather goods from Colombia. Offers excellent quality handbags and wallets from Italy as well as travel accessories. Offers the Limited Land Collection. Received a Best of Bermuda Gold Award in 2004.

❑ **Voilé:** *Butterfield Place Shopping Concourse, 67 Front Street, Tel. 4441-295-2112, ext. 120.* This award-win-ning (Best of Bermuda Gold Award in 2004) shop includes top quality imported leather bags by Longchamp (Paris) and men's and women's shoes produced by Johnson & Murphy. Excellent displays and service.

LIQUOR AND LIQUEURS

❑ **Gosling Brothers, Ltd.:** *33 Front Street (corner of Front and Queen streets), Tel. 441-295-1123. Also has branch shops.* Oper-ating in Bermuda since 1806, Gosling's is an institution. In-deed, this family-operated company is Bermuda's oldest business house and larg-est exporter of Bermuda products. It of-fers an excellent range of wines as well as produces its own labels of famous liquors – Gosling's Black Seal® Rum (www.black seal.com), Gosling's Gold Bermuda Rum (www.goslingsgold.com), and Gosling's Rum Swizzle. The Black Seal® Rum has become synonymous with Bermuda – a key ingredient in Bermuda's popular fish chowder, Bermuda Rum Swizzle, and the  famous Dark'n Stormy cocktail. These and other rums, li-queurs, whiskies, champagnes, and wines also are available farther east along Front Street at Gosling's **Black Seal Shop** (97 Front Street), which also includes exclusive designer cloth-ing, gifts, and accessories. A special Bermudian drink, Black Seal rum is often mixed with Barritt's Ginger Beer (an ac-quired local taste) to make Bermuda's famous Dark'n Stormy cocktail. If you are traveling by cruise ship, you can purchase liquor "in-bond" (duty free) at Gosling's and have them de-liver it free (little effort since the shop is located within 100 feet of the cruise terminal) to your ship. Air travelers are well advised to purchase the famous Gosling's liquors and liqueurs at the **Gosling's Duty Free** shop in the airport departure lounge.

❑ **Burrows Lightbourn:** *East Broadway (eastern continuation of Front Street, Tel. 441-295-0176. Also has branch shops.* This also is one of Bermuda's largest wine and spirits merchants. It offers a good range of wines, liquors, liqueurs, and beers. It also allows visitors to purchase liquors "in-bond" and will deliver in-store purchases to cruise ships.

BOOKS

❑ **The Bookmark:** *Phoenix Centre, 3 Reid Street, Tel. 441-295-3838.* Representing Bermuda's largest bookstore, The Bookmark offers an excellent selection of books from the United States and England as well as a special book section focusing on Bermuda.

CUBAN CIGARS

❑ **Cuarenta Bucaneros:** *The Continental Building, 25 Church Street, Tel. 441-295-4523. Website: www.cigarbox.bm or www.cigarbox bermuda.com.* This shop specializes in top quality Cuban cigars, It supplies many of Bermuda's shops, restaurants, hotels, and corporate executives with several famous brands direct from the factories in Havana – Romeo y Julieta, Cohiba, Montecristo, and Hoyo de Monterrey. It also will deliver directly to your hotel as well as offers online shopping via www.cigarbox.bm. Beware, however, the U.S. Customs may seize these purchases if declared when entering the United States.

❑ **Chatham House:** *Corner of Front and Burnaby streets, Tel. 441-292-8422.* Offers a good selection of excellent quality Cuban cigars – Romeo y Julieta, Cohiba, Punch, Partagas, Hoyo de Monterrey, Montecristo, Bolivaar, H Upmann, and others.

St. George's Best Shops

As we noted earlier, most shops in St. George, which are concentrated around King's Square and along Water and Duke of York streets, are branches of major shops and department stores in Hamilton which are primarily oriented to cruise ship passengers who frequently visit this quaint historical town during the cruise season. Most shops with brief descriptions are detailed in the above section on Hamilton.

JEWELRY AND WATCHES

❏ **Crisson Jewellers:** *York Street, Tel. 441-297-0672, and Water Street, Tel. 441-297-0107.* Specializes in famous brand-name watches, such as Rolex, Tag Heuer, Omega, Ebel, Movado, Rado, Raymond Weil, Tissot, Longines, Seiko, Citizen, and Swiss Army, that are reputed to be 30 percent below retail prices in the United States.

❏ **E. R. Aubrey:** 20 *East York Street (next to Police Station), Tel. 441-297-5059.* Specializes in tanzanite (Bermuda's largest source), loose stones, and gold and silver jewelry set in diamonds and precious stones. Offers inexpensive lines of jewelry as well as promotes numerous sales and give-aways.

CHINA, CRYSTAL, AND GLASSWARE

❏ **Bluck's:** *Water Street, Tel. 441-297-0476.* Offers top quality china, crystal, and glassware.

❏ **Vera P. Card:** *Water Street, Tel. 441-295-1729.* Offers special collections of china, porcelain, glassware, clocks, gifts, and jewelry. Includes an extensive collection of Lladró, M.I. Hummel figurines, Swarovski crystal, and other lines of fine crystal and glass. A jewelry section includes gold and sterling silver jewelry set with stones and Majorca pearls.

PERFUMES AND FRAGRANCIES

❏ **Peniston Brown and Company Ltd.:** *6 Water Street, on corner of King's Square.* Famous for its extensive line of perfumes and fragrances.

ANTIQUES

❏ **Antique Garden:** 20 *West Duke of York Street, Tel. 441-297-0901 or e-mail: antiquegarden@logic.bm.* This two-story house is jam-packed with antiques and collectibles from England and local estates – china, glassware, mugs, pictures, lamps, books, and furniture. Be prepared for a disorienting experience – it may take you some time for your eyes to get focused on what is definitely a unique collection of varying quality treasures and trash!

❑ **Pickwick Mews:** *6 Duke of York.* This small and newly renovated cottage includes antique and reproduction furniture,
paintings, and Chinese and Japanese boxes.

Arts, Crafts, and Gifts

❑ **Carole Holding:** *King's Square.* Look for inexpensive paintings and lithographs by Carole Holding as well as numerous
attractive gift, souvenir, and household items that are popular with visitors – chopping boards, bone china mugs, kitchen
towels, glass ornaments, T-shirts, jams, banana leaf dolls and
angels, Bermuda Spa body scrub, ceramic tableware, and Bermuda cedar items.

❑ **Dockside Glass:** *Corner of Bridge and Water streets, Tel./Fax
441-297-3908. Open daily from 9am to 5 pm during the winter and
from 9am to 9pm during the summer.* This is a small version of
the **Dockyard Glassworks** and **Bermuda Rum Cake Factory**
which is based at the Royal Naval Dockyard. You can sample
nine different rum cake flavors, watch glass artists produce
Bermuda longtails and tiny tree frogs, and shop for several
colorful and creative glass creations on display in this cottage
shop.

Clothing and Accessories

❑ **Crown Colony Shop:** *Somers Wharf, Water Street.* This is our
favorite women's clothing store in St. George. Offers an attractive selection of sweaters, hats, slacks, women's wear,
and accessories with similar selections as found at The English Sports Shop and Cécile. Includes Lilly Pulitzer fashions.

❑ **Cow Polly East:** *Somers Wharf, Water Street.* A nice small boutique offering clothing, picture frames, boxes, hats, jewelry,
neckties, and attractive handbags from the Philippines.

❑ **English Sports Shop:** *Somers Wharf, Water Street.* This inviting
waterfront shop offers similar fashionable items as found in
its shop in Hamilton – shirts, shorts, footwear, jeans, caps,
hats, sweaters, swimsuits, and T-shirts.

❑ **Taylors Clothing Shop:** *Water Street.* Part of The Sports Shop.
Specializes in sweaters, knits, woolens, and hats.

❑ **A. S. Cooper & Sons:** *Somers Wharf, Water Street.* Includes
both men's and women's clothes and accessories as well as
gift items.

Royal Naval Dockyard's Best Shops

The Royal Naval Dockyard also has many branch shops of Hamilton-based shops along with several specialty shops only found in this area's unique shopping, market, and art complex. The Clocktower Mall has the largest concentration of shops followed by the Bermuda Crafts Market and Bermuda Arts Centre.

Art and Photography

❑ **Bermuda Arts Centre:** *Maritime Lane, Royal Naval Dockyard. Open daily, 10am to 5pm. Tel. 441-234-2809, Fax 441-234-0540, or e-mail: artcentre@ibl.bm. Website: www.artbermuda.bm.* Located next to the Bermuda Craft Market and across from the Bermuda Maritime Museum, this small but innovative art venue includes changing art exhibits, working studios, and booths selling paintings, ceramics (by Barbara Finsness), cards, books, and prints. Look for the studios of **Jonah Jones** (oil painter), **Chesley Trott** (wood sculptor), and **Lynn Morrell** (jewelry, textile, and mixed media artist). The exhibition hall changes shows every six weeks.

❑ **Chesley Trott:** *Bermuda Arts Center, Maritime Lane, Royal Naval Dockyard. Open daily, 10am to 5pm. Tel. 441-234-0313 or e-mail: ctjet@northrock.bm.*  Chesley Trott is one of Bermuda's premier wood carvers and sculptors who is especially known for his work in Bermuda cedar. However, he is a very multi-faceted artist who also works with ebony, teak, fiddlewood, silk oak, mahogany, and American black walnut as well as bronze. He also occasionally paints. You'll usually find this very personable artist-in-residence (since 1991) at work in his studio turning out has latest wood creations, which are primarily elongated abstract figures.

❑ **Michael Swan Gallery:** *Unit 3/16 Clocktower Mall, RN Dockyard, Tel. 441-234-3128, Fax 441-234-3164, or e-mail: mswan@ibl.bm. Website: www.michaelswan .com.* Michael Swan is one of Bermuda's  most popular young artists. An airbrush artist who works in acrylic, his works are instantly recognizable. He captures many of Bermuda's striking architectural scenes and it greenery through the use of warm pastels, light, and shadows. His gallery includes his many prints as well as craft items, wearables, and jewelry produced by other local and international artists and craftspeople.

❑ **Picturesque Gallery:** *Clocktower Shopping Mall, Tel. 441-234-3342, Fax 441-295-1326, or e-mail:* _rskinner@ibl.bm_. *Website:* _www.picturesquebermuda.com_. Showcases the photographic work of Roland Skinner.

ARTS AND CRAFTS

❑ **Bermuda Craft Market:** *Cooperage Building, 4 Freeport Road, next to the Bermuda Arts Centre, Tel. 441-234-3208. Open Monday through Saturday, 10am to 5pm, and Sunday, 11am to 5pm. Closed on Christmas Day and Good Friday.* Includes several vendor stalls offering Bermuda-made rum cakes, jams, pepper sauce, painted glass, dolls, jewelry, ceramics, T-shirts, cedar boxes (**Bermuda Cedar** by Lynette Titterton), quilts, jewelry, Christmas ornaments, ceramics, small paintings, wearable art, and wickerwork. A good place to learn about local crafts and meet craftspeople or learn how to contact them.

❑ **Bermuda Clayworks:** *Located immediately northeast of the Clocktower Mall along Camber Road and just before the Dockyard Glassworks. Tel. 441-234-3136, Fax 441-234-3136, or e-mail:* _clayworks@ibl.com_. *Website:* _www.bermudaclayworks.com_. This is a combination ceramic factory, workshop/studio, and shop that produces uniquely designed colorful ceramic plates, bowls, cups, and other utilitarian and decorative pieces. The shop allows visitors to produce their own pottery – look for the "Paint Your Own Pottery" studio on the left rear side of the shop – a great  family activity for those who enjoy hands-on arts and crafts.

❑ **Dockyard Glassworks:** *Camber Road at Dockyard Terrace, Tel. 441-234-4216 or Fax 441-234-3813. Website:* _www.dockglass.com_. *Open daily from 8am to 6pm and from 8am to 10pm when cruise ships are in dock.* Located in the same expansive building with its other business – Bermuda Rum Cake Company – this combination glass factory and retail shop enables visitors to leisurely watch artists firing glass and then making it into unique collectible art glass pieces (plates, bowls, vases, tiny tree frogs, "honeymoon hogs," and multicolored fish and birds) as well as shop in its adjacent factory shop. You also wander next door to sample the nine different flavors of rum cakes. The place can get very hot given the blasting furnaces that overheat this building space.

GIFTS, SOUVENIRS, FRAGRANCIES

❑ **Dockyard Linens:** *Clocktower Mall, Tel. 441-234-3871.* This small shop offers fine Bermuda linens, tea towels, and various gift items.

❑ **A.S. Cooper & Sons:** *Clocktower Mall. Tel. 444-295-3961. Website: www.coopersbermuda.com.* Specializes in ceramics and souvenirs. Includes a good collection of Wedgwood products.

❑ **The Littlest Drawbridge:** *24 Clocktower Mall, Tel. 441-234-6214. Website: www.littlestdrawbridge.free.bm.* Includes a nice selection of Bermuda cedar and other handcrafted gift items from around the world – bookmarks, postcards, desk accessories, boxes, vases, goblets, bowls, sachets, and cedar essential oil and incense cones. The cedar objects are made from the indigenous, fragrant (follow your nose to this tiny shop), and increasingly rare Juniperus Bermudiana tree.

❑ **Wadsons:** *Clocktower Mall, Tel. 441-295-3025.* Located at the very end of the mall, Wadsons offers relatively inexpensive T-shirts, souvenirs, and gifts. Look for their "10% Off" coupons on purchases of $10 or more, which are printed in the local tourist literature, such as *Preview Bermuda* and *This Week in Bermuda.* If you can't find a coupon, ask for 10% discount anyway, since you now know about their ongoing discount!

JEWELRY

❑ **E. R. Aubrey:** *Clocktower Mall. Tel. 441-234-5688.* Heavily marketed to tourists as the least expensive jewelry store in Bermuda (offers a price guarantee – they will not be undersold!), this branch shop offers a large selection of rings, earrings, pendants, bracelets, and loose stones. They also offer a free loose tanzanite stone with every purchase.

❑ **Crisson:** *Clocktower Mall.* Specializes in name-brand jewelry and watches.

CLOTHING AND ACCESSORIES

❑ **Calypso:** *Clocktower Mall.* Offers upscale imported clothes, beachwear, and accessories for discerning shoppers.

FOODS

❑ **Bermuda Rum Cake Factory:** *1 Maritime Lane, Tel. 441-234-4216, Fax 441-234-3813, or e-mail: mail@bermudarumcakes.com. Website: www.bermudarumcakes.com.* Sharing an expansive building with Dockside Glassworks, the Bermuda Rum Cake Factory bakes nine different rum cakes, using Gosling's Black Seal rum, in its "The Cakery." You can watch them baking as well as taste samples of the different rum cakes. The flavors include traditional black rum, rum and ginger, rum swizzle, banana rum, coconut rum, classic coffee, and rich, dark chocolate rum. They also produce a Bermuda Gold and Fruit Cake. You also can find their cakes at Dockside Glass (St. George), Gosling's Duty Free (Airport), The Airport Gift Shops, Hamilton Princess Lobby Shop, A. S. Cooper's (Hamilton), and Fresh Produce (Southampton Princess).

❑ **Bermuda Craft Market:** *4 Freeport Road, Tel. 441-234-3208, Fax 441-234-3327, or e-mail: bdacraftmkt@northrock.bm.* Includes a limited selection of rum cakes, jams, and pepper sauces among its many arts and crafts (see above "Arts and Crafts" section).

Beyond the Towns

You'll find a few shops and galleries elsewhere on the island. Most of these shops are found in the shopping arcades of major hotels and resorts, at artists' home studios, and in the international airport.

❑ **The Birdsey Studio:** *5 Stowe Road, Paget, Tel. 441-236-6658 or Fax 441-236-9123. Open 10:30am to 1pm in season, but appointments always recommended to avoid disappointment.* Alfred Birdsey, Bermuda's first and most famous modern artist, died in 1996 at the age of 84. His daughter, Jo Birdsey Linberg, a painter in her own right and now Artist-in-Residence, runs The Birdsey Studio. Visitors to this place have an opportunity to meet the artist and acquire her paintings, which reflect the modern and impressionistic style of her father. She produces impressionistic landscapes, figurative paintings, and whimsical animals in oils and watercolors. Prices range from $700 to $1,000 for oils and from $50 to $350 for watercolors. You also can purchase note card reproductions of her father's famous paintings.

❑ **The Lisa Quinn Studio:** *Wing Cottage, 9 Tribe Road #3, Southampton, Tel. 441-238-1438, Fax 441-238-0667, or e-mail: lisaqb@mailcity.com. Website: www.thelisaquinnstudio.com. Open Tuesday to Saturday, 10am to 4pm. Wine reception every Tuesday evening from 5:30 to 7:30pm (but call to confirm).* Located within walking distance of the Reefs Hotel Resort on the picturesque South Shore, this traditional two-story cheerful cottage turned friendly studio showcases the beautiful and vibrant watercolors and lithographs of local artist Lisa Quinn, who focuses on architecture, floral, landscape, Provence, and still life themes.

❑ **The Bermuda Perfumery Gardens:** *212 North Shore Road (North Shore Road and Harrington Sound Road), Bailey's Bay, Tel. 441-293-0627, Fax 441-293-8810, or e-mail: cmcurtis@ibl.bm.* This factory produces Lili fragrances for men (Cedarwood, Bravo!, Navy Lime, Bambu) and women (Jasmine, Oleander, Easter Lily, Passion Flower, Bermudiana, Frangipanni). Visitors can take a free tour of the factory to observe how the perfumes are made, enjoy the colorful and fragrant gardens, and shop in the charming Calabash Gift Shop. Admission to the gardens is $1.50.

❑ **Calypso:** *Shopping arcade at the Elbow Beach Bermuda resort, 60 South Shore Road, Paget,* Includes an attractive selection of ceramics, clothing, hats, handbags, women's sportswear, scarves, neckties, women's slippers, and Longchamp bags.

❑ **Gosling's Duty Free:** *International Airport.* Visitors departing from Bermuda by air can purchase in this duty- free shop Gosling's signature rums, liquors, and rum cakes.

14 Special Shopping Experiences

Many visitors to Bermuda discover that there's more to shopping in Bermuda than the standard retail store and shopping mall environments. Here are some special shopping experiences that you may want to consider during your stay in Bermuda:

❑ Become a creative artisan for an hour by making your own pottery at the "Paint Your Own Pottery Studio" at the **Bermuda Clayworks** (Royal Naval Dockyard).

❑ Sample nine different Bermuda rum cakes (made from 100 percent Black Seal Rum) and watch baking in "The Cakery" of the **Bermuda Rum Cake Company** (Royal Naval Dockyard). Samples also are available at **Dockside Glass** in St. George.

❑ Watch glass making and demonstrations of artists creating unique art glass at **Dockyard Glassworks** (Royal Naval Dockyard) and **Dockside Glass** (St. George).

❑ During the month of June, visit **A.S. Cooper & Sons** in Hamilton to watch demonstrations by representatives from Wedgwood (see front cover photo) and Belleek Darian as they work with fine porcelain and china.

❑ Watch jewelers at work crafting unique jewelry designs at **Kirk's** in Hamilton.

❑ Have custom jewelry made by working with the talented designers at **Walker Christopher**, **Kirk's**, and **Solomon's**, as well as see the unique Bermuda jewelry collection designed by **Astwood Dickinson** in Hamilton.

❑ Meet artists, watch them at work in studios, and buy directly from them at the **Bermuda Arts Centre** (Royal Naval Dockyard), **Carole Holding** (Hamilton), **The Birdsey Studio** (Paget), and the **Lisa Quinn Studio** (Southampton).

❑ Spend an evening exploring the various arts and crafts of vendors who set up shop along the streets during **Harbour Nights** (Hamilton on Wednesdays) and **Heritage Nights** (St. George on Tuesdays) during the cruise ship season (April to September). Get your and your family's faces painted by local artists and photographed during the festive Harbour Nights in Hamilton.

❑ Explore the **Bermuda Craft Market** (Royal Naval Dock yard) for unique gifts and souvenirs produced by Bermuda's many artisans. Talk to them about their works and life as an artist in Bermuda.

❑ Visit the perfume factory and gardens at the **Bermuda Perfumery Gardens** (Bailey's Bay) to see the making and marketing of Bermuda fragrancies.

❑ Take the informative **Art and Architectural Tour** (starts at 10am every Tuesday) sponsored through the Bermuda National Gallery (www.bng.bm) in Hamilton before making any major art purchases in Bermuda.

❑ Discover the unique stone sculptures of Shona artists and learn about Zimbabwe's art scene from the engaging Dusty Hind at the **Crisson & Hind Fine Art Gallery** in Hamilton. Buy here and you're likely to add lots of weight to your luggage!

❑ Search for the unique banana leaf dolls and banana leaf angel tree ornaments produced by **Ronnie Chameau**.

❑ Discover the distinctive handcrafted Christmas ornaments, jewelry, and gift items produced by **Heidi Augustinovi** and available at A. S. Cooper and Sons and the Bermuda Craft Market, or call 441-236-8011.

8

Finding Your Best
Place to Stay

G IVEN BERMUDA'S reputation as an attractive tourist and business destination, you will find a good range of quality accommodations. These include large elegant resort-type hotels, charming inns and bed and breakfasts (B&Bs), and romantic cottage colonies, small hotels, guesthouses, apartments, and clubs. Each has its own particular character and appeal to different types of visitors. Some are large corporate properties that emphasize proper hotel service while others are small family-owned properties with very personal service, including home-made meals and afternoon tea. If you enjoy small and intimate boutique properties, Bermuda will not disappoint you with its many delightful choices.

On the other hand, if you want a complete resort experience – fine restaurants, shopping, entertainment, spa, golf, tennis, beaches, scuba diving, snorkeling, boating, and parasailing – Bermuda's large resort hotels will more than meet your needs and exacting standards for resort-style accommodations.

Costs and Bargains

As we noted earlier, cruise ship passengers stay onboard in Bermuda at bargain rates, because of their relatively inexpensive approach to Bermuda. However, if you arrive by air, the cost of ground accommodations in Bermuda can range considerably, from a low of $100 a night for a very basic B&B, guesthouse, or apartment during the off season to over $900 a night for upscale cottages and hotel resorts during the high season. Most visitors can expect to pay between $200 to $600 a night during the high season, which for most properties runs from April 1st through October 31st.

There are several things air travelers can do to cut the costs of accommodations in Bermuda:

1. **Plan to visit Bermuda during the off season**, which runs from November 1st through March 31st. While some properties close during this slow period, others substantially discount their standard rack rates by as much as 50 percent. Always ask about specials and extra discounts during this period.

2. **Focus on less expensive alternative accommodations,** such as B&Bs, inns, cottages, suites, and apartments. However, some of these alternatives can be very pricey, running up to $400 a night.

3. **Consider buying a travel package** (see Chapter 3) that combines air, accommodations, and meals.

4. **Contact a property directly and ask for any special rates.** Special rates could relate to a membership (AAA, AARP, military, government) or a promotion. If none, ask for a discount. Calling a toll-free number will often take you into a general reservation system where you will be quoted the full rack rate. Front desks of properties always have more flexibility with prices than reservation systems. However, specials and discounts are very limited during the high season when many properties can command their advertised rack rates.

5. **If traveling with a family, book an apartment** with cooking facilities that can substantially cut your cost of both accommodations and dining out.

PART III

In Pursuit of Pleasures

6. **Switch from an American Plan to a European Plan** (see below), or vice versa, depending on which one best meets your dining needs.

7. **Ask about "Dine Around Programs"** which enable guests with prepaid meal plans to sample restaurants of different properties rather than incur additional costs of dining outside their hotels. Top properties, such as the Pompano Beach Club, Cambridge Beaches, Ariel Sands, and Coco Reef, participate in such programs.

8. **Explore online hotel booking sites** to compare discounted rates on Bermuda hotels. For starters, try www.hotel.com, www.tripadvisor.com, www.bermudahotel.com, www.ho teladvisor.com, www.hotel-caribbean.com, www.bermuda .wheretostay.com, and our own www.travel-smarter.com.

For updated information on accommodation rates and packages, visit the Bermuda Tourism website:

www.bermudatourism.com

Also, contact a travel agent for special accommodations rates or call 1-800-BERMUDA.

When you book accommodations in Bermuda, keep in mind three additional cost factors:

1. A 7¼% government Occupancy Tax will be added to your room bill.

2. A 10% Resort Levy (service charge) will be added to your room bill.

3. Food may or may not be included in your room rate, depending on which plan you select. Here are the major options:

   - **American Plan (AP):** Also known as "full board," this plan includes three meals a day.

   - **Modified American Plan (MAP):** Also called "half-board," this plan includes breakfast and dinner.

   - **Bermuda Plan (BP):** This includes a full American or English breakfast.

- **Continental Plan (CP):** This includes a continental breakfast that primarily consists of bread, jam, and coffee or tea.

- **European Plan (EP):** Room only – no meals.

Be sure to clarify any of these and other additional costs and plans before you book your accommodations. Otherwise you may be in for some unexpected surprises and expensive disappointments, especially if you enjoy dining in local restaurants but have already paid for your meals at your hotel or resort. If, for example, you choose the most expensive alternative – the American Plan – everything will be prepaid and you won't need to sample any of the local restaurants identified in Chapter 9. The European Plan will always be the cheapest alternative for accommodations but you will have to spend more on dining, which can become a costly expense. The American Plan makes sense if you are staying at a relatively self-contained property where there are few restaurants nearby. However, if you are staying in Hamilton or St. George, you may want to go with the European Plan and dine outside your property. In addition, you may not have a choice of plan during the high season since many properties automatically book guests under the Modified American Plan. With dinner already paid for, you may be reluctant to venture beyond your hotel to try some of the wonderful restaurants we outline in Chapter 9. If this is your situation, check on the availability of a "Dine Around Program" through your property.

Selecting Your Best Location

Which type of accommodations you choose can make a big difference in how well you enjoy your Bermuda holiday. Indeed, Bermuda offers several styles of accommodations, depending on your needs and goals.

Hotels in Hamilton, which are our first choice, are ideal for business people and those who wish to do lots of shopping, dining, sightseeing, and people watching as well as have access to convenient transportation to other parts of the island. You won't run out of things to see and do when you stay in and around Hamilton.

If you just want to relax on the beach, go golfing, or participate in water sports, you may want to book a beachfront resort property on the South Shore. Some properties are more secluded, romantic, and quaint than the much larger and more public resort complexes. You may feel somewhat captive at these places, with limited things to see and do after a day or two of self-indulgence.

If you are traveling with children, consider staying at a property that also offers kids' programs, such as the Fairmont Hamilton Princess, the Fairmont Southampton, and the Wyndham Bermuda Resort and Spa.

You may want to try different styles of properties – stay three days in a Hamilton hotel and another three days at a beachfront cottage colony, resort, or apartment.

Different Types of Properties

For your convenience, we identify the major properties in Bermuda by both type and location. We strongly recommend visiting the website of each property; exploring various properties that are annotated on www.bermuda-online.org, www.bermudasbest.com, www.bermuda4u.com, www.fodors.com, and www.frommers.com; and checking out their current rates at www.bermudatourism.com. If a property does not have a website, search for it by name on www.google.com, www.yahoo.com, or www.ask.com. In most cases you will be able to pull it up on one of several online booking sites, which will include details and photos as well as pricing and reservation information. Examining properties in this manner will give you some sense of what you can expect if you stay at particular properties.

BED AND BREAKFAST

❑ **Edgehill Manor** (residential near Hamilton City)
P.O. Box HM 1048
Hamilton HM EX, Bermuda
Tel. 441-295-7124
Fax 441-295-3850
E-mail: bmarshal@ibl.com

❑ **Erith Guest House** (Paget)
15 Pomander Road
Paget PG 05, Bermuda
Tel. 441-232-1827
E-mail: kcampbel@ibl.com
Website: www.erithguesthouse.com

❑ **Granaway Guest House & Cottage**
(Harbour Road, Warwick)
P.O. Box WK 533
Warwick WK BX, Bermuda
Tel. 441-256-3747
Fax 441-236-3749
E-mail: info@granaway.com
Website: www.granaway.com

❑ **Greene's Guest House** (Southampton)
P.O. Box SN 395
Southampton SN BX, Bermuda
Tel. 441-238-0834
Fax 441-238-8980
E-mail: greenesguesthouse@yahoo.com

❑ **Hi-Roy** (off North Shore Road, Pembroke)
22 Princess Estate Road
Pembroke HM 04, Bermuda
Tel. 441-292-0808

❑ **Little Pomander Guest House** (Hamilton Harbour,
Hamilton City, Pembroke)
P.O. Box HM 384
Hamilton HM BX, Bermuda
Tel. 441-236-7635
Fax 441-236-8332
E-mail: litpomander@cwbda.bm
Website: www.littlepomander.com

❑ **Royal Heights Guest House**
(Lighthouse Hill, Southampton)
P.O. Box SN 144
Southampton SN BX, Bermuda
Tel. 441-238-0043
Fax 441-238-8445
E-mail: royalheights@ibl.bm

❑ **Salt Kettle House** (Salt Kettle, Paget)
10 Salt Kettle Road
Paget PG 01, Bermuda
Tel. 441-236-0407
Fax 441-236-8639

INNS

❑ **Aunt Nea's Inn at Hillcrest** (St. George)
P.O. Box GE 96
St. George's GE BX, Bermuda
Tel. 441-297-1630
Fax 441-297-1908
E-mail: frontdesk@auntneas.com
Website: www.auntneas.com

❑ **Fordham Hall Guest House**
(Pitts Bay Road, Hamilton City, Pembroke)

P.O. Box HM 248
Hamilton HM CX, Bermuda
Tel. 441-295-1551
Fax 441-295-3906
E-mail: fordham@northrock.bm

❑ **Loughlands** (South Road, Paget)
79 South Road
Paget PG 03, Bermuda
Tel. 441-236-1255

❑ **Oxford House** (Woodbourn Avenue,
Hamilton City, Pembroke)
P.O. Box HM 374
Hamilton HM BX, Bermuda
Tel. 441-295-0503 or 800-548-7758 (USA)
Fax 441-295-0250
Website: www.oxfordhouse.bm

SMALL COTTAGES, SUITES, AND APARTMENTS

❑ **Blue Horizons** (Warwick)
93 South Road
Warwick WK 10, Bermuda
Tel. 441-236-6350 or 800-637-4116 (USA)
Fax 441-236-9151
E-mail: blu@bspl.bm

❑ **Burch's Guest Apartments** (Devonshire)
110 North Shore Road
Devonshire FL 03, Bermuda
Tel. 441-292-5746 or 800-637-4116 (USA)
Fax 441-295-3794
E-mail: bur@bspl.bm

❑ **Dawkings Manors** (Paget)
P.O. Box PG 34
Paget PG BX, Bermuda
Tel. 441-236-7419 or 800-637-4116 (USA)
Fax 441-236-7088
E-mail: dawkinsmanorhotel@ibl.bm
Website: www.bermuda-charm.com

❑ **Garden House** (Sandys)
4 Middle Road, Somerset Bridge
Sandys SB 01, Bermuda
Tel. 441-234-1435
Fax 441-234-3006

❏ **Grape Bay Cottages** (Grape Bay, Paget)
P.O. Box HM 1851
Hamilton HM HX, Bermuda
Tel. 441-295-7017 or 800-637-4116 (USA)
Fax 441-286-0563
E-mail: grapebaycottages@northrock.bm
Website: www.bermuda.com

❏ **La Casa Del Masa** (residential area, Pembroke)
P.O. Box HM 2394
Hamilton HM GX, Bermuda
Tel. 441-292-8726
Fax 441-295-4447

❏ **Mazarine By the Sea** (North Shore, Pembroke)
P.O. Box HM 5153
Hamilton HM NX, Bermuda
Tel. 441-292-1690
Fax 441-292-9077
E-mail: mazarinebythesea@ibl.com

❏ **Ocean Terrace** (Southampton)
P.O. Box SN 501
Southampton SN BX, Bermuda
Tel. 441-238-0019 or 800-637-4116 (USA)
Fax 441-238-4673

❏ **Palmetto Suites** (Smith's)
P.O. Box FL 54
Smith's FL BX, Bermuda
Tel. 441-293-2323
Fax 441-293-8761
E-mail: jamaral@palmettosuites.com
Website: www.palmettosuites.com

❏ **Robin's Nest** (Pembroke)
10 Vale Close
Pembroke HM 04, Bermuda
Tel. 441-292-4347 or 800-637-4116 (USA)
Fax 441-292-4347
E-mail: robinsnest@cwbda.bm

❏ **South View Cottage** (Southampton)
9 Bowe Lane
Southampton SN 04, Bermuda
Tel. 441-238-0064

❑ **Syl-Den Apartments** (Warwick)
8 Warwickshire Road
Warwick WK 02, Bermuda
Tel. 441-238-1834 or 800-637-4116 (USA)
Fax 441-238-3205
E-mail: syl@bspl.bm

❑ **Vienna Guest Apartments** (Warwick)
63 Cedar Hill
Warwick WK 06, Bermuda
Tel. 441-236-3300 or 800-637-4116 (USA)
Fax 441-236-6100
E-mail: vienna@ibl.bm
Website: www.bermuda.com

LARGE COTTAGES, SUITES, AND APARTMENTS

❑ **Astwood Cove** (Warwick)
49 South Road
Warwick WK 07, Bermuda
Tel. 441-236-0984
Fax 441-236-1164
E-mail: astwoodcove@northrock.bm

❑ **Brightside Apartments** (Smith's)
P.O. Box FL 319
Smith's FL BX, Bermuda
Tel. 441-292-8410
Fax 441-295-6968
E-mail: brightside@ibl.bm
Website: www.bermuda.com

❑ **Clairfont Apartments** (Warwick)
P.O. Box WK 85
Warwick WK BX, Bermuda
Tel. 441-258-0149
Fax 441-238-3503
E-mail: clairfont@ibl.bm

❑ **The Clear View Suites** (Hamilton)
Sandy Lane
Hamilton Parish CR 02, Bermuda
Tel. 441-293-0484 or 800-468-9600 (USA)
Fax 441-293-0267
E-mail: otrott@northrock.bm
Website: www.bermuda-online.org/clearview.htm

❑ **Greenbank & Cottages** (Paget)
P.O. Box PG 201
Paget PG BX, Bermuda
Tel. 441-236-3615 or 800-637-4116 (USA)
E-mail: grebank@ibl.bm
Website: www.bermudamall.com

❑ **Marley Beach Cottages** (Paget)
P.O. Box PG 278
Paget PG BX, Bermuda
Tel. 441-236-1143, ext. 46, or 800-637-4116 (USA)
Fax 441-236-1984
E-mail: mar@bspl.bm
Website: www.netlinkbermuda.com/marley

❑ **Munro Beach Cottages** (Southampton)
P.O. Box SN 99
Southampton SN BX, Bermuda
Tel. 441-234-1175 or 800-637-4116 (USA)
Fax 441-234-3528
E-mail: munro@northrock.bm
Website: www.munrobeach.com

❑ **Paraquet Guest Apartments** (Paget)
P.O. Box PG 173
Paget PG BX, Bermuda
Tel. 441-236-5842
Fax 441-236-1665

❑ **Rosemont** (Hamilton City, Pembroke)
P.O. Box HM 37
Hamilton HM AX, Bermuda
Tel. 441-292-1055 or 800-367-0040 (USA)
Fax 441-295-3913
E-mail: rosemont@ibl.bm

❑ **Sandpiper Apartments** (Warwick)
P.O. Box HM 685
Hamilton HM CX, Bermuda
Tel. 441-236-7093 or 800-637-4116 (USA)
Fax 441-236-3898
E-mail: sandpiper@ibl.bm

❑ **Valley Cottage & Apartments** (Paget)
P.O. Box PG 214
Paget PG BX, Bermuda
Tel. 441-236-0628 or 800-637-4116 (USA)

Fax 441-236-3895
E-mail: rsimons@northrock.bm

❑ **The Wharf Executive Suites** (Paget)
1 Harbour Road
Paget PG 01, Bermuda
Tel. 441-232-5700
Fax 441-232-4008
Website: www.wharfexecutivesuites.com

PRIVATE CLUBS

❑ **Coral Beach & Tennis Club** (South Road, Paget)
34 South Road
Paget PG 04, Bermuda
Tel. 441-236-2233
Fax 441-236-1878
E-mail: coralbch@ibl.bm
Website: www.bermudasbest.com

❑ **Mid Ocean Club** (South Road, Tucker's Town)
P.O. Box HM 1728
Hamilton HM GX, Bermuda
Tel. 441-293-0330
Fax 441-293-8837
E-mail: midoceanclub@ibl.bm

COTTAGE COLONIES

❑ **Ariel Sands** (South Road, Devonshire)
P.O. Box HM 334
Hamilton HM BX, Bermuda
Tel. 441-236-1010 or 800-468-6610 (USA)
E-mail: reservations@CWBDA.bm
Website: www.arielsands.com

❑ **Cambridge Beaches** (Sandys)
30 King's Point Road
Somerset MA 02, Bermuda
Tel. 441-234-0331 or 800-468-7300 (North America)
Fax 441-234-3352
E-mail: cambridge@ibl.bm
Website: www.cambridgebeaches.com

❑ **Fourways Inn** (Middle Road, Paget)
P.O. Box PG 294
Paget PG BX, Bermuda

Tel. 441-236-6517 or 800-962-7654
Fax 441-236-5528
E-mail: fourways@ibl.bm

❑ **Horizons & Cottages** (South Road, Paget)
P.O. Box PG 198
Paget PG BX, Bermuda
E-mail: horizons@ibl.bm
Website: www.bermudasbest.com

❑ **Pink Beach Club & Cottages** (Smith's)
P.O. Box HM 1017
Hamilton HMDX, Bermuda
Tel. 441-293-1666 or 800-355-6161 (USA/Canada)
E-mail: info@pinkbeach.com
Website: www.pinkbeach.com

❑ **St. George's Club Hotel and Timesharing**
(Rose Hill, St. George's)
P.O. Box GE 92
St. George's GE BX, Bermuda
Tel. 441-297-1200
Fax 441-297-8003
E-mail: stgcluboperations@ibl.bm
Website: www.StGeorgeClub.com

❑ **Willowbank** (Ely's Harbour, Sandys)
P.O. Box MA 296
Sandys MA BX, Bermuda
Tel. 441-234-1616 or 800-752-8495 (USA)
Fax 441-234-3375
E-mail: reservations@willowbank.bm
Website: www.willowbank.bm

SMALL HOTELS

❑ **Hamilton Hotel & Island Club Hotel
and Timesharing** (Langton Hill, Pembroke)
P.O. Box HM 1738
Hamilton, HM GX, Bermuda
Tel. 441-295-5608 or 800-203-3222 (USA/Canada)

❑ **Harmony Club** (South Road, Paget)
P.O. Box PG 299
Paget PG BX, Bermuda
Tel. 441-236-5500 or 888-427-6664 (USA/Canada)
Fax 441-236-2624

E-mail: reservation@harmonyclub.com
Website: www.harmonyclub.com

❑ **Newstead Hotel** (Harbour Road, Paget)
P.O. Box PG 196
Paget PG BX, Bermuda
Tel. 441-256-6060 or 800-468-4111 (USA/Canada)
Fax 441-236-7454
E-mail: reservations@newsteadhotel.com

❑ **Pompano Beach Club** (Southwest, Southampton)
36 Pompano Beach Road
Southampton SB 03, Bermuda
Tel. 441-234-0222 or 800-343-4155 (USA/Canada)
Fax 441-234-1694
E-mail: pompano@ibl.bm
Website: www.pompanobeachclub.com

❑ **The Reefs** (South Road, Southampton)
56 South Road
Southampton SN 02, Bermuda
Tel. 441-238-0222 or 800-742-2008 (USA/Canada)
Fax 441-238-8372
E-mail: reefsbda@ibl.bm
Website: www.TheReefs.com

❑ **Rosedon** (Pitt Bay Road, Hamilton City, Pembroke)
P.O. Box HM 290
Hamilton HM AX, Bermuda
Tel. 441-295-1640 or 800-742-5008 (USA)
Fax 441-295-5904
E-mail: rosedon@ibl.bm
Websites: www.rosedonbermuda.com

❑ **Royal Palms Hotel & Restaurant**
(Rosemont Avenue, Hamilton City, Pembroke)
P.O. Box HM 499
Hamilton HM CX, Bermuda
Tel. 441-292-1854 or 800-678-0783 (USA)
Fax 441-292-1946
E-mail: reservations@royalpalms.bm
Website: www.royalpalms.bm

❑ **Stonington Beach Hotel** (South Shore, Paget)
P.O. Box HM 523
Hamilton HM CX, Bermuda
Tel. 441-236-5416 or 800-457-5000 (USA/Canada)

E-mail: stonington@northrock.bm
Website: www.stoningtonbeach.com

❑ **Surf Side Beach Club** (South Shore, Warwick)
P.O. Box WK 101
Warwick WK BX, Bermuda
Tel. 441-236-7100 or 800-553-9990 (USA/Canada)
Fax 441-236-9765
E-mail: surf@ibl.bm
Website: www.surfside.bm

❑ **Waterloo House** (Pitt Bay Road, Hamilton City,
Pembroke)
P.O. Box HM 333
Hamilton HM BX, Bermuda
Tel. 441-295-4480 or 800-468-4100 (USA)
Fax 441-295-2585
E-mail: waterloo@ibl.bm
Website: www.bermudasbest.com

RESORT HOTELS

❑ **Elbow Beach Bermuda** (South Shore, Paget)
P.O. Box HM 455
Hamilton HM BX, Bermuda
Tel. 441-236-5535 or 800-544-3526 (USA)
Fax 441-236-8045
Website: www.mandarinoriental.com

❑ **The Fairmont Hamilton Princess**
(Pitt Bay Road, Hamilton City, Pembroke)
P.O. Box HM 837
Hamilton HM CX, Bermuda
Tel. 800-441-1414
Fax 506-877-3160
E-mail: hamilton@fairmont.com
Website: www.fairmont.com/hamilton

❑ **Fairmont Southampton** (South Shore, Southampton)
P.O. Box HM 1379
Hamilton HM FX, Bermuda
Tel. 800-441-1414 (USA/Canada)
Fax 506-877-3160
E-mail: southampton@fairmont.com
Website: www.fairmont.com

❑ **Grotto Bay Beach Resort & Tennis Club** (Hamilton)
11 Blue Hole Hill
Hamilton CR 04, Bermuda
Tel. 441-293-8333 or 800-582-3190 (USA)
Fax 441-293-2306
E-mail: lsgrottobay@ibl.bm
Website: www.grottobay.com

❑ **Wyndham Bermuda Resort & Spa**
(South Shore, Paget)
6 Sonesta Drive
Southampton SN 02, Bermuda
Tel. 441-238-8122 or 800-WYNDHAM
Fax 441-238-8463
Website: www.wyndham.com

Best of the Best

We have our own personal favorites (see map on page 63) based on several properties we have stayed at or visited for inspection. If you want to experience the best of the best in accommodations, consider staying at these fine properties that are found throughout the island.

❑ **The Fairmont Hamilton Princess**: *HM CX Bermuda, Tel. 441-295-3000, Fax 441-295-2616, or 800-441-1414. E-mail: hamilton@fairmont.com. Website: www.fairmont.com/hamilton.*
The Fairmont Hamilton Princess has been considered a gem

of the island since its opening in 1885. Its recent renovation makes it as luxurious as it is historic. Combining British elegance and Bermudian charm, the Fairmont Hamilton Princess provides first-class facilities to both business and leisure travelers alike. Its location in downtown Hamilton, a short walk from the main shopping district, makes it a perfect choice for those with business to conduct or with a major interest in shopping. For guests wanting the city location of the Fairmont Hamilton Princess combined with the offerings of a resort, a complimentary ferry service may be taken advantage of, taking guests to its sister property, The Fairmont Southampton. A 20-minute scenic ferry ride within the calm water of the lagoon ends by dropping guests near a bus stop from where they take a hotel shuttle bus to the Southampton to enjoy a variety of resort activities.

The Fairmont Hamilton offers 410 guestrooms, including 43 suites, which provide remote cable color TV, in-room safe, stocked mini-bar, voice mail, iron/ironing board, hair dryer, alarm clock radio, coffee/tea maker, high-speed and/or dial-up Internet access. Choose the Fairmont Gold Wing and additional amenities are provided: private check-in, complimentary deluxe continental breakfast, concierge service, and an exclusive spacious lounge surround Fairmont Gold Guests with enhanced comfort and personalized service. Guest rooms in this wing feature marble bathrooms, fine furnishings, and premier in-room amenities. The lounge provides computers with complimentary Internet access.

The Explorers Camp offers a program of supervised activities for youngsters five years and older. The camp is open from 9am and 5pm daily during peak season; off-peak season hours are 12pm to 5pm daily. Children 7 years and older may stay for evening activities, Tuesday to Saturday from 6:30pm to 10:30pm.

Heritage Court offers a cosmopolitan setting for evening cocktails, afternoon tea, or select from a menu featuring classic Bermudian dishes. *Heritage Court* garnered a "Best of Bermuda" award for its afternoon tea. If you have afternoon tea, you may want to skip dinner! *Harley's Restaurant*, "Best of Bermuda Gold Award" winner offers international fare or enjoy the same choice of cuisine under the Bermuda Sky at *Harley's Terrace*. *HP's* offers freshly baked pastries and a selection of Seattle's Best Coffee® in its dining area or "to go." Fitness Facility; Business Center; Conference/Banquet Facilities.

❑ **The Fairmont Southampton**: *101 South Shore Road, P.O. Box HM 1379, Hamilton HM FX, Tel. 441-238-8000, Fax 441-238-8968, or 800-441-1414. E-mail: southampton@fairmont.com. Website: www.fairmont.com.* Situated on the highest point on the island, The Fairmont Southampton is the resort hotel sister to the in-town Fairmont Hamilton Princess. Guests at either property have full access to the offerings of both properties and can travel between them on a complimentary 20-minute scenic ferry ride on the calm waters within the reef. The 593 guestrooms and suites offer balconies, walk-in closets, mini-bar, in-room-safe, remote cable color television, iron/ironing board, hairdryer, clock radio with alarm, coffee/tea-making facilities, bathrobes, voice mail and dataport with Internet access. Fairmont Gold, located on the 6th floor, offers additional amenities: private check-in area, private lounge offering computers with complimentary use of Internet, complimentary deluxe continental breakfast, afternoon tea, hor d'oeuvres, and honor bar. Guestrooms have either ocean or harbor views.

Wickets is a casual family restaurant featuring a potpourri of international cuisine offering both buffets and à la carte dining. *Windows on the Sound* offers a panoramic view of the Great Sound and serves a full American breakfast and a traditional Bermuda Sunday brunch. *Newport Room*, an award-winning restaurant recipient of an AAA Four-Diamond Award, serves modern French cuisine. *The Wine Cellar*, with the unique atmosphere of an old English pub, features nightly entertainment, billiards, and televised sports, and promotes a variety of fine spirits, wine, and beer. *Jasmine* offers afternoon tea as well as salads, sandwiches, pizza, and light fare. *Waterlot Inn* is a free-standing 330-year-old inn (built in 1670) located on the harbor and accessible by hotel trolley. It is the recipient of an AAA Four-Diamond Award and serves Mediterranean cuisine. The *Explorers Camp* offers a program of supervised activities for youngsters 5 years and older. Its offerings for young guests is the same as at the Fairmont Hamilton Princess. (See section on Explorers Club under Fairmont Hamilton Princess.)

The new world-class Willow Stream – The Spa at Fairmont Southampton – features luxury surroundings fused with Bermuda's premier spa therapies. The spa facility includes a beautiful indoor pool that almost feels as if you are outside. The Fairmont Southampton Golf Club, located on the hotel grounds, is deemed the world's most scenic and challenging par-3 executive course and is a perennial *Golf Digest Place to Play* award winner. Six other off-site golf courses are available for play with advance arrangements. Fitness Facilities and an array of water sports; Business Center; Conference/Banquet Facilities.

❑ **Waterloo House**: *100 Pitts Bay Road, Hamilton, HMBX, Bermuda, Tel. 441-295-4480, Fax 441-295-2585, or 800-468-4100. E-mail: waterloo@ibl.bm. Website: www.bermudasbest.com.* Overlooking Hamilton Harbour and a short walk from the business district and center for shopping in Hamilton, Waterloo House is a stone manor house built in 1815. The inn, a Relais & Chateaux property, extends to include a few adjacent historical buildings that were once used as warehouses. Each of the 30 unique deluxe guestrooms and suites is decorated with antiques and artwork. Spacious bathrooms include heated towel racks. Some have Jacuzzis. Two deluxe one-bedroom suites are available in a waterfront cottage. Guestrooms offer remote-control air conditioners, in-room safe, and an electric trouser press. Guests enjoy a complimentary full breakfast. The inn's public areas are well decorated and contain quality art.

The Wellington Room serves delicious meals in an elegant setting, or dine waterside on the *Poinciana Terrace*. Enjoy cocktails in the *Lone Room Bar* or afternoon tea in the garden or flagpole terrace. Long-term guests may choose to try one of the restaurants of a sister property: Horizons & Cottages or Coral Beach & Tennis Club. Guests may also choose to enjoy The Coral Beach & Tennis Club's championship tennis courts, fitness center with personal trainer, European Spa, or beach.

❑ **Ariel Sands**: *34 South Shore Road, Devonshire, P.O. Box HM 334, Hamilton HM BX, Bermuda, Tel. 441-236-1010, Fax 441-236-0087, or 800-468-6610. E-mail: reservations@arielsands.com. Website: www.arielsands.com.* Nestled into 14 acres on Bermuda's South Shore, Ariel

Sands offers ocean views from every cottage, a beach for swimming or sunning, a long list of on-property amenities, and Bermudian hospitality. Owned by the Dill family and boasting Michael Douglas as a shareholder and frequent guest, (Michael's mother, Diana, is a Dill), Ariel Sands is a member of the Bermuda Collection – a select group of some of the island's top small hotels and cottage colonies. Ariel Sands received a *Top 10* award in *Travel and Leisure's* World's Best Awards 2002, in "Hotel Services for Hotels in Bermuda, Bahamas, and the Caribbean."

Ariel Sands offers 47 deluxe guestrooms, suites and cottages with either king or twin-size beds. Guestrooms are decorated in soft, muted tones and configured differently from one another, but most have nicely proportioned tile bathrooms. A small refrigerator is provided – ready to be stocked with items of the guest's choosing from convenience stores. Bathrobes, hairdryer, iron/ironing board, coffeepot with coffee are provided, as are color cable television and radio in each guestroom. VCR is available on request with a rental library. Direct-dial telephone with modem capability is also available in each guestroom. Each guestroom has a private balcony, porch, or patio with ocean views.

There is a large double-sided fireplace in the main building. Massage, health and beauty treatments, and a hair salon are available. Along with ocean swimming, there are two naturally fed seawater pools and a heated freshwater pool and two tennis courts lit for night play. Health Facilities; Business Facilities; Restaurant; Conference/Banquet Facilities.

❑ **Elbow Beach Bermuda**: *60 South Shore Road, Paget PG 04, P.O. Box HM 455, Hamilton, HM BX, Bermuda, Tel. 441-236-3535, Fax 441-236-8043, or 800-223-7434. Website: www.man darinoriental.com.* The historic Elbow Beach Hotel, enjoys a beautiful South Shore setting on a pink sand beach just five minutes from Hamilton and 25 minutes from the airport. A member of *The Leading Hotels of the World* and managed by the Mandarin Oriental Hotel Group, Elbow Beach offers two kinds of hotel experiences. Some guests may prefer a classic Bermuda cottage colony experience, while others may opt for the main hotel with the conveniences and luxuries it provides.

The over-90-year-old, four-story main building, painted a Bermudian shade of yellow with crisp white trim, offers 131 guestrooms and one penthouse suite. The cottage colony consists of 104 guestrooms set amidst the grounds and gracefully arranged winding down the hill from the main building through an assemblage of exotic plants and manicured lawns to the beach. Amenities in most guestrooms include TV, clock/radio, in-room safe, electronic mini-bar, ironing board/iron, bathrobes, and hairdryer. Guestrooms in the main building feature high-speed Internet connection, virtual network and visual tele-conferencing capabilities, and overnight complimentary shoeshine.

The signature restaurant, *Seahorse Grill,* features New Bermudian Cuisine. The *Veranda Bar,* Bermuda's first rum bar, also features a cigar room, and serves cocktails, beverages, and a menu of light selections. *Blue Point* is a poolside grill serving burgers, island fish, and other patio fare with alfresco seating and ocean views. *Lido,* located above the beach, offers an eclectic menu with Mediterranean touches. *Mickey's Beach Bistro & Bar,* located on the beach, serves casual fare and is open from May until October. *The Sea Breeze Café* offers alfresco dining overlooking the beach. *Deep* is a state-of-the-art nightclub facility. A champagne and wine list is available as well as a fun cocktail list.

Stunning ocean views from individual balconies are the perfect backdrop to the newly featured spa's six private self-contained suites. The luxurious spa has Asian accents, yet a distinct island feel enhanced by signature Bermudian treatments. *Pollock Shields,* a sunken wreck, lies 60 feet beneath the surface and is accessible via a shore dive. Fitness Facility along with tennis, golf, and water sports; Business Facilities; Conference/Banquet Facilities.

❑ **The Reefs**: *56 South Shore Road, Southampton SNO2, Bermuda, Tel. 441-238-0222, Fax 441-238-8372. E-mail: reefsbda@ibl.bm. Website: www.thereefs.com.* Nestled into a cove above a private beach, The Reefs offers 65 guestrooms, suites, and private cot-tages. Most are unique and differ from one another in configuration and/or decor. Each is tastefully decorated in island tones or prints. Amenities include refrigerator, in-room safe, iron/ironing board, coffee maker, bathrobes, and hairdryer. Suites and cot-tage suites have TV/VCR/DVD. A small TV/VCR may be available from the front desk on request, but can only play videos. The Clubhouse has a cable television available for guest viewing.

Grill 56, the more formal dining room, requires men wear a jacket on most nights. *Coconuts,* located on the deck overlooking the beach, has a more relaxed atmosphere and offers alfresco dining for both lunch and dinner. The four-course set dinner menu offers a mix of Cajun and Caribbean flavors. You may want to experience dining on the sand below Coconuts for a unique and beautiful setting. Only 16 guests (for a surcharge) are afforded this opportunity each evening during the summer season. *Ocean Echo* offers alfresco dining with ocean views on the main terrace. The dinner menu features a variety of unique items off the grill. All guests are invited for *Afternoon Tea* served daily in the lounge. Fitness Center and water activities; two tennis courts, golf on nearby courses.

❏ **Pink Beach Club and Cottages:** *P.O. Box HM 1017, Hamilton HM DX, Bermuda, Tel. 441-293-1666, Fax 441-293-8935, or 800-335-6161. E-mail: info@pinkbeach.com. Website: www.pinkbeach.com.* Located on the South Shore, nestled on

16½ acres of rolling hills with tropical gardens and overlooking two pink sand coral beaches, Pink Beach Club is the Bermuda cottage hideaway most people would picture if asked to imagine what Bermuda looks like – pink cottages trimmed in white and accented with forest green. A member of the *Small Luxury Hotels of the World*, the property is comprised of 16 cottage buildings, which house 94 guestrooms and suites. The majority of accommodations at Pink Beach Club and Cottages are cottage-style suites and junior suites, with all but three offering ocean views. Cottage deluxe rooms and ocean view junior suites are spacious one-room suites that feature a living room/bedroom combination. All other guestroom categories are one-bedroom suites which feature a bedroom and a separate living room area. Guestrooms are decorated in soft pastel shades, with new cherry wood furniture in old English style – blending tropical ambiance with British traditional elegance. Botanical prints hang above the bed, and oriental carpets soften the tile floors. Guest suites have spacious Italian marble bathrooms accommodating double sinks and a soaking tub, and large dressing areas as well as oversized terraces. Guestrooms are equipped with hairdryer, robes, in-room safe, a mini refrigerator or access to a full kitchen, coffee maker, iron/ironing board, direct dial phones, and a private terrace or patio with chaise lounges and a table and chairs.

Dining venues at Pink Beach Club and Cottages provide guests with the choice of dining in comfortable elegance at the *Bermudiana*, a formal, indoor, ocean front dining room (serving dinner) and *The Breakers*, a smart casual, outdoor, a la carte restaurant (serving breakfast, lunch, and dinner). Floor-to-ceiling windows in the Bermudiana offer panoramic ocean views. The menu changes daily, but Bermuda's trademark fish chowder and rockfish are regulars on the menu. Guests may choose to have a full, hot English breakfast in the privacy of their own cottage, served by a personal housekeeper. A traditional English afternoon tea is served each day in the *Hibiscus Lounge*, and guests can sample the island's popular cocktails at the *Cedar Bar*.

Pink Beach Club and Cottages features two pink sand beaches and a heated swimming pool, two tennis courts, ping pong tables and a snooker table. Snorkeling equipment is included in the nightly rate and mopeds can be rented on property. For golf enthusiasts, the hotel is just minutes away from two championship golf courses. Tee times are easily arranged. Hilltop Cottage houses a complete fitness center. Two massage therapists are on-property for in-cottage massages and spa treatments. The concierge will assist with arranging sightseeing tours, deep-sea fishing charters, sailing, scuba diving, glass-bottom boat cruises, or whatever available activity the guest desires. The helpful, friendly staff seem truly dedicated to making guests feel so at home they never want to leave.

❑ **Cambridge Beaches:** *30 King's Point Road, Somerset MA02, Bermuda, Tel. 441-234-0331, Fax 441-234-3352, or 800-468-7300. E-mail: cambridge@ibl.bm. Website: www.cambridgebeach es.com.* Cambridge Beaches is an exclusive hideaway resort situated on a 25-acre peninsula with five private beaches overlooking Mangrove Bay and Long Bay and just a few minutes walk from Somerset Village. The 94 cottage-style guestrooms and suites (18 new deluxe guestrooms and suites were added in 2001) feature large private beach or garden view terraces. Some guestrooms have fireplaces. Marble bathrooms have Jacuzzzis. Choose from two gourmet restaurants, an outdoor dining terrace, and a luncheon patio. Classic and nouveau Bermudian-influenced Continental cuisine. Facilities include indoor and outdoor pools, three tennis courts, extensive marina, putting and croquet, and fully equipped spa.

❑ **Pompano Beach Club:** *36 Pompano Beach Road, Southampton SB03, Bermuda, Tel. 441-234-0222, Fax 441-234-1694, or 800-343-4155. E-mail: pompano@ibl.bm. Website: www.pompanobeach club.com.* Located on the southwest shore overlooking the ocean, Pompano Beach Club offers nine pink and white low-rise cottages. Each cottage has several spacious guestrooms and suites with large bathrooms. Balconies overlook the ocean. Breakfast and dinner are served in the *Cedar Room Restaurant* overlooking the sea. Lunch is served on the pool terrace. Private beach. Oceanside freshwater heated pool, wading pool and two outdoor Jacuzzis. Complimentary shuttle service to/from the bus and nearby Rockaway ferry stop. Scooter rentals available.

❑ **Horizons and Cottages:** *33 South Shore Road, P.O. Box PG 198, Paget PGBX, Bermuda, Tel. 441-236-0048, Fax 441-236-1981, or Toll Free 800-468-0022. E-mail: horizons@ibl.bm. Website: www.bermudasbest.com.* A Relais & Chateaux property, Horizons & Cottages is an estate with cottages dotted across 25 acres of grounds overlooking the ocean. Bermuda's oldest cottage colony has 13 one- and two-story pink and white cottages housing 48 spacious guestrooms and suites. Unexpected "extra" amenities include an electric trouser press and heated towel racks. Several guest units have fireplaces. Breakfast and dinner are served in the *Middleton Room* during the winter months, with lunch served in the *English Pub*. In the summer months breakfast and dinner are alfresco on the *Ocean Terrace* with lunch served on the pool patio. There are weekly outdoor barbecues on the *Barbeque Terrace.* Tennis courts, nine-hole golf course, 18-hole putting green, freshwater pool. Use of private beach, sports facilities, fitness center and beauty spa at the Coral Beach & Tennis Club.

❑ **Newstead Hotel:** *Harbour Road, P.O. Box PG 196, Paget, Bermuda, Tel. 441-236-6060, Fax 441-236-7454, or 800-468-4111. E-mail: reservations@newsteadhotel.com.* Located at the edge of a scenic harbor and recently renovated, the Newstead is a delightful full-service inn. A traditional Bermuda manor house filled with antiques and surrounded by several cottage-style wings, the Newstead offers 42 harbor and garden-view guestrooms. Electric trouser press and heated towel racks are amenities beyond most guests' expectations. Indoor restaurant with water views and *Noah's* (outdoor restaurant) and bar. Large lounge with fireplace. Private dock with deep-water swimming. Heated pool, tennis courts, putting green, Cybex mini-gym, spa. Ten-minute ferry ride to Hamilton.

❑ **Rosedon:** *Pitts Bay Road, P.O. Box HM 290, Hamilton HM AX, Bermuda, Tel. 441-295-1640, Fax 441-295-5904, or 800-742-5008. E-mail:* <u>rosedon@ibl.bm</u>. *Website:* <u>www.rosedonbermuda.com</u>. Located across the street from the Fairmont Hamilton Princess, the Rosedon is a small hotel (or large guesthouse) with old-world character and charm and an attentive staff. The main house, built in 1906, has colonial guestrooms with an island flavor and a wide verandah overlooking gardens. The modern verandah guestrooms in the rear open onto the pool. The main house has two large lounges with TV and a self-service honor bar. Breakfast can be served in the guest's room, on the verandah, or at poolside and is included with the rate. There is afternoon tea, but no restaurant on premises. Heated pool; access to tennis courts and golf courses nearby; water sports and boating easily arranged. Five minute walk to Hamilton shopping or ferry ride.

Each of the above recommended properties can be found in the following parishes, going from west to east:

Sandys Parish

- Cambridge Beaches

Southampton Parish

- Fairmont Southampton
- The Reefs
- Pompano Beach Club

Paget Parish

- Elbow Beach
- Horizons and Cottages
- Newstead

Pembroke Parish/Hamilton City

- Fairmont Hamilton Princess
- Rosedon
- Waterloo House

Devonshire Parish

- Ariel Sands Beach Club

Smith's Parish

- Pink Beach Club and Cottages

9

Dining Right

I N ADDITION TO SHOPPING, dining is one of the major highlights of visiting Bermuda. You'll discover many different dining venues and cuisines among the island's more than 150 restaurants. A few restaurants are truly memorable, especially for their waterfront views and ambience. Some boast very inventive chefs who combine local and international cuisines into many excellent dishes.

A Changing Dining Scene

Bermuda seems to have an over-abundance of award-winning restaurants, which may or may not be all that deserving. Most restaurants are operated by owner chefs or run by a restaurant management group, such as the Little Venice Group.

The basic realities of dining in Bermuda do not encourage and support great restaurants and chefs. For example, many visitors staying at local properties are on prepaid meal plans that cover two or three meals a day (Modified American Plan or American Plan). Others end up dining in their hotels because of the inconvenience and high cost of local transportation at night – $20 to

$40 to take a taxi to and from a restaurant, if either their hotel or the restaurant are outside Hamilton. With the exception of the wonderful restaurants at the Elbow Beach Bermuda, Fairmont Southampton, The Reefs, and the Pink Beach Club along the South Shore, few hotel restaurants have incentives to provide top quality cuisine and service. Like cruise ship passengers who dine onboard several times a day, most hotels have captive audiences. Also, few Bermuda restaurants draw top international chefs, except for a few visiting chefs at major hotel resorts, since most properties do not have sufficient clientele to support such expensive expertise year round.

Nonetheless, you will find many chefs in Bermuda with lots of international experience, and the numbers of such chefs are growing. Bermuda even hosts an annual Culinary Arts Festival that attracts celebrity chefs from North America and Europe. Compared to 10 years ago, Bermuda's dining scene has definitely changed for the better.

Bermuda does have a few excellent restaurants that offer fine food and unique and romantic dining experiences. Over 70 percent of these restaurants are found in Hamilton City where visitors staying in nearby hotels or on cruise ships can easily walk to at night. If you are staying elsewhere, you may find dining in these restaurants to be inconvenient at night. Shoppers and businesspeople staying in and around Hamilton City are in a good position to enjoy these restaurants.

In general, the cost of dining out is relatively expensive in Bermuda but not more than you might pay at an above average restaurant in major U.S. cities, such as New York, Boston, and Washington, DC. For example, the average cost of dining at a top restaurant such as The Lido at the Elbow Beach Bermuda is $60 to $80 per person, including beverage. In fact, we find the cost of dining in Bermuda to be reasonable compared to other costs incurred while visiting this island. If you've recently dined in London or Paris, Bermuda's restaurants will look like bargains! Indeed, everything is relative to where you've been.

Local Cuisine and Best Choices

Bermudian cuisine tends to be very eclectic, drawing major influences from British, American, African, Portuguese, and Asian cooking. A Bermudian breakfast, for example, consists of boiled, salted codfish prepared with a bacon-tomato sauce served with boiled potatoes, hard-boiled eggs, bananas, and slices of avocado. You can sample this unique breakfast at several Sunday brunches in Bermuda.

Most restaurants serve a combination of local and international foods, with a bias toward American, British, Italian, and French dishes. Since most food must be imported to Bermuda, you may want to try local dishes that incorporate fresh sea catches, especially Bermuda rockfish, spiny Bermuda lobster ("guinea chick"), wahoo (red snapper) steak, shark, yellowfin tuna, fish chowder, and mussel pie. Other popular local dishes include Hoppin' John (black-eyed peas and rice), cassava pie, conch chowder, shark hash, Portuguese red bean soup, and codfish and potatoes for Sunday brunch.

When in doubt what best to order from the menu, always ask your waiter for recommendations. Ask what the restaurant is especially noted for, or what's really cooking well that day, rather than take potluck from names of familiar or unfamiliar dishes on the menu. Most waiters will identify their best dishes if asked to do so. If they can't differentiate what's really good coming from the kitchen, or if they only steer you to the most expensive items on the menu, chances are nothing is particularly outstanding and you'll be just as well off taking potluck.

Local dining venues include elegant dining rooms, waterfront and alfresco restaurants, trattorias, garden patios and terraces, cafes, pubs, and bars. You won't find a McDonald's, Burger King, or KFC in Bermuda!

Dining Tips, Customs, and Issues

Especially during high season, you are advised to make dinner reservations well in advance at top restaurants. Most restaurants are open for dinner from 6 to 10pm. The majority of diners arrive between 7 and 9pm and stay until closing.

Sunday brunch is a local dining tradition at several properties. It usually involves a large buffet with some local specialties, such as codfish and potatoes. The best Sunday brunch is found at the Waterlot Inn (Fairmont Southampton).

Bermuda's top restaurants prefer (recommend but seldom require) men to wear a jacket, although many restaurants are relaxing this requirement to smart casual. Always check on a restaurant's dress code when you book a reservation.

Many restaurants permit smoking, which can be irritating to nonsmokers who prefer nonsmoking dining environments. Some, such as The Waterlot Inn, even advertise enjoying a rich cigar at the end of your fine meal – a great way to finish off your evening as well as unappreciative guests around you! However, several restaurants do have nonsmoking sections and a few are 100-percent smoke-free. If smoking is a dining issue with you, be sure to ask before being seated at a restaurant.

Several properties serve the traditional formal English tea from 3 to 5pm. One of the best ($39.00) is found at the Fairmont Hamilton Princess. Some properties turn this ritual into an informal local high tea practice by serving it to guests dressed in their swimming suits around the pool.

Many restaurants offer excellent selections of wine. In fact, restaurants in Bermuda are reputed to have received more *Wine Spectator* awards per square mile than anywhere else in the world, save for Manhattan.

Since most restaurants automatically add a 15-percent service charge to your bill, there is no need to leave a tip. However, be careful when you sign your credit card charge slip, which may suggest otherwise. Most places use the same paper charge slips as found in U.S. restaurants. These slips have an extra "Tip" line immediately following the subtotal. Some visitors automatically add a tip because of this suggestive line and thus end up double-tipping. Just cross out the tip line and make the subtotal your total. If you've received extraordinary service that you wish to reward with a separate tip, leave cash so your waiter will receive your special tip directly.

Four upscale hotels sponsor a "Dine Around Program" – Pompano Beach Club, Cambridge Beaches, Ariel Sands, and The Reefs. Visitors staying at any one of these four properties on a prepaid dining plan can dine at any of the member resort restaurants without paying extra, other than their drinks. Other properties also have started similar programs, especially during the off season. Check with the Bermuda Department of Tourism, especially their Visitors' Service Bureaus (see Chapter 2), on the latest dine-around programs.

For the latest information on restaurants in Bermuda, including reviews, links, and some sample menus, we recommend visiting these websites:

- www.bermudadining.com
- www.diningbermuda.com
- www.bermuda-online.org/restaurants.htm
- www.bermudarestaurants.com
- www.bermuda4u.com
- www.bermudatourism.com
- www.fodors.com
- www.frommers.com

Unique Dining Experiences

Two of our most memorable dining experiences in Bermuda are in the elegant dining room of the Waterloo House (Wellington Room) and dining barefoot on the beach at The Reefs. Both places have a special ambience as well as offer excellent dishes and attentive service.

❑ **The Wellington Room:** *Waterloo House, Pitts Bay Road, Hamilton City, PEMBROKE, Tel. 441-295-4480. Reservations essential for dinner. Open for both lunch (noon-2:30pm) and* *dinner (7-9:30pm).* This is truly one of Bermuda's most memorable restaurants where great food, service, and ambience come together. Housed in one of Bermuda's most elegant small hotels (a Relais & Châteaux property) and facing Hamilton Harbour, the Wellington Room offers both terrace and indoor dining. The well-appointed English dining room, with its red interior, red and white striped wood chairs, and fireplace, offers an intimate setting for one of Bermuda's best dining experiences. The food here is simply outstanding as is the service and the extreme attention to detail. Individual dishes look like works of art! The menu includes numerous tasty fish dishes, such as baked red rockfish, tiger prawns, house blackened red snapper, and poached lobster and crawfish. Also check out the marinated duck breast,

grilled beef tenderloin steak, and Jack Daniels glazed rack of lamb. Try the wonderful appetizers and soups, especially the lobster bisque and the nicely spiced Chilean sea bass tandor. The Wellington Room also offers one of Bermuda's longest wine lists. If you only dine in one restaurant outside your hotel, make sure you put the Wellington Room at the top of your "must dine here" list!

❑ **Coconuts:** *The Reefs, 56 South Shore Road, SOUTHAMPTON, Tel. 441-238-0222. Reservations essential.* This seasonal restaurant (open from April through November) has one of the most beautiful oceanfront settings in Bermuda. Wedged between rocky cliffs and an inviting sandy beach, the restaurant has two alfresco sections: one attached to the hotel and the other literally in the sand on the beach. The real special treat here is get-

ting one of the six tables set up on the beach for a unique dining experience. Patrons leave their shoes and socks on the rack up above at the main restaurant and are escorted barefoot to their candlelit table in the sand. The water literally laps just a few feet away from your table, and the sounds of chirping tree frogs add to the charming beachfront ambience. Patrons are served a four-course meal with four to six choices within each course. While you may not remember the dishes, which are respectable, the service here is excellent and the whole dining-on-the-beach experience is outstanding. The cost is just under $100 per person.

Other memorable dining experiences are most likely found with these fine restaurants, which we will shortly feature:

- Ascot
- Fourways
- Fresco
- La Coquille
- Seahorse Grill
- The Newport Room
- Tom Moore's Tavern
- Waterlot Inn

Bermuda's 36 Best Restaurants

While the dining scene in Bermuda is constantly changing, the following restaurants have received good reviews during the past two years:

❏ **Aqua:** *Ariel Sands Hotel, 34 Shore Road, DEVONSHIRE, Tel. 441-236-1010. Open daily 8-10am, 12:30-2:30pm, and 6:30-9:30pm. Reservations required.* This is Michael Douglas's oceanfront

restaurant featuring fusion-style cuisine, with special emphasis on Bermudian, international, and Italian dishes. Under the direction of chef Claudio Vigilante, this restaurant continues to receive excellent reviews. Its wonderful oceanfront setting and ambience are especially memorable aspects of this casual restaurant and definitely set it apart from other restaurants in Bermuda. This is a very eclectic restaurant. House specialties include rockfish and lamb, and the popular bento box for dessert. Try the Thai-spiced *tuna à la niçoise* served in a coconut. Expensive.

❏ **Ascots:** *Royal Palms Hotel, 24 Rosemont Avenue, HAMILTON CITY. Tel. 441-295-9644. Open for lunch Monday through Friday, 12noon-2:30pm, and for dinner Monday through Saturday, 6:30-10pm.* Located in a spacious old mansion on the edge of the city in a residential area (just a few minutes walk from downtown Hamilton), this Italian and French restaurant is especially noted for its fresh fish, the use of fresh ingredients, and several creative dishes. The menu changes regularly, but the emphasis on fine gourmet cuisine is consistent as is the excellent service and wonderful ambience. Dine under the stars or in an elegant dining room. Expensive.

❏ **Barracuda Grill:** *5 Burnaby Hill, HAMILTON CITY, Tel. 441-292-1609 or Fax 441-292-8354. Open for lunch, Monday through Friday, 12noon to 2:30pm, and dinner, daily from 5:30-10pm.* Formerly the Fisherman's Reef and centrally located in downtown Hamilton (above the Hog Penny), this fresh seafood restaurant is known for its contemporary style, linen-covered tables, and colorful walls and paintings. Serves excellent seafood dishes, including grilled rockfish and steamed lobster. Expensive.

❏ **Beethoven's Restaurant & Bar:** *Clocktower Building, ROYAL NAVAL DOCKYARD, Tel. 441-234-5009. May through October, open Sunday to Wednesday from 9am to 6pm and Thursday to Saturday from 11am to 9pm. November to April open daily from 9am to 5pm.* Owned and operated by two Swiss chefs, this casual yet intimate Swiss and Mediterranean restaurant is a good dining choice throughout the day (breakfast, lunch, and dinner) when visiting the Royal Naval Dockyard area. Offers both indoor and outdoor dining, including afternoon tea. Try the fish chowder, sandwiches, and specials for lunch. The interesting menu at dinner includes lemon pepper tuna steak, Maryland crab cakes, and oriental chicken. Moderate.

❏ **Bermudiana Dining Room:** *Pink Beach Club and Cottages, 1 N South Shore, Tuckers Town, SMITH'S, Tel. 441-293-1666. Open daily for dinner, 6:30 to 9pm. Website: www.pinkbeach.com. Jacket required for dinner.* This lovely dining room in the Club House overlooks the picturesque salmon and white cottages as well as the ocean. Guests staying at the Pink Beach Club and Cottages are in for a real treat since this sophisticated fine dining restaurant is included in their room rate. However, many people from the outside make this one of their choice restaurants because of the inviting cuisine, views, ambience, entertainment, and exacting service. Talented London chef Joanne Bainbridge changes the international menu daily. Dinner is a very satisfying gastronomic five-course affair. Includes an extensive wine list, specialty coffees, and nightly entertainment from April to December. Expensive.

❑ **Bistro J:** *102 Chancery Lane, HAMILTON CITY, Tel. 441-296-8546. Open Monday through Saturday, 12noon to 2:30pm and 6-10pm.* Located along one of the city's charming alleys, the imaginative menu here changes daily. You can't go wrong with the fresh local seafood and homemade pastas and desserts. A good place to ask about their best dishes for the day. Offers an extensive wine list, including wines by the glass. Moderate.

❑ **Café Gio:** *Water Street, opposite the Post Office, ST. GEORGE, Tel. 441-297-1307. Open daily 11:30am to 2:30pm and 6:30 to 10pm.* Formerly San Giorgio's, this friendly Italian and increasingly international eatery is known for its excellent food and service, waterfront setting, and great views of the charming old town of St. George. Moderate.

❑ **Carriage House:** *22 Water Street, Somers Wharf, ST. GEORGE, Tel. 441-297-1730. Open daily from 11:30am to 2:30pm and 5:30 to 9:30pm.* Sunday brunch from noon to 2pm. Located in a charming 18th-century brick carriage house with a harbor-front patio, this popular restaurant offers casual and international dining. Especially noted for its wide selection of salads, a sandwich board, and à la carte menu for lunch. Both indoor and outdoor candelit dining on the waterside patio at night. Serves an early-bird four-course dinner from 5:30 to 6:45pm. Moderate.

❑ **Chopsticks Restaurant:** *88 Reid Street, HAMILTON CITY, Tel. 441-292-0791. Open Monday through Friday for lunch, 12noon to 2:30pm, and daily for dinner, 5 to 11pm.* If you're looking for Chinese and Thai food, Chopsticks is the place to dine. Offers excellent Szechuan, Cantonese, Hunan, Mandarin, and Thai dishes. Try the jade chicken, green curry chicken, scrimp in lobster sauce, beef in oyster sauce, and duck in red curry. Moderate.

❑ **Coconuts:** See description on pages 160-161 under "Unique Dining Experiences."

❑ **Fourways:** *Fourways Inn and Cottage Colony, Middle Road, PAGET, Tel. 441-236-6517. Website: www.fourwaysinn.com. Open daily 7 to 10pm. Jacket and tie required. Reservations required.* Housed in a well appointed 18th-century manor house, this restaurant is consistently one of Bermuda's top gourmet restaurants which often draws international celebrities, American politicians, and European royalty. Especially noted for its seafood dishes, Chateaubriand, veal sauteed in lemon butter, roasted rack of lamb, grilled filet mignon, and special soufflés for dessert. Includes an incredible wine list that will take you deep into their cellar of more than 7,500 bottles of wine. Dining also available on the lovely Palm Court terrace. Excellent and understated service. Expensive before wine and very expensive thereafter – but very special.

❑ **Fresco's Restaurant & Wine Bar:** *Chancery Lane (off Front Street), HAMILTON CITY, Tel. 441-295-5057. Open Monday through Friday for lunch, 12noon to 2:30pm, and Monday through Saturday for dinner, 6:30 to 10:30pm. Wine bar open Monday through Saturday, 5pm to 1am.* This popular and casual bistro, noted for its inventive Mediterranean dishes with Bermudian influences, excellent service, and nice ambience, also boasts Bermuda's only wine bar. Try their signature pork filet mignon and sea scallop dishes as well as their freshly baked chocolate mousse cake. Includes a courtyard for alfresco dining. Moderate.

❑ **Harbourfront:** *21 Front Street West, HAMILTON CITY, Tel. 441-295-4207. Open Monday through Saturday for lunch, 11:45am to 2:30pm, and dinner, 6-10pm.* Located across from the ferry terminal and overlooking scenic Hamilton Harbour from its second floor balcony, this popular Continental restaurant also has a sushi bar and grill room. Features sushi lunch buffets on Mondays ($24) and a sushi happy hour. Known for its fresh seafood, pasta, meat, poultry, and game dishes. Moderate to expensive.

❑ **Hog Penny Restaurant and Pub:** *5 Burnaby Hill, HAMILTON CITY, Tel. 441-292-2534. Open daily for lunch, 12noon to 3pm, and dinner, 5:30 to 10pm, and extended hours during the cruise ship season (April through September). Early-bird dinner available daily from 5:30 to 7pm. Includes nightly entertainment until 1am.* This is one of Bermuda's dining and drinking institutions, popular with both locals (including celebrity Catherine Zeta-Jones) and visitors. A combination British and Bermudian pub, it serves traditional pub fare for lunch – shepherd's pie, tuna salad, fish and chips, and steak-and-kidney pie. The dinner menu includes fresh fish of the day, nice cuts of Angus beef, and Indian curries. Lots of draft beer and ale gets consumed here. Moderate.

❑ **House of India:** *Park View Plaza, 57 North Street, HAMILTON CITY, Tel. 441-295-6450. Open Monday through Friday for lunch (buffet), 11:30am to 2:30pm, and daily for dinner, 5:30 to 9:45pm.* One of Bermuda's two Indian restaurants, the House of India specializes in Northern Indian cuisine. Offers a good variety of chicken, beef, lamb, and vegetarian dishes. Diners can specify the degree of spiciness they desire in each dish.

❑ **La Coquille:** *Pembroke Hall, 40 Crow Lane, HAMILTON CITY, Tel. 441-292-6122. Open daily for lunch, 12noon to 2:30pm, and Monday through Saturday for dinner, 6:30 to 10pm.* Located at the Bermuda Underwater Exploration Institute and overlooking Hamilton Harbour, this remains one of Bermuda's best French and Mediterranean restaurants, which competes well with Monte Carlo (see below). Its sophisticated menu and international staff emphasize fine dining. Chef Serge Bottelli uses local produce to create his own version of Provençal cuisine. For dinner, try the sauteed breast of duck in black-berry sauce, mushroom ravioli in celery root dressing, mari-nated veal T-bone, marinated salmon topped with blood or-ange vinaigrette, and grilled lamb in rosemary sauce. Expen-sive.

❑ **La Trattoria Restaurant and Pizzeria:** *22 Washington Lane, HAMILTON CITY, Tel. 441-295-1877. Open Monday through Friday for lunch, 11:30am to 3:30pm and daily for dinner, 5:30 to 10:30pm.* This simple but fun and fast restaurant serves pizza baked in its wood-burning oven, excellent pastas, and nu-merous Italian dishes, including fresh fish. Moderate.

❑ **Lido Restaurant:** *Elbow Beach Bermuda, Lido Complex, 60 South Road, PAGET, Tel. 441-236-9884 or e-mail:* _conciergeelbow@mohq. com_. *Open daily for dinner from 6:30 to 10pm. Website:* _www.man darinoriental.com/bermuda_. Located above the beach, this newly renovated restaurant (damaged by Hurricane Fabian in Sep-tember 2003 and reopened in May 2005) offers an innovative menu of local seafood specialties with Mediterranean touches. Try the madako octopus carpaccio in soy lime dressing, or the seared wild salmon in a light curry sauce, with lobster ravioli. Patrons receive free entrance to the popular Deep nightclub next door. Expensive.

❑ **Little Venice:** *Bermudiana Road, HAMILTON CITY, Tel. 441-295-3503. Open for lunch Monday through Friday, 11:35am to 3pm, and for dinner daily from 6:30 to 10pm.* Popular with both locals and visitors, for over 30 years this restaurant has served tasty regional Italian food. Try the delicious medley of local seafood (*casseruola di pesce dello chef*), fish chowder, calamari, grilled swordfish, homemade ravioli, and spaghetti with seafood. Terrace dining available. Moderate.

❑ **Lobster Pot & Boat House Bar:** *6 Bermudiana Road, HAMILTON CITY, Tel. 441-292-6898. Open for lunch Monday through Friday, 11:30am to 3pm, and dinner daily from 5:30 to 11pm.* This is one of Bermuda's oldest and most popular seafood restaurants which boasts nautical themes and a rustic atmosphere. Offers a good selection of fresh seafood, including tasty Bermuda fish chowder, pan-fried local fish topped with bananas and almonds, Maine and spiny Caribbean lobsters, and platters of hogfish, wahoo, rockfish, and tuna prepared to your specifications. Moderate.

❑ **L'Oriental:** *32 Bermudiana Road, HAMILTON CITY, Tel. 441-296-4477. Open daily for dinner from 6 to 11:30pm. Reservations highly recommended.* Specializing in Asian fusion cuisine, this popular restaurant includes a teppanyaki table where chefs prepare sizzling meats and fish. It also includes an excellent sushi, oyster, salmon, and caviar bar. Its extensive menu includes such favorites as soft shell crab futomaki, scallops in ginger and chili sauce, and shrimp teppanyaki. You can dine under the pagoda, on the outside terrace, or at the teppanyaki table or sushi bar. It shares its kitchen with Little Venice, which is next door, and part of the Little Venice Group. Moderate.

❑ **Mediterraneo Bar and Ristorante:** *39 Church Street, HAMILTON CITY, Tel. 441-296-9046. Open Monday through Friday from 11am to midnight and Saturdays from 5pm to midnight.* Offers a sumptuous selection of seafood, pasta, pizza, meat, and chicken dishes. Moderate.

❑ **Mickey's Beach Bistro and Bar:** *Elbow Beach Bermuda, 60 South Road, PAGET, Tel. 441-236-9107. Open daily for lunch, from 12noon to 4pm and for dinner from 6 to 11pm. Website: www.mandarinorien tal.com/bermuda.* Located on the beach, this is alfresco dining at its best. Offers an inventive menu with such specialties as gratinated crab cake Bayou, rigatoni with bay scallops, pappardelle with sausage, seared lemon sole sauteed shrimp "Tuscan Style," seafood paella, and swordfish. Expensive.

❑ **Monte Carlo:** *9 Victoria Street (behind City Hall car park), HAMILTON CITY, Tel. 441-295-5453, or e-mail: montecarolo@nor throck.bm. Open for lunch Monday through Friday, 12noon to 2:30pm, and dinner Monday through Saturday, 6 to 10:30pm.*

Website: www.montecarlobermuda.com. This popular Italian and Mediterranean restaurant specializes in dishes from southern France and Italy. Especially known for its excellent bouillabaisse, filet of tuna, rack of lamb, and veal scallopini. Well known for its pastas, desserts, and excellent service. Moderate.

❑ **The Newport Room:** *Southampton Princess Hotel, South Road, SOUTHAMPTON, Tel. 441-238-8000. Open daily for dinner from 7 to 10pm. Jacket and tie required. Reservations essential.* This is one of Bermuda's very best French and Continental restaurants with an upscale nautical setting reminiscent of a royal yacht. The inventive and regularly changing menu includes numerous tempting fresh seafood, steak, and game dishes. If available, try the Armagnac flamed lobster, jack rabbit with wild mushrooms, tenderloin of beef infused with truffle juice, mint glazed rack of lamb, or Bermudian lobster stuffed with salmon mousse. Excellent service. Expensive.

❑ **Port O'Call:** *87 Front Street, HAMILTON CITY, Tel. 441-295-5373. Open for lunch Monday through Friday, 12noon to 2:30pm, and dinner daily, 6 to 11pm.* Popular for both lunch and dinner, this casual restaurant specializes in fresh Bermuda seafood and steaks. Try the curried lobster, grilled shrimp, yellowfin tuna with salsa, and rack of lamb. Includes an excellent wine selection. Offers both inside and alfresco dining options with a harbor view. Moderate.

❑ **Portofino:** *20 Bermudiana Road, HAMILTON CITY, Tel. 441-292-2375. Open for lunch Monday through Friday, 11:30am to 3pm, and dinner daily, 6pm to midnight (closes at 11pm on Sunday).* For more than 25 years this popular trattoria has specialized in northern and southern Italian cuisine. Especially noted for its fresh local fish, imported calamari and clams, pizza, homemade pasta, daily risotto, cannelloni, lasagna, veal parmigiana, and chicken cacciatore. Do check out their daily specials, which tend to be very good. Moderate.

❑ **Primavera:** *69 Pitts Bay Road, HAMILTON CITY, Tel, 441-295-2167. Open for lunch Monday Through Friday, 11:45am to 2:30pm, and dinner daily, 6:30 to 10:15pm.* This has long been one of Bermuda's most popular Italian restaurants for excellent seafood dishes. Known for its tortellini Primavera, black ravioli with lobsters, beef carpaccio with Parmesean, baby clams, and chicken cacciatore. Includes a sushi bar and extensive wine list. Excellent service.

❏ **Rosa's Cantina:** *121 Front Street, HAMILTON CITY, Tel. 441-295-1912. Only daily from 12noon to 1am.* If you're hankering for Tex-Mex food, mariachi music, and reasonable prices, this is the place to visit. This kid-friendly restaurant (children get balloons, crayons, and paper to play with) serves chili, burritos, nachos, tacos, enchiladas, beef and chicken fajitas, big Texas steaks, and an excellent mesquite-grilled rib-eye steak. Inexpensive to moderate.

❏ **Rustico Restaurant and Pizzeria:** *8 North Shore Road, Flatts Village, HAMILTON PARISH, Tel. 441-295-5212 or e-mail: rustico@northrock.bm. Website: www.primaverarestaurant.com. Open daily for lunch, 11:45am to 2:30pm, and dinner, 6:15-10pm.* This relatively new restaurant (opened in March 2001) is located in the picturesque fishing community of Flatts Village, about 15 minutes east of Hamilton City, and across from the Bermuda Museum, Aquarium, and Zoo. Its light Mediterranean-Asian menu includes excellent salads, thin-crust pizza, fresh seafood dishes, pasta, and burgers and fries. Try the fresh carpaccio. Moderate.

❏ **Seahorse Grill:** *Elbow Beach Bermuda, 60 South Road, PAGET, Tel. 441-236-3535. Open daily for breakfast, from 7 to 11am, and for dinner, from 6:30 to 10pm. Website: www.mandarinoriental.com/ bermuda.* This award-winning contemporary Bermudian restaurant is under the direction of one of Bermuda's most innovative chefs, Scott Connor. The creative menu includes such pleasers as grilled fish chowder, braised beef short ribs with taro gnocchi, poached lobster with mango and chile aioli, and seared scallops and Maine lobster. Includes an excellent wine list. Expensive.

❏ **Tio Pepe:** *117 South Shore Road, Horseshoe Bay, SOUTHAMPTON, Tel. 441-238-1897. Open daily from 11am to 10:30pm during May through September and 12noon to 10pm during off season months.* Conveniently located near Horseshoe Bay and the Fairmont Southampton Princess, this Italian eatery serves well portioned pizza, pasta, and several traditional Italian dishes. Includes three indoor dining rooms and an outdoor terrace. Moderate.

❏ **Tom Moore's Tavern:** *Walsingham Lane, Walsingham Bay, HAMILTON PARISH, Tel. 441-293-8020. Website: www.tommoo res.com. Open daily for dinner from 7 to 10pm. Closed from January 5th to February 1st. Jacket required. Reservations essential.* This fine dining French and Continental restaurant serves classic French and Italian cuisine in an historic residence dating from

1652 and lovingly restored into a gourmet restaurant in 1985. The specialty here is fresh seafood – lobsters, rockfish, scallops, and yellow-tail. The kitchen also is noted for its excellent versions of sirloin steak, lamb chops, roast duckling, and quail with heavy sauces. One of Bermuda's finest restaurants for a truly memorable dining experience. Expensive.

❑ **Tuscany:** *95 Front Street, HAMILTON CITY, Tel. 441-292-4507. Open for lunch Monday through Friday, 12noon to 2pm, and for dinner daily, 6:30 to 10:30pm.* Many diners, including local chefs, who frequent this place, consider this to be the best Italian restaurant in Bermuda for ambience, food, and service. Serves excellent pizza, fish, veal, and pasta dishes. Try the pan-fried rockfish in lemon-butter and herb sauce, portobello mushroom with tiger prawns, and the fresh fish of the day. Dining inside and on the veranda, which overlooks Front Street and Hamilton Harbour. Moderate.

❑ **Waterlot Inn:** *Fairmont Southampton Princess, 101 South Shore Road, SOUTHAMPTON, Tel. 441-238-8000. Open daily for dinner, 6:30 to 9pm. Famous Sunday brunch buffet from 12noon to 2pm. Closed January and February. Reservations required.* This is one of Bermuda's best and most memorable fine dining restaurants for Continental and Bermudian cuisine. Located in a 325-year-old converted warehouse and inn along the ocean, this two-story well-appointed restaurant has several cozy dining rooms. The food here is outstanding. Try the Bermuda fish chowder, pan-fried Bermuda fish, grilled rack of lamb, bouillabaisse, veal shank, and the wonderful desserts. Serves one of the best Sunday brunch in Bermuda, including a live Dixieland jazz quintet.

❑ **The Wellington Room:** See description on pages 159-160 under "Unique Dining Experiences."

❑ **Whaler Inn:** *Fairmont Southampton Princess, 101 South Shore Road, SOUTHAMPTON, Tel. 441-238-8000. Open daily during May through September for lunch (12noon to 2:30pm) and dinner (6:30 to 9:30pm); open daily during October to April for dinner only from 6:30 to 9:30pm. Reservations recommended.* This famous seafood restaurant is beautifully located on a cliff overlooking the ocean and beach. It offers a good selection of fresh game fish, such as shark, mahimahi, wahoo, yellowfin tuna, and barracuda, which can be broiled, sauteed in butter, or pan-fried. Try the key lime cheesecake for dessert.

The Quick Restaurant Directory

For your convenience when visiting different parts of the island and looking for good places to dine, we've rearranged the above 36 recommended restaurants by both location and cuisine:

Restaurant	Location	Cuisine
❏ Aqua	Devonshire	Bermudian/International
❏ Ascots	Hamilton	Italian/French
❏ Barracuda Grill	Hamilton	Seafood
❏ Beethovan's	Dockyard	Swiss/Mediterranean
❏ Bistro J	Hamilton	Seafood/Pasta
❏ Bermudiana	Smiths	International
❏ Café Gio	St. George	Italian
❏ Carriage House	St. George	International
❏ Chopsticks	Hamilton	Chinese/Thai
❏ Coconuts	Southampton	International
❏ Fourways	Paget	International/Seafood
❏ Fresco's	Hamilton	Mediterranean
❏ Harbourfront	Hamilton	Continental/Asian
❏ Hog Penny	Hamilton	British/Bermudian
❏ House of India	Hamilton	Indian
❏ La Coquille	Hamilton	French/Mediterranean
❏ La Trattoria	Hamilton	Italian
❏ Lido	Paget	International/Seafood
❏ Little Venice	Hamilton	Italian
❏ Lobster Pot	Hamilton	Seafood
❏ L'Oriental	Hamilton	Asian Fusion
❏ Mediterraneo	Hamilton	Mediterranean
❏ Monte Carlo	Hamilton	Italian/Mediterranean
❏ Newport Room	Southampton	French/Continental
❏ Port O'Call	Hamilton	Seafood
❏ Portofino	Hamilton	Italian
❏ Primavera	Hamilton	Italian
❏ Rosa' Cantina	Hamilton	Tex-Mex
❏ Rustico	Flatts Village	Mediterranean
❏ Seahorse Grill	Paget	Bermudian
❏ Tio Pepe	Southampton	Italian
❏ Tom Moore's	Walsingham Bay	French/Continental
❏ Tuscany	Hamilton	Italian
❏ Waterlot Inn	Southampton	Bermudian/Continental
❏ Wellington Room	Hamilton	Bermudian/Continental
❏ Whaler Inn	Southampton	Seafood

Pubs, Bars, and Nightly Entertainment

Bermuda has several pubs, bars, and nightly entertainment venues that also serve food. We outline the major such places in the final section of Chapter 10 under "Entertainment."

What More to See and Do

B ERMUDA HAS MANY THINGS to see and do in addition to shopping and dining. In this final chapter we highlight Bermuda's major attractions for those who enjoy sightseeing, hiking, beaches, golf, tennis, birding, horseback riding, water sports, nightly entertainment, or simply being pampered.

Sightseeing

Many visitors enjoy renting a motor scooter to explore the island on their own. Others hire a taxi or take buses and ferries to explore the island's major highlights. Whatever your mode of transportation, be sure to pick up a copy of *Bermuda: East to West*, which is published by the Bermuda Department of Tourism and should be available through various Visitors' Service Bureaus in Hamilton, St. George, and Royal Naval Dockyard. This booklet breaks down Bermuda's major sights by parish and includes useful maps and descriptions of the island's major highlights. Much of this information also can be found under the "What to

Do" section of their website: www.bermudatour ism.com.

Since Bermuda is rich in history and preserves it well in museums, you can expect to see lots of old structures and visit several museums. One of the most interesting island walks is the Railway Trail, an old abandoned rail line, that snakes from one end of the island to the other and offers wonderful views of the island at a leisurely pace. We note different sections of the Railway Trail in our summary of attractions for each parish. Here are over 100 things you can see and do in the island's nine parishes and three towns. We've highlighted in bold the most popular and interesting attractions:

St. George's Parish/Town of St. George

- Barber's Alley
- Bermudian Heritage Museum
- Bermuda National Trust Museum (Globe Hotel)
- Bridge House (Art Gallery)
- The *Deliverance*
- Ducking Stool
- Old Rectory
- Somers Garden
- St. George's Historical Society Museum, Printery, and Garden
- **St. Peter's Church**
- The State House
- The Statue of Sir George Somers
- Town Hall
- Tucker House Museum
- Unfinished Church
- **Walking tour of King's Square and Water and Duke of York streets**

St. George's Parish

- Ferry Reach
  - Bermuda Biological Station for Research
  - Brunt Point Fort
  - Ferry Island Fort
  - Martello Tower
- Forts of the East End
  - Alexandra Battery
  - Fort St. Catherine
  - Gates Fort

- Railway Trail: St. George's to Ferry Reach
- St. David's Island and Southside
  - Carter House
  - Clearwater Beach
  - Fort Popple
  - St. David's Battery
  - St. David's Lighthouse

Hamilton Parish

- Bermuda Aquarium, Natural History Museum, and Zoo (in Flatts Village)
- Bermuda Glassblowing Studio & Showroom
- Bermuda Perfumery
- Bermuda Railway Museum
- Blue Hole Park
- Bridge House Gallery
- **Crystal Caves**
- Flatts Village
- Flatts Bridge & Inlet
- Railway Trail: Coney Island to Flatts Village
- Shelly Bay Park
- Walsingham Nature Reserve

Smith's Parish

- Devil's Hole Aquarium
- John Smith's Bay Park
- Spittal Pond Nature Reserve
- **Verdmont House**

Devonshire Parish

- Arboretum
- Devonshire Bay Park
- Devonshire Marsh
- Old Devonshire Parish Church
- Palm Grove Garden
- Palmetto Park
- Railway Trail: Flatts Inlet to Palmetto Road

Pembroke Parish/City of Hamilton

- Albuoy's Point
- **Art and Architectural Tour**
- Barr's Bay Park
- **Bermuda Cathedral (Cathedral of the Most Holy Trinity)**

- Bermuda National Library and Bermuda Historical Society Museum
- Cabinet Building and Senate Chamber
- Cenotaph
- **Fort Hamilton**
- Government House
- **Hamilton City Hall and Arts Centre** (includes the
- Bermuda National Gallery and the Bermuda Society of Arts Gallery)
- Par-la-Ville Park
- Perot Post Office
- Sessions House (House of Assembly) and Jubilee Clock Tower
- St. Andrew's Presbyterian Church
- St. Theresa's Cathedral
- Victoria Park
- **Walking tour of Pitts Bay Road, Front Street, and Church Street**

Pembroke Parish

- Admiralty House Park
- **The Bermuda Underwater Exploration Institute**
- Clarence Cove
- Pembroke Marsh and Parson's Road Playground

Paget Parish

- **Botanical Gardens, Camden, and**
- **Masterworks Foundation**
- **Elbow Beach Park**
- Paget Marsh
- Railway Trail: Trimingham Hill, Paget to
- Dunscombe Road, Warwick
- Waterville House

Warwick Parish

- Ashwood Park
- Christ Church
- Railway Trail: Warwick to Southampton section
- South Shore Park
- Warwick Long Bay Park

Southampton Parish

- Church Bay Park
- **Gibbs' Hill Lighthouse Park**
- **Horseshoe Bay Park**

- Railway Trail: Southampton to Sandys
- South Shore Park
- Whale Bay Battery/West Whale Bay Fort

Sandys Parish

- Heydon Trust Estate
- Hog Bay Park
- Lagoon Park – Ireland Island South
- Royal Naval Cemetery
- **Royal Naval Dockyard**
- **Scaur Hill Fort and Park**
- Somerset Bridge
- Somerset Long Bay Park & Nature Reserve
- Somerset Village
- Springfield & Gilbert Nature Reserve
- St. James' Anglican Church

Sandys Parish/Royal Naval Dockyard Complex

- Bermuda Arts Centre
- **Bermuda Maritime Museum**
- Bermuda Clayworks
- Bermuda Craft Market
- Clocktower Building
- Cooperage
- Dockyard Glassworks & Bermuda Rum Cake Factory
- Railway Trail: Somerset Bridge to Somerset Village
- Victualling Yard

If you are traveling with children, the following sites and activities especially appeal to young people:

- Bermuda Aquarium, Natural History Museum, and Zoo
- Bermuda Maritime Museum
- Bermuda Railway Trail
- Crystal Caves
- Devil's Hole Aquarium
- Gibbs' Hill Lighthouse Park

Hiking and Birding

If you love hiking and bird watching, Bermuda will not disappoint you. Hikers can spend a good day or two following the popular Bermuda Railway Trail that runs nearly 21 miles, from one end of the island to another. Operating from 1931 to 1948, the Bermuda Railway includes many interesting sights along the way. As noted in the previous section, Bermuda Department of

Tourism's *Bermuda: East to West* includes information on each section of the trail. Also, ask for a copy of the *Bermuda Railway Trail Guide*, which can be found at the Visitors' Service Bureaus. Bermuda's many parks and beaches also offer excellent hiking opportunities.

Several parks and marshes afford opportunities to observe Bermuda's large bird population, especially during the January through March migration season. Look for eastern warblers, egrets, herons, fork-tailed flycatchers, martins, doves, cardinals, cahows, and gray-and-white petrel. Some of best places for bird watching are Paget March (Paget Parish). Walsingham Trust (Hamilton Parish), and Spittal Pond (Smith's Parish). Hikers taking the Bermuda Railway Trail will pass near these key sites.

Exploring Coves, Caves, and Beaches

Bermuda boasts several beautiful pink beaches that are variously used for sunbathing, swimming, snorkeling, or just walking. The pink-colored sand comes from a mixture of shell particles, coral pieces, and calcium carbonate which become wet. If you stay along the South Shore, you may have direct access to some of the island's most popular beaches. Properties with some of the best beaches include the Pink Beach Club and Cottages, Ariel Sands Beach Club, Fairmont Southampton, Elbow Beach Bermuda, and The Reefs.

Many of Bermuda's beaches are public and can be reached by bus. Some are parts of public parks. Others are rocky coves and inlets with small stretches of beach. The larger public beaches have lifeguards, rest rooms, showers, changing facilities, water sports, beach gear rental shops, and snack shops. Some beaches are unsafe for swimming and thus are best used for sunbathing and walking. If you are using public transportation to reach the beaches, be sure to pick up a copy of *Bermuda's Guide to Beaches and Transportation* at the Visitors' Service Bureaus.

Going from east to west by parish, Bermuda's major beaches include:

St. George's Parish

- Achilles Bay
- St. Catherine's Beach (Gates Bay)
- **Tobacco Bay**

Hamilton Parish

- Shelley Bay

Smith's Parish

- **Job Smith's Bay**

Paget Parish

- **Elbow Beach**

Warwick Parish

- Astwood Cove
- Jobson's Cove
- Stonehole Bay
- Warwick Long Bay

Southampton Parish

- Chaplin Bay
- Church Bay
- **Horseshoe Bay**

Sandy's Parish

- Somerset Long Bay
- West Whale Bay

Bermuda's best and most photographed beach, which also is very crowded during the high season, is found along the South Shore at Southampton's Horseshoe Bay. In fact, Discovery's Travel Channel recently identified Horseshoe Bay Beach as the world's second best beach. Other top beaches, which are less crowded, include Wafer Rocks Beach, Port Royal Cove, and Peel Rock Cove.

Playing Golf and Tennis

Golf enthusiasts love playing several of Bermuda's spectacular nine- and 18-hole golf courses. The island's eight golf courses represent the world's largest number of golf courses per square mile. Green fees for nonmembers playing 18 holes run between $55 and $200, depending on the golf course and time of week.

Caddy fees are about $25 per bag and golf cart rentals run around $25. Lessons are usually available from $50 to $90 an hour. Proper attire, such as Bermuda shorts and a shirt with collar, is required at most golf courses.

The island's four best and most popular 18-hole golf courses are highlighted in bold:

- **Belmont Hills Golf Club**
  Warwick Parish
  www.belmonthills.com

- **Fairmont Southampton Golf Club**
  Hamilton Parish
  www.fairmont.com/southampton

- Mid Ocean Club
  St. George's Parish
  www.themidoceanclubbermuda.com

- Ocean View Golf Course
  Devonshire Parish

- **Port Royal Golf Course**
  Southampton Parish

- Riddell's Bay Golf and Country Club
  Warwick Parish
  www.riddellsbay.com

- **St. George's Golf Club**
  St. George Parish

- Tucker's Point Club
  Hamilton Parish
  www.tuckerspoint.com

Golf tournaments are held throughout the year, with most being open to qualifying amateurs and professionals. The Bermuda Open at the Port Royal Golf Course in October is the island's most prestigious annual international golf tournament. For details on golf in Bermuda, including courses, membership, tournaments, and instruction, be sure to visit these websites:

- **Bermuda Golf Association**
  www.bermudagolf.com

- **Bermuda Junior Golf Association**
  http://juniorgolf.free.bm

- **Bermuda Goodwill Golf Tournament**
  www.bermudagoodwill.org

- **Bermuda-Online**
  www.bermuda-online.org/golf.htm

Also, pick up a copy of *Bermuda Golfing and Tournaments*, which is free through the Visitors' Service Bureaus, as well as visit the

"Golf" section of the island's official tourism website: www.bermudatourism.com/golf. This website also includes information on golf courses, vacations, cruises, tour operators, tournaments, and tee times (you can schedule online through this website).

Tennis is a very popular sport in Bermuda. Indeed, tennis lovers will find many excellent tennis facilities at both public and private clubs. Many of the courts operate both day and night. Rates normally run from $4 to $6 per hour or per play, plus equipment rental. Lessons run from $20 to $30 for 30 minutes. Most major hotels and resorts have tennis courts, rent equipment, and offer tennis lessons. Like golf courses, proper attire is required for most tennis courts, including mandatory tennis whites at a few courts. Some of the best places to play tennis include:

- **Cambridge Beaches**
  Sandys Parish
  www.cambridgebeaches.com

- **Castle Harbour Resort**
  Hamilton Parish

- **CoCo Reef Resort**
  Paget Parish
  www.cocoreefbermuda.com

- **Coral Beach and Tennis Club** (private/guests)
  Paget Parish

- **Elbow Beach Bermuda Tennis Courts**
  Paget Parish
  www.mandarinoriental.com/bermuda

- **Fairmont Southampton Tennis Facility**
  Southampton Parish
  www.fairmont.com

- **Government Tennis Stadium**
  Pembroke Parish

- **Port Royal Golf Club**
  Southampton Parish

- **Fairmont Southampton**
  Southampton Parish
  www.fairmont.com/southampton

- **Wyndham Bermuda Resort and Spa**
  Southampton Parish
  www.wyndham.com

For information on tennis tournaments and upcoming events, visit the website of the Bermuda Lawn Tennis Association: www.blta.bm.

Participating in Watersports

Surrounded by beautiful waters and reefs, Bermuda is a water enthusiast's paradise. Indeed, except in the winter months, consider taking advantage of Bermuda's many opportunities to experience the richness and excitement of its waters.

INTRODUCTIONS AND OVERVIEWS

For a good overview of Bermuda's maritime history, be sure to visit the **Bermuda Maritime Museum** at the Royal Naval Dockyard. You can also swim with the dolphins at **Dolphin Quest Bermuda** (www.dolphinquest.org) which is part of the museum. Also, check out the **Bermuda Underwater Exploration Institute** (www.buei.org), which is located on East Broadway just outside of the City of Hamilton, as well as the **Bermuda Aquarium, Museum, and Zoo** at 40 North Shore Road, Flatts Inlet, Hamilton Parish (www.bamz.org). Novices may want to take advantage of a unique Bermudian diving experience – the **Bermuda Bell Diving** (5 North Shore Road, Flatts Inlet, www.belldive.bm) takes visitors offshore to a shallow ocean site where they are outfitted with large custom-made underwater helmets for walking along the ocean floor to enjoy undersea gardens and feed the fish.

SCUBA DIVING

Bermuda offers numerous opportunities for sailing, fishing, snorkeling, wind surfing, and scuba diving. Experienced divers enjoy Bermuda's clear warm waters with visibility of over 150 feet. They can explore many underwater caves and more than 400 shipwrecks that are found within the 200 square miles of coral reefs surrounding the islands. Some of these shipwrecks date from the 1600s. The best time for diving is from April to November.

Several PADI-certified companies offer diving courses and excursions:

- **Blue Water Divers & Watersports**
  Robinson's Marina, Sandys
  Tel. 441-234-1034
  www.divebermuda.com

- **Dive Bermuda**
  Tel. 441-295-9485
  www.bermudascuba.com

- **Fantasea Diving/South Side Scuba**
  Darrell's Wharf, Paget
  Tel. 441-236-6339
  www.fantasea.bm

- **Nautilus Diving Ltd.**
  Southampton Princess Hotel
  Tel. 441-238-2332

- **Scuba Look**
  Warwick Parish
  Tel. 441- 293-7319

BOATING

Boaters have numerous opportunities to explore the waters surrounding Bermuda. Power and sail boat rentals can be arranged through the following companies:

- **Dockyard Boat Rentals**
  Royal Naval Dockyard, Sandys
  Tel. 441-234-0300

- **Mangrove Marina Ltd.**
  Cambridge Road
  Sandys Parish
  Tel. 441-234-0914

- **Pompano Beach Watersports**
  Pompano Beach Club
  Southampton Parish
  Tel. 441-234-0222

- **South Side Watersports**
  Hamilton Parish
  Tel. 441-293-2915

- **Race's Boatyard**
  Crow Lane
  Paget Parish
  Tel. 441-292-1843

Chartered and skippered yachts can be arranged through the following companies:

- **Bermuda Barefoot Cruises**
  Tel. 441-236-3498
  www.bermudabarefootcruises.com

- **Bermuda Caribbean Yacht Co.**
  Tel. 441-238-8578

- **Golden Rule Cruise Charters**
  Tel. 441-238-1962

- **Ocean Wind Charters**
  Tel. 441-238-0825
  www.myparadise.com/
  oceanwinds.htm

- **Rance's Boatyard**
  Tel. 441-292-1843

- **Salt Kettle Boat Rentals**
  Tel. 441-236-4863

- **Salt Kettle Yacht Charters**
  Tel. 441-235-1929

- **Sand Dollar Cruises**
  Tel. 441-236-1967

Fishing

Fishing is another attractive sport for visitors to Bermuda. The waters around Bermuda are great for catching blue marlin, yellowfin tuna, blackfin tuna, pompano, wahoo, snapper, grouper, barracuda, greater amberjack, porgy, billfish, and parrotfish. The best time of year for fishing is May through November. Several companies offer both deep sea and short fishing adventures. Half day fishing trips can cost from $50 to $150 per person. Chartering a boat for a day can run from $700 for a half day to over $1,500 for a full day, depending on the size of the boat. Contact the following companies for information on sportfishing in Bermuda:

- **Albatross Fishing Charters**
  Tel. 441-297-0715
  E-mail: albatross@ilb.bm

- **Andrea Christine Charters**
  Tel. 441-237-3048
  www.andreachristine.com

- **Atlantic Spray Fishing Charters**
  Tel. 441-735-9444
  www.atlanticspraycharters.bm

- **Baxter's Reef Fishing**
  Tel. 441-234-2963
  E-mail: baxtersreef@northrock.bm

- **Bermuda Sportsfishing**
  Tel. 441-295-2380

- **Eureka Fishing Charters**
  Tel. 441-734-2400
  www.bermudashorts.bm/eureka

- **In Excess**
  Tel. 441-236-7446
  www.bermudashorts.bm/inexcess

- **Knock Down Charters**
  Tel. 441-236-3551
  www.knockdowncharters.com

- **Mako Charters**
  Tel. 441-295-3620
  www.fishbermuda.com/mako

- **Overproof Charter Fishing**
  Tel. 441-335-5663
  www.overprooffishing.com

- **Playmate Charters**
  Tel. 441-292-7131
  www.playmatefishing.com

- **Sea Wolfe Sportfishing**
  Tel. 441-234-1832
  www.sportfishbermuda.com

For information on shore fishing, including renting rod, reel, and tackle, contact:

- **Mangrove Marine**
  Somerset Bridge, Sandys
  Tel. 441-234-091

- **Windjammer Watersports**
  Royal Naval Dockyard: 441-234-0250
  Cambridge Beaches: 441-234-0250
  E-mail: windjammerbda@northrock.bm

For information on annual fishing tournaments, contact the Bermuda Department of Tourism (www.bermudatourism.com) as well as the following websites centered on promoting the annual Bermuda Big Game Classic and the Bermuda Triple Crown Billfish Classic:

- **Bermuda Big Game Classic**
  www.bermudabiggameclassic.com

- **Bermuda Triple Crown Billfish Classic**
  www.bermudatriplecrowns.com

SNORKELING

Bermuda's beaches and clear shallow waters and numerous coral reefs are perfect for snorkeling expeditions. Most of the major public beaches we discussed earlier will rent snorkels, masks, and fins. One of the favorite beaches for snorkeling is Church Beach in Southampton. In addition to the unique undersea walk sponsored by **Bermuda Bell Diving** (5 North Shore Road, Flatts Inlet, www.belldive.bm), the following companies arrange snor-

keling trips. Some also offer additional services, such as touring the islands, swimming, kayaking, windsurfing, water skiing, and walking underwater:

- **Bermuda Water Sports**
  Tel. 441-293-2640

- **Bermuda Water Tours Ltd.**
  Tel. 441-236-1500

- **Blue Hole Water Sports**
  Tel. 293-2915
  www.blueholewater.bm

- **Michael Hayward's Snorkeling Adventures**
  Tel. 441-236-9894

- **Longtail Sailing**
  Tel. 441-292-0282

- **Pitman's Snorkeling**
  Tel. 441-234-0700

- **Reef Roamers**
  Tel. 441-292-8652

- **Sand Dollar Cruises**
  Tel. 441-234-1434

- **Sea Trek Tours**
  Tel. 441-335-5183

- **Undersea Walk**
  Tel. 441-234-2861
  www.hartleybermuda.com

- **Underwater Wonderworld**
  Tel. 441-292-4434

WATER-SKIING AND PARASAILING

Several companies can outfit you for both water-skiing and parasailing in the many bays, sounds, and harbors. Most companies also will provide instruction for around $50 a half hour:

- **Bermuda Island Parasail Company**
  Tel. 441-232-2871

- **Bermuda Waterski Centre**
  Tel. 441-234-3354

- **Fantesea Diving**
  Tel. 441-293-2543

- **Nautilus Diving**
  Tel. 441-238-2332

- **Skyrider Bermuda Ltd.**
  Tel. 441-234-3019

- **South Side Scuba**
  Tel. 441-293-2915

- **South Side Watersports**
  Tel. 441-236-6339

- **St. George's Parasail Water Sports Ltd.**
  Tel. 441-297-1542

SEA ADVENTURES

A few companies also offer a variety of interesting sea adventures. Check out these companies for different types of programs:

- **Blue Water Safari**
  Tel/Fax 441-236-5599
  www.bluewatersafari.com

- **Hat-Trick Catamaran Sailing**
  Tel. 441-235-5077

- **Robinson's Boston Whalers**
  Tel. 441-234-0914

- **Sea Venture Watersports**
  Tel. 441-238-6881
  www.jetskibermuda.com

- **WildCat Adventure Tours**
  Tel. 441-293-7433

- **Windjammer Watersports**
  Tel. 441-234-0250

Riding Trails and Beaches By Horse

Visitors can rent horses for riding along supervised trails only. Trails are found along the north coast and in South Shore Park. Bermuda's largest riding facility is the **Spicelands Riding Centre**, which is located in Warwick Parish (Tel. 441-238-8212, website: spicelandriding.com) and operates along the South Shore. Riding times are Monday through Friday, 6:30am, 8:30am, 10:30am, 4pm, and 6pm, and Saturday and Sunday at 6:30am, 8:30am, and 10:30am. It charges $60 for a one-hour walk-pace horseback ride on scenic trails to Bermuda's sandy dunes that lead to pink sand beaches. A more energetic ride – Dunes on Horseback with trotting and cantering – is available on Monday, Wednesday, and Friday and costs $120 per person. From December 1 to March 31, visitors also can ride along the beach. Beach rides are available Monday through Friday from May to October.

The **Bermuda Riding for the Disabled Equestrian Centre** (Warwick Parish, Tel. 441-238-7433, website: www.windreach. org) provides free riding opportunities for people with disabilities in a special facility. They welcome donations.

Being Pampered at Spas

If you really want to pamper yourself during your stay in Bermuda, schedule some spa treatments. Similar to major hotels and resorts around the world, many of Bermuda's properties now offer spa facilities. At least eight major spas offer a variety of treatments and therapies: body massage, hydrotherapy, cathioderme facial, or manicure and pedicure. The island's three major destination spas include:

- **Cedars Spa**
  Wyndham Bermuda Resort and Spa
  Southampton Parish
  Tel. 441-238-8122, ext. 3218
  www.wyndham.com

- **The Spa at the Elbow Beach Bermuda**
  Elbow Beach Bermuda
  Paget Parish
  Tel. 441-239-8900
  www.mandarinoriental.com

- **Willow Stream Spa**
  The Fairmont Southampton
  Southampton Parish
  Tel. 441-239-6924
  www.fairmontspahotelsandresorts.com

Major day spas include:

- **Spa at Ariel Sands**
  Ariel Sands Beach Club
  Devonshire Parish
  Tel. 441-235-5300
  www.arielsands.com/amenities/spa.htm

- **Coolwaters Spa and Salon**
  Water Street
  Town of St. George
  Tel. 441-297-1528

- **Inner Sanctum Urban Spa**
  Pitts Bay Road
  Pembroke Parish
  Tel. 441-296-9009

- **The Ocean Spa at Cambridge Beaches**
  Cambridge Beaches
  Somerset, Sandys Parish
  Tel. 441-234-3636
  Website: www.cambridgebeaches.com

- **The Coral Beach Spa**
  34 South Road
  Paget Parish
  Tel. 441-239-7222

- **Face and Body Day Spa**
  Bermudiana Arcade
  27 Queen Street
  City of Hamilton
  Tel. 441-292-8081

- **Gillian's**
  14 South Road
  Devonshire Parish
  Tel. 441-232-0496

- **The Hideaway at Surf Side**
  90 South Road
  Warwick Parish
  Tel. 441-238-5738
  Website: www.surfside.bm

- **Serenity Massage & Body Treatment**
  The Pompano Beach Club
  36 Pompano Road
  Southampton Parish
  Tel. 441-234-0222, ext. 218

- **Strands Day Spa**
  31 Reid Street
  City of Hamilton
  Tel. 441-295-0353
  Website: www.strands.bm

- **Total Fitness Centre**
  24 Brunswick Street
  City of Hamilton
  Tel. 441-295-0087

Enjoying Entertainment

While sedate Bermuda is not known for its evening entertainment, you will find a few places to enjoy nightlife, from pubs and bars to nightclubs. During the high season, many of the bars and lounges at the major hotels, such as the Elbow Beach, Fairmont Southampton, Wyndham, and the Reefs, offer live entertainment and shows.

Pubs and bars include lots of drinking along with some live musical entertainment and happy hours with discounted drinks. Some have $10 to $25 cover charges, depending on the entertainment. The major pubs and bars include:

- **The Beach**
  Front Street
  City of Hamilton
  Tel. 441-292-0219

  Bar with street view.
  Open until 3am.

- **Blue Juice**
  Bermuda House Lane
  City of Hamilton
  Tel. 441-292-4507

  Patio bar with disco.
  Open daily, 11am to
  3am.

- **Café Continental**
  16 Burnaby Street
  City of Hamilton
  Tel. 441-292-3284

  Wine bar.

- **Casey's Cocktail Lounge**
  Queen Street
  City of Hamilton
  Tel. 441-292-9994

  Loud music. Open
  Monday to Saturday,
  10am to 10pm.

- **Clay House Inn**
  77 North Shore Road
  Devonshire
  Tel. 441-292-3193

  Caribbean-style
  music and shows.

- **Coconut Rock**
  20 Reid Street
  City of Hamilton
  Tel. 441-292-1043

  Restaurant and two
  lively bars with music
  videos. Open daily,
  1:30pm to 1am.

- **Docksider**
  Front Street
  Hamilton
  Tel. 441-296-3333

  Pub with three bars
  and pool room. Happy
  hour, 5-7pm.Open daily,
  11am to 1am.

- **Fairmont Hamilton
  Hotel Terrace**
  Pitts Bay Road
  Tel. 441-295-3000

  Happy hour and live
  music, 5-9pm.

- **Flanagan's**
  Emporium Building
  69 Front Street
  City of Hamilton
  Tel. 441-295-8299

  Irish pub and sports
  bar offering good
  musical entertainment.
  Happy hour, 5-7pm.
  Open daily, 11am to 1am.

- **Fresco's**
  Chancery Lane
  City of Hamilton
  Tel. 441-295-5058

  Wine bar. Attracts
  young professionals.

- **Frog & Onion Pub**
  Royal Naval Dockyard
  Sandys Parish
  Tel. 441-234-2900
  www.frogandonion.bm

  Located in the old
  cupperage (barrel
  factory). Open daily,
  11:30am to 1am.

- **Henry VII**
  South Shore Road
  Southampton
  Tel. 441-238-1977

  Pub with nightly entertainment, including comedy acts. Open daily, 6pm to 1am.

- **Hog Penny**
  Burnaby Street
  City of Hamilton
  Tel. 441-292-2534

  Pub with nightly entertainment daily from 9:45pm to 1am.

- **M R Onions**
  Par-la-Ville Road
  City of Hamilton
  Tel. 441-292-5012

  Restaurant, bar, and Internet cafe.

- **North Rock Brewing Company**
  South Shore Road
  Devonshire Parish
  Tel. 441-236-6633
  www.bermudashorts.bm/northrock

  Locally produced beer and food.

- **Pickled Onion**
  Front Street
  City of Hamilton
  Tel. 441-295-2263
  www.thepickledonion.com

  Great happy hour with live music. Open daily, 11:30am to 1am (3am on Saturdays and Sundays).

- **The Porch**
  Front Street
  City of Hamilton
  Tel. 441-292-4737

  Good harbor views and entertainment.

- **Robin Hood Pub**
  Richmond Road
  Pembroke Parish
  Tel. 441-295-3314

  Sports bar popular with expats. Open daily, 11am to 1am (opens 12noon on Sunday).

- **Swinging Doors**
  Court Street
  City of Hamilton
  Tel. 441-293-9267

  Bar
  Open until 3am.

- **Swizzle Inn**
  Bailey's Bay
  Blue Hole Hill
  (close to airport)
  Tel. 441-293-9300
  www.swizzleinn.com

  Serves the popular Rum Swizzle drink. Open daily, 11am to 1am (closed first two weeks of January).

- **Veranda Bar**
  Elbow Beach Bermuda
  Paget Parish
  Tel. 441-236-3535

Upscale piano bar.

Bermuda has four major nightclubs for live music, dancing, and special shows. Most require smart casual attire. All stay open until 3am:

- **Club 40**
  119 Front Street
  City of Hamilton
  Tel. 441-292-9340

Open Tuesday through Saturday, 10pm to 3am.

- **Deep**
  Elbow Beach Bermuda
  Paget Parish
  Tel. 441-236-3535

Luxurious state-of-the-art nightclub for the sophisticated crowd. Open Monday through Saturday, 10pm to 3am.

- **Hilly's**
  123 Front Street
  City of Hamilton
  Tel. 441-295-1370

- **Ozone Night Club and The Lucky Strike Casino**
  Emporium Building
  69 Front Street
  City of Hamilton
  Tel. 441-292-3379

Trendy nightclub with small casino attached. Open 9:30pm to 3am.

- **The Spinning Wheel**
  Court Street
  City of Hamilton
  Tel. 441-292-7799

For more information on Bermuda's nightlife, visit these websites:

www.entertainmentbermuda.com
www.blackandcoke.com
www.bermudamusic.com
www.oasisbermuda.com

Bermuda also boasts more classical and cultural forms of entertainment – concerts, musical performances, ballet, dance presentations, and theatrical performances of the Bermuda Philharmonic, Bermuda Musical and Dramatic Society, Bermuda Civic Ballet, Gilbert and Sullivan Society, Menuhin Foundation, and other groups. It also hosts the Bermuda Music Festival and the Bermuda Festival Fringe. Check with the Visitors' Service Bureaus or your hotel concierge for the times and locations of such cultural presentations, performances, and festivals.

Index

Maps

Bermuda, 63
Hamilton, 67
Royal Naval Dockyard, 72
St. George, 70

Bermuda

A

A & J Sports Cards, 89, 99, 115
A.S. Cooper & Sons, 88, 89, 94, 95, 98, 113-114, 117, 121, 124, 127
A.S. Cooper Man, 117
Accessories, 94-95, 116-118, 121, 125
Accommodation(s):
    apartments, 132, 139-141
    bed and breakfast, 135-136
    Bermuda, 13
    best, 131-155
    booking, 133
    booking sites, 133
    costs, 132-133
    cottage colonies, 141-142
    dining around programs, 133
    Hamilton, 134
    inns, 136-137
    kids' programs, 135
    large cottages, 139-141
    off-season, 54-55, 132
    parishes, 154-155
    plans, 133-134
    private clubs, 141
    resort hotels, 144-145
    small cottages, 137
    small hotels, 142-144
ACE Gallery, 97
Airline(s):
    alternative, 31-32
    costs, 31-32
    discount, 31, 52
    packages, 35
Airport, 26-27
Anthony Pettit, 99, 115
Antique Garden, 99, 120
Antiques, 99-100, 114-115, 120
Apartments, 132, 139-141

Archie Brown, 117
Architecture, 60, 87
Ariel Sands, 148-149
Art:
    galleries, 121-124
    quality, 107-111
    scene, 84
Art and Architectural Tours, 68, 96, 108, 128
Artists, 96, 107, 128
Arts and crafts:
    Hamilton, 114
    Royal Naval Dockyards, 123-124
    St. George, 121
Aston & Gunn, 95, 116
Astwood Dickinson Jewellery, 89, 92, 93, 94, 105

B

Barbara Finsness, 100, 122
Bargains, 11, 81-82, 132-133
Bars, 190-194
Beaches, 177-178
Bed and breakfast, 135-136
Bermuda Aquarium, Museum, and Zoo, 182
Bermuda Arts Centre, 79, 88, 93, 96, 98-99, 122-123
Bermuda Bell Diving, 182
Bermuda Cedar, 123
Bermuda Clayworks, 88, 98, 123, 127
Bermuda Craft Market, 79, 88, 90, 123, 125, 128
Bermuda Department of Tourism, 38-39
Bermuda Maritime Museum, 73, 88, 182
Bermuda National Gallery, 96, 107-108
Bermuda Perfumery Gardens, 94, 126, 128
Bermuda Rum Cake Company, 100, 124, 125, 127
Bermuda shorts, 25
Bermuda Society of Arts, 96, 108
Bermuda Tourism, 51, 133
Bermudiana, 84, 97-99
Bicycles, 45
Birding, 177

Birdsey Studio, 96, 97, 125-126
Black Seal Shop, 119
Bluck's, 95, 111-112, 120
Boating, 183-184
Books, 119
Bookmark, 119
Britain, 22-23
Bronzes, 108
Buildings, 87
Buses, 44
Business, 7, 8, 60, 82-83
Burrows Lightbourn Ltd., 101, 119
Butterfield Place Shopping Concourse, 89

C

Calabash Gift Shop, 94
Calypso, 88, 95, 116-117, 126, 127
Cambridge Beaches, 152-153
Caribbean, 4
Carole Holding, 88, 97, 101, 109-110, 114, 121
Cars, 9, 42
Cash, 84
Cécile, 88, 94, 115-116
Cedar, 111
Character, 1-8
Chatham House, 119
Chefs, 157
Chesley Trott, 111, 122, 123
Children, 176
China, 95-96, 120
Christmas decorations, 98, 114, 128
Church Street, 68, 103
Climate, 8, 23-24
Clocktower Mall, 79, 88, 98, 122
Clothes, 24
Clothing, 94-95, 115-117, 121, 125
Coconuts, 160-161
Collectibles, 99-100, 115-116
Collections, 84
Commissions, 83
Competition, 80
Consolidation, 82-83
Cooper's Cachet, 93, 96, 98, 107, 113, 114
Cost of living, 58-59
Costs:
    anticipated, 52-54
    Bermuda, 8
    cutting, 54-56
    high, 14
Cottage colonies, 141-142
Coupons, 82
Coves, 177-178
Cow Polly East, 95, 121
Crafts, 97-99, 114-115, 123-124
Craftspeople, 12
Credit cards, 84
Crisson, 78, 88, 93, 94, 104, 120, 125
Crisson & Hind Fine Art Gallery, 97, 110-111, 128
Crown Colony, 95, 117, 121

Cruise:
    deals, 33-34, 54
    ships, 3, 6, 8, 14, 32-34, 74
    shoppers, 78, 83, 90-91
Crystal, 95-96, 107, 120
Cuarenta Bucaneros, 119
Cuban Cigars, 119
Culture, 28, 194
Cuisine, 157-158
Customs:
    Bermuda, 27
    United States, 56-57

D

Department stores, 89-90
Desert Rose, 89
Desmond Fountain Gallery, 89, 96, 97, 108
Devonshire Parish, 64
Dine Around Programs, 133, 159
Dining:
    costs, 157-158
    customs, 158-159
    hotel/resort, 133-134
    programs, 133, 159
    scene, 156-171
    tips, 158-159
    unique, 159-161
    websites, 159
Disabled, 46
Discounts, 84, 94
Dockside Glass, 121, 127
Dockyard Glassworks, 88, 98, 121, 123-124, 127
Dockyard Linens, 124
Documents, 26
Dolphin Quest Bermuda, 182
Dress, 25
Driving, 9, 43-44
Duke of York Street, 70
Duties, 93

E

E.R. Aubrey, 88, 93, 105-106, 120, 125
Economy, 8, 60-62
Elbow Beach Bermuda, 149-150
Electricity, 48
Emporium Building, 89
English Sports Shop, 88, 94, 95, 116, 121
Entertainment, 5, 7, 34, 190–194
Expatriates, 51, 61
Exports, 22

F

Face painting, 90, 128
Fairmont Hamilton Princess, 145-146
Fairmont Southampton, 146
Families, 48
Ferries, 45
Festivals, 48
Fishing

deep sea, 184-185
shore, 185
tournaments, 185-186
Food products, 100, 125
Fragrances (see Perfumes)
French Connection, 117
Front Street, 66-69, 85, 103

G
Gallery Ltd., 89
Geography, 3, 58-59
Gift items, 97-99, 114-115, 124
Glassware, 95-96, 120
Golf:
courses, 179-180
holidays, 36-37
tour operators, 37
tournaments, 180
Gosling Brothers, 101, 118-119
Gosling's Duty Free, 119, 126
Gourmet products, 100
Graham Foster, 97, 108
Guides, 46-47

H
Hamilton:
best shops, 102-119
city of, 60-61, 66-68
entertainment, 190-194
map of, 67
parish of, 62
sightseeing, 68
staying in, 14
Harbour Nights, 29, 80, 90, 127
Harbourmaster, 100, 118
Harrington Jewellers, 89
Heidi Augustinovi, 128
Heritage House, 96, 99, 109, 114
Heritage Nights, 29, 71, 80, 90, 127
Heritage Passport, 55
Hiking, 177
History, 21-23
Home products, 114-115
Homes, 59-60
Honeymoons, 6, 37-38
Horizons and Cottages, 153
Horseback riding, 188
Horse-drawn carriages, 45
Hotels (see Accommodations):
Hours:
business, 28
Hamilton, 28-29
shop, 28-29
special, 29
Royal Naval Dockyard, 79
St. George, 29

I
Ian MacDonald-Smith, 111
Industry, 22
Inns, 136-137
Insurance:
businesses, 60

companies, 30
travel, 29-30
Internet:
shopping on, 93-94
sites, 51-52
Irish Linen Shop, 100, 107
iShopAroundTheWorld.com, xxiv, 17-18, 20-21, 203
Island Shop (see The Island Shop)
Islands, 59

J
Jewelry:
bargains, 82
custom, 103, 105, 127
duties on, 93
local, 103
quality, 103-107
shops, 92-93, 120, 124-125
theme, 105
repairing, 93
Jonah Jones, 123
Just Clicked Gallery, 97, 111

K
Kids' programs, 135
King's Square, 70
Kirk's Jewelry, 89, 93, 105, 127

L
Language, 27-28
Leather goods, 100, 118
Limestone, 60
Linens, 100, 107, 127
Liquor, 101, 118-119
Lisa Quinn Studio, 96, 97, 126
Littlest Drawbridge, 124
Location, 3, 8, 59
Longchamp, 100
Louis Vuitton, 89, 100
Luggage, 100, 118
Lynn Morrell, 93, 123

M
Manners, 5
Maps:
Bermuda, 63
Hamiton, 67
Royal Naval Dockyard, 72
St. George, 70
Markets, 90
Marks & Spencer, 89, 117
Marriage (see Weddings)
Masterworks Foundation Gallery, 97, 108
Meal plans, 133-134
Merchandise, 84
Michael Swan Gallery, 88, 96, 97, 122-123
Mini-buses, 45
Money, 47
Motor scooters, 43

N

New Heritage House Gallery, 96-97, 109, 115
Newstead Hotel, 153-154
Nightclubs, 193
Nightlife:
    Bermuda, 5, 7, 190–194
    cruise, 34

O

One Cellar Lane, 89
Onion Jacks Trading Post, 100
Outerbridge Sherry Peppers, 101

P

Packing, 24-25, 91
Paget Parish, 65
Paint Your Own Pottery Studio, 124, 127
Paintings, 96-97
Parasailing, 187
Parishes, 9, 62-66
Peniston Brown and Company, 94, 114, 120
People, 9
Perfumes, 94, 114, 120, 124
Perot Post Office, 115
Photography, 96-97, 111, 122-123
Pickwick Mews, 121
Picturesque Gallery, 88, 97, 111, 123
Pink Beach Club and Cottages, 151-152
Pitts Bay Road, 68
Planning, xxiv
Pleasures, 12-13, 129-194
Pompano Beach Club, 153
Population, 3, 58, 61-62
Pottery, 124
Predictability, 3
Preparation, 21-57
Prices:
    best, 80
    comparison, 79
    competitive, 80, 88
    fixed, 80, 84
Private clubs, 141
Products, 84
Pubs:
    Bermuda, 190-193:
    dining at, 55
Pulp & Circumstance Gifts, 98

R

Races, 9
Reading, 51-52
Reef Gift Shop, 98
Reefs Resort (see The Reefs)
Reid Street, 68, 103
Resort hotels, 144-145
Resort wear, 24
Resorts, 131-155
Restaurants:

Bermuda, 13
    best, 159-171
    directory to, 160
Riding, 188
Roland Skinner, 97
Ronnie Chameau, 98, 128
Rosedon, 154
Royal Naval Dockyard:
    best shops, 122-125
    character, 87
    community, 71-73
    cruise ships, 87, 90
    cruises at, 74
    history, 71, 87
    hours, 79
    map of, 72
    shopping, 79, 87-88
    shops, 122-126
Royall Lyme, 94
Rum Cake Factory, 88

S

Safety, 29
Sailing (See Boating)
Sales, 78, 82
Sandy's Parish, 65-66
Scuba Diving, 182-183
Sculptures, 96-97, 110
Sea adventures, 187-188
Seasons, 23-24
Security, 29
Shipping, 110
Shop(s):
    branch, 85
    hours, 79
    recommended, 16-17
Shoppers:
    art, 83-84
    cruise ship, 83
    savvy, 83
Shopping:
    activity, 7
    audiences, 78
    bargain, 78
    bargains, 81-82
    centers, 88-89
    choices, 77
    classes, 78-79
    collections, 84
    commissions, 83
    comparative, 15, 80, 88
    consolidation, 82-83
    costs, 79
    coupons, 82
    cruise ship, 77-78, 90-91
    cultures, 79-81
    focus, xxii-xxiv
    fun, 80
    hotel, 88
    hours, 79
    locations, 85-91
    opportunities, 78
    prices, 80-81

quality, 12, 17, 78, 81, 92-128
recommended, 16
resort, 88
rules, 11
sales, 82
savings, 79
skills, 16
special, 127-128
strategies, 77-84
Sunday, 79
tax free, 81
upscale, 77
Sightseeing:
    Bermuda, 172-173
    Devonshire Parish, 174
    Hamilton City, 68, 175
    Hamilton Parish, 174
    Paget Parish, 175
    Pembroke Parish, 165
    Royal Naval Dockyard, 176
    Sandy's Parish, 176
    Smith's Parish, 174
    Southampton Parish, 176
    St. George Town, 173
    St. George's Parish, 173-174
    Warwick Parish, 175
Smiths Department Store, 83
Smith's Parish, 64
Snorkeling, 186-187
Solomon's Fine Jewelry, 93, 104
Somers Wharf, 87, 89
Southampton Parish, 65
Souvenirs, 124
Spas, 188-190
St. George:
    architecture, 87
    best shops, 119-121
    cruise ships, 80, 87
    Heritage Night, 29, 80, 87
    history, 69
    hours, 29
    Kings Square, 87
    map of, 69
    shopping, 80, 87
    sightseeing, 69-71
    Somers Wharf, 87
    town, 69-71
St. George's Parish, 62
Stamps, 116
Stefanel, 95, 117
Sunday brunches, 158
Swiss Timing, 94

T
Tableware, 95-96, 114
Taylors Clothing Shop, 121
Taxes, 27, 47-48, 57, 81
Taxi:
    companies, 46
    costs, 42-43, 45-46, 91
    drivers, 28
Tea, 158
Temperature Guarantee program, 24

Tennis, 180-181
The Island Shop, 78, 89, 98, 100, 113
The Reefs, 150-151
Time:
    hours, 28
    zones, 28
Tipping, 47, 159
Tour:
    golf, 37
    guides, 28
Tourism, 8, 22, 58
Tourist offices, 37-38
Tournaments, 48-50
Trails, 188
Transportation:
    costs, 27, 43-46, 91
    international, 30-34
    island, 14:
    options, 9-10, 42-46
Travel:
    deals, 35-36
    focus, xxii-xxiv
    guides, 52
    literature, 41
    packages, 132
    websites, 50-51
Travel-shopping, 10-12
Treasures, 10-12
Trimingham's and Smiths, xxiv, 83

U-Y
USA3000, 31, 52, 54
Vera P. Card, 88, 95, 98, 112-113, 120
Visitors' Service Bureaus, 41, 90
Voilé, 89, 100, 118
Wadsons, 98, 124
Walker Arcade, 89
Walker Christopher, 93, 103-104
Washington Mall, 89
Watches, 93-94, 120
Water, 48, 56, 59
Water Street, 70
Waterloo House, 147-148
Water-skiing, 187
Watersports, 6, 181-188
Websites:
    accommodations, 135
    airline, 31, 35
    Bermuda, 42, 50-51
    Bermuda Tourism, 38
    cruise ship, 32-35
    entertainment, 194
    golf, 37
    insurance, 30
    restaurant, 159
    tour package, 35-36
    travel deals, 17-18
    travel-shopping, 17-18
    U.S. Customs, 56
    wedding, 38
Weddings, 3, 37-38
Wellington Room, 159-160
Wine, 56, 159

World Heritage Site, 69
Workforce, 61
Yachts, 183-184

Featured Restaurants

Aqua, 161
Ascots, 162
Barracuda Grill, 162
Beethoven's Restaurant & Bar, 162
Bermudiana Dining Room, 162
Bistro J, 163
Café Gio, 163
Carriage House, 163
Chopsticks Restaurant, 163
Coconuts, 160-161
Fourways, 163-164
Fresco's Restaurant & Wine Bar, 164
Harbourfront, 164
Hog Penny Restaurant & Pub, 164
House of India, 165
La Coquille, 165
La Trattoria Restaurant & Pizzeria, 165
Lido Restaurant, 165
Little Venice, 165-166
Lobster Pot & Boat House Bar, 166
L'Oriental, 166
Mediterraneo Bar and Ristorante, 166
Mickey's Beach Bistro & Bar, 166
Monte Carlo, 166-167
The Newport Room, 167
Port O'Call, 167
Portofino, 167
Primavera, 167
Rosa's Cantina, 168
Rustico Restaurant & Pizzeria, 168
Seahorse Grill, 168
Tio Pepe, 168
Tom Moore's Travern, 168-169
Tuscany, 169
Waterlot Inn, 169
Wellington Room, 159-160
Whaler Inn, 169

The Authors

WINSTON CHURCHILL put it best – *"My needs are very simple – I simply want the best of everything."* Indeed, his attitude on life is well and alive amongst many of today's travelers. With limited time, careful budgeting, and a sense of adventure, many people seek both quality and value as they search for the best of the best.

Ron and Caryl Krannich, Ph.Ds, discovered this fact of travel life over 20 years ago when they were living and working in Thailand as consultants with the Office of the Prime Minister. Former university professors and specialists on Southeast Asia, they discovered what they really loved to do – shop for quality arts, antiques, and home decorative items – was not well represented in most travel guides, which primarily focused on sightseeing, hotels, and restaurants. While some guidebooks included a small section on shopping, they only listed types of products and names and addresses of a few shops, many of questionable quality. And budget guides simply avoided quality shopping altogether, as if shopping was a travel sin!

The Krannichs knew there was much more to travel than what was represented in travel guides. Avid collectors of Asian, South Pacific, Middle Eastern, African, and Latin American arts, antiques, and home decorative items, they learned long ago that one of the best ways to learn about another culture and meet its talented artists and craftspeople was by shopping for local products. In so doing, they also acquired some wonderful products, met many interesting and talented individuals, and helped support the continuing development of local arts and crafts.

But they quickly learned shopping in many countries was very different from shopping in North America and Europe. In the West, merchants nicely display items, identify prices, and periodically run sales. At the same time, shoppers in the West can easily do comparative shopping, watch for sales, and trust quality and delivery; they even have consumer protection! Americans and Europeans in other parts of the world face a shopping culture based on different principles. Like a fish out of water, they make many mistakes: don't know how to bargain, avoid purchasing large items because they don't understand shipping, and are frequent victims of scams and rip-offs, especially in the case of gems and jewelry. To shop a country right, travelers need to know how to find quality products, bargain for the best prices, avoid scams, and ship their purchases with ease. What they most need is a combination travel and how-to book that focuses on the best of the best.

In 1987 the Krannichs inaugurated their first shopping guide to Asia – *Shopping in Exotic Places* – a guide to quality shopping in Hong Kong, South Korea, Thailand, Indonesia, and Singapore. Receiving rave reviews from leading travel publications and professionals, the book quickly found an enthusiastic audience amongst other avid travel-shoppers. It broke new ground as a combination travel and how-to book. No longer would shopping be confined to just naming products and identifying names and addresses of shops. It also included advice on how to pack for a shopping trip (take two suitcases, one filled with bubble-wrap), comparative shopping, bargaining skills, and shopping rules. Shopping was serious stuff requiring serious treatment of the subject by individuals who understood what they were doing. The Krannichs subsequently expanded their work into a series of travel-shopping guides on Hong Kong, Thailand, Indonesia, Singapore and Malaysia, Australia and Papua New Guinea, the South Pacific, and the Caribbean.

Beginning in 1996, the series took on a new look as well as an expanded focus. Known as the *Impact Guides* and appropriately titled *The Treasures and Pleasures of . . . Best of the Best*, new editions covered Hong Kong, Thailand, Indonesia, Singapore,

Malaysia, Paris and the French Riviera, and the Caribbean. In 1997 and 1999 new volumes appeared on Italy, Hong Kong, and China. New volumes for 2000-2005 included India, Australia, Thailand, Myanmar, Hong Kong, Singapore, Bali, Egypt, Brazil (Rio and São Paulo), Vietnam, Cambodia, Turkey, Mexico, South Africa, and Santa Fe and Taos.

The Impact Guides now serve as the major content for a travel website called iShopAroundTheWorld.com.

While the primary focus remains shopping for quality products, the books and website also include useful information on the best hotels, restaurants, and sightseeing. As the authors note, *"Our users are discerning travelers who seek the best of the best. They are looking for a very special travel experience which is not well represented in other travel guides."*

The Krannichs' passion for traveling and shopping is reflected in their home, which is uniquely designed around their Asian, South Pacific, Middle East, North African, and Latin American art collections and which has been featured on CNN and in the *New York Times*. *"We're fortunate in being able to create a living environment which pulls together so many wonderful travel memories and quality products,"* say the Krannichs. *"We learned long ago to seek out quality products and buy the best we could afford at the time. Quality lasts and is appreciated for years to come. Many of our readers share our passion for quality shopping abroad."* Their books also are popular with designers, antique dealers, and importers who use them to source products and suppliers.

While the Impact Guides keep the Krannichs busy traveling to exotic places, their travel series is an avocation rather than a vocation. The Krannichs also are noted authors of more than 40 career books (see page vi), some of which deal with how to find international and travel jobs. The Krannichs also operate one of the world's largest career resource centers. Their works are available in most bookstores or through the publisher's online bookstore: www.impactpublications.com.

If you have any questions or comments for the authors, please direct them to:

Ron and Caryl Krannich
IMPACT PUBLICATIONS
9104 Manassas Drive, Suite N
Manassas Park, VA 20111-5211 USA
Fax 703-335-9486
E-mail: krannich@impactpublications.com

Feedback and Recommendations

W E WELCOME FEEDBACK and recommendations from our readers and users. If you have encountered a particular shop or travel experience, either good or bad, that you feel should be included in future editions of this book or on www.ishoparoundtheworld. com, please send your comments by e-mail, fax, or mail to:

Ron and Caryl Krannich
IMPACT PUBLICATIONS
9104 Manassas Drive, Suite N
Manassas Park, VA 20111-5211 USA
Fax 703-335-9486
E-mail: krannich@impactpublications.com

More Treasures
and Pleasures

THE FOLLOWING TRAVEL guides can be ordered directly from the publisher. Complete this form (or list the titles), enclose payment, and send your order to:

IMPACT PUBLICATIONS
9104 Manassas Drive, Suite N
Manassas Park, VA 20111-5211 (USA)
Tel. 1-800-361-1055 (orders only)
703-361-7300 (information) Fax 703-335-9486
E-mail: info@impactpublications.com
Online bookstore: www.impactpublications.com

All prices are in U.S. dollars. Orders from individuals should be prepaid by check, moneyorder, or credit card (Visa, MasterCard, American Express, and Discover). We accept credit card orders by telephone, fax, e-mail, and online. If your order must be shipped outside the United States, please include an additional US$4.00 per title for air mail shipping. Orders usually ship within 48 hours. For more information on the authors, travel resources, and international shopping, visit www.impact publications.com and www.ishoparoundtheworld.com.

Qty.	TITLES	Price	TOTAL
Bermuda Travel			
___	Bermuda Guide	$14.95	_____
___	Fodor's Bermuda	$16.00	_____
___	Frommer's Bermuda	$16.99	_____
___	Treasures and Pleasures of Bermuda	$16.95	_____
The Impact Guides			
___	Treasures and Pleasures of Australia	$17.95	_____
___	Treasures and Pleasures..Bali & Lombok	$18.95	_____

___	Treasures and Pleasures of Egypt	$16.95 ___
___	Treasures and Pleasures of Hong Kong	$16.95 ___
___	Treasures and Pleasures of India	$16.95 ___
___	Treasures and Pleasures of Mexico	$19.95 ___
___	Treasures and Pleasures of Paris	$18.95 ___
___	Treasures and Pleasures of Rio/São Paulo	$13.95 ___
___	Treasures and Pleasures of Santa Fe/Taos	$18.95 ___
___	Treasures and Pleasures of Singapore	$18.95 ___
___	Treasures and Pleasures of South America	$23.95 ___
___	Treasures and Pleasures of Southern Africa	$19.95 ___
___	Treasures and Pleasures of Thailand and Myanmar	$21.95 ___
___	Treasures and Pleasures of Turkey	$16.95 ___
___	Treasures and Pleasures of Vietnam and Cambodia	$16.95 ___

SUBTOTAL – – – – – –- $_____

❏ Virginia residents add 5% sales tax $_____
❏ Shipping/handling ($5.00 for the first
  title and $2.00 for each additional book) $_____
❏ Additional $4.00 per title if shipping outside U.S. $_____

TOTAL ENCLOSED – – – – – $_____

SHIP TO:

Name_____

Address_____

Phone Number:_____

PAYMENT METHOD:

❏ I enclose check/moneyorder for $ _____
  made payable to IMPACT PUBLICATIONS.

❏ Please charge $ _____ to my credit card:
❏ Visa   ❏ MasterCard   ❏ American Express   ❏ Discover

Card #_____Expiration date: ___/ ___

Signature_____

Discover the Best
Online Travel Deals!

WWW.TRAVEL-SMARTER.COM

- **Hotels**
- **Airlines**
- **Car Rentals**
- **Cruises**
- **Vacation packages**
- **Golf holidays**
- **Travel insurance**
- **Last minute travel deals**

For the very best deals – up to 70% discounts – click onto **HOT RATES** and **HOT DEALS**. This website also is rich with travel services, content, and tools, including:

- e-cards
- city guides
- currency converter
- flight tracker
- and much more

The same travel deals can by accessed through your one-stop travel-shopping website:

Keep in Touch . . .
On the Web!

www.impactpublications.com
www.ishoparoundtheworld.com
www.travel-smarter.com
www.winningthejob.com
www.veteransworld.com
www.exoffenderreentry.com